Lecture Notes in Computer Science 13484

More information about this series at https://link.springer.com/bookseries/558

Gabriel Zachmann · Mariano Alcañiz Raya ·
Partrick Bourdot · Maud Marchal ·
Jeanine Stefanucci · Xubo Yang (Eds.)

Virtual Reality and Mixed Reality

19th EuroXR International Conference, EuroXR 2022
Stuttgart, Germany, September 14–16, 2022
Proceedings

 Springer

Editors
Gabriel Zachmann (iD)
University of Bremen
Bremen, Germany

Partrick Bourdot
University of Paris-Saclay
Orsay Cedex, France

Jeanine Stefanucci
University of Utah
Salt Lake City, UT, USA

Mariano Alcañiz Raya (iD)
Universitat Politècnica de València
Valencia, Spain

Maud Marchal
INSA, IRISA
University of Rennes
Rennes Cedex, France

Xubo Yang
Shanghai Jiao Tong University
Shanghai, China

ISSN 0302-9743   ISSN 1611-3349 (electronic)
Lecture Notes in Computer Science
ISBN 978-3-031-16233-6   ISBN 978-3-031-16234-3 (eBook)
https://doi.org/10.1007/978-3-031-16234-3

This Springer imprint is published by the registered company Springer Nature Switzerland AG
The registered company address is: Gewerbestrasse 11, 6330 Cham, Switzerland

Preface

We are pleased to present in this LNCS volume the scientific proceedings of the 19th EuroXR International Conference (EuroXR 2022), organized by the Virtual Dimension Center (VDC), Fellbach, Germany, and held during September 14–16, 2022.

Prior EuroXR conferences (under the name of EuroVR until 2020) were held in Bremen, Germany (2014); Lecco, Italy (2015); Athens, Greece (2016); Laval, France (2017); London, UK (2018); Tallinn, Estonia (2019); Valencia, Spain (2020, virtual); Milano, Italy (2021, virtual). This series of conferences was initiated in 2004 by the INTUITION Network of Excellence in Virtual and Augmented Reality, supported by the European Commission until 2008. From 2009 through 2013, EuroVR was embedded in the Joint Virtual Reality Conferences (JVRC).

The focus and aim of the EuroXR conferences is to present, each year, novel results and insights in virtual reality (VR), augmented reality (AR), and mixed reality (MR), commonly referred to under the umbrella of extended reality (XR), including software systems, immersive rendering technologies, 3D user interfaces, and applications. EuroXR also aims to foster engagement between European industries, academia, and the public sector, to promote the development and deployment of XR techniques in new and emerging, but also existing, fields. To this end, all EuroXR conferences include not only a scientific track but also an application-oriented track, with its own proceedings.

Since 2017, the EuroXR Association has collaborated with Springer to publish the proceedings of the scientific track of its annual conference. In order to maintain the scientific standards to be expected from such a conference, we established a number of committees overseeing the process of creating a scientific program: the scientific program chairs, leading an International Program Committee (IPC) made up of international experts in the field, and the EuroXR academic task force.

For the 2022 issue, a total of 37 papers had been submitted, out of which 13 papers were accepted (six long, five medium, and two short papers). This amounts to an acceptance rate of 35%. The selection process was based on a double-blind peer-review process; each paper was reviewed by three members of the IPC, some with the help of external expert reviewers. Based on those review reports and the scores, the scientific program chairs took the final decision and wrote a meta-review for each and every paper.

This year, the scientific program of EuroXR and, hence, this LNCS volume, is organized into five sections: XR Interaction, XR and Neurodevelopmental Disorders, Algorithms for XR, Modeling Scenes for XR, and Scientific Posters. The latter section contains short papers accompanying the poster presentations, which present work in progress or other scientific contributions, such as ideas for unimplemented and/or unusual systems. These short paper contributions were, nonetheless, reviewed by three members of the IPC.

In addition to the regular scientific papers track, EuroXR invited three keynote speakers: Anthony Steed (University College London, UK), Giuseppe Riva (University of Milan, Italy), and Bruce Thomas (University of South Australia, Australia). In additon, there were keynote speakers in the application track along with the paper presentations. Furthermore, the conference hosted demo sessions and lab tours.

We would like to thank all the IPC members and external reviewers for their insightful reviews, which helped ensure the high quality of papers selected for the scientific track. Furthermore, we would like to thank the application chairs, demos and exhibition chairs, and the local organizers of EuroXR 2022.

We are also grateful to the team at Springer for their support and advice during the preparation of this LNCS volume.

July 2022

Gabriel Zachmann
Mariano Alcañiz Raya
Patrick Bourdot
Maud Marchal
Jeanine Stefanucci
Xubo Yang

Organization

General Chairs

Christoph Runde   Virtual Dimension Center, Germany
Kiyoshy Kiokawa   Osaka University, Japan
Frank Steinicke   University of Hamburg, Germany

Scientific Program Chairs

Mariano Alcañiz Raya   Universitat Politècnica de València, Spain
Patrick Bourdot   Université Paris-Saclay, CNRS, LISN, VENISE, France
Maud Marchal   IRISA-INSA Rennes, France
Jeanine Stefannuci   University of Utah, USA
Xubo Yang   Shanghai Jiao Tong University, China
Gabriel Zachmann   University of Bremen, Germany

Application Program Chairs

Arcadio Reyes-Lecuona   University of Malaga, Spain
Manfred Dangelmaier   Fraunhofer IAO, Germany
Kaj Helin   VTT, Finland
Jérôme Perret   Haption, France
Nicholas Polys   Virginia Tech, USA
Wolfgang Schäfer   ZHAW School of Management and Law, Switzerland

Demos and Exhibition Chairs

Frédéric Noël   Grenoble Institute of Technology, France
Matthieu Poyade   Glasgow School of Art, UK
Giannis Karaseitanidis   ICCS, Greece
Kayvan Mirza   Optinvent, France

Organization Team

Christoph Runde   Virtual Dimension Center, Germany
Diána Kretschmar   Virtual Dimension Center, Germany
Ioannis Alexiadis   Virtual Dimension Center, Germany

Vitor Macedo	Virtual Dimension Center, Germany
Jonas Gröpl	Virtual Dimension Center, Germany
Patrick Bourdot	Université Paris-Saclay, CNRS, LISN, VENISE, France
Mariano Alcaniz Raya	Universitat Politècnica de València, Spain
Arcadio Reyes-Lecuona	University of Malaga, Spain
Frédéric Noël	Grenoble Institute of Technology, France
Gabriel Zachmann	University of Bremen, Germany

International Program Committee

Mariano Alcañiz	Universidad Politécnica Valencia, Spain
Angelos Amditis	ICCS, Greece
Ferran Argelaguet	Inria Rennes, France
Sara Arlati	Italian National Research Council, Italy
Josep Blat	Universitat Pompeu Fabra, Spain
Andrea Bönsch	RWTH Aachen University, Germany
Pierre Boulanger	University of Alberta, Canada
Ronan Boulic	EPFL, Switzerland
Patrick Bourdot	Université Paris-Saclay, France
Antonio Capobianco	Université de Strasbourg, France
Julien Castet	Immersion, France
Weiya Chen	Huazhong University of Science and Technology, China
Irene Chicchi Giglioli	Universidad Politécnica Valencia, Spain
Sue Cobb	University of Nottingham, UK
Volker Coors	HFT Stuttgart, Germany
María Cuevas-Rodríguez	Universidad de Málaga, Spain
Manfred Dangelmaier	Faunhofer IAO, Germany
Angelica De Antonio	Universidad Politecnica de Madrid, Spain
Lucio De Paolis	University of Salento, Italy
Thierry Duval	IMT Atlantique, France
Peter Eisert	Humboldt-Universität zu Berlin, Germany
John Ahmet Erkoyuncu	Cranfield University, UK
Antonio Fernández	Universidad Castilla–La Mancha, Spain
Manuel Hernandez	Manusamozika, Spain
Francesco Ferrise	Politecnico di Milano, Italy
Jakub Flotyński	Poznań University of Economics and Business, Poland
Issei Fujishiro	Keio University, Japan
Akemi Galvez	Universidad de Cantabria, Spain
Pascual Gonzalez	Universidad Castilla–La Mancha, Spain
Daniel Gonzalez-Toledo	University of Malaga, Spain

Contents

XR Interaction

Designing Functional Prototypes Combining BCI and AR for Home Automation

Hakim Si-Mohammed[1,2]([envelope])[iD], Coralie Haumont[2], Alexandre Sanchez[2],
Cyril Plapous[3], Foued Bouchnak[3], Jean-Philippe Javaudin[3],
and Anatole Lécuyer[2][iD]

[1] Univ. Lille, CNRS, Centrale Lille, UMR 9189 CRIStAL, 59000 Lille, France
`hakim.simohammed@univ-lille.fr`
[2] Inria, Univ. Rennes, IRISA, CNRS, Rennes, France
`anatole.lecuyer@inria.fr`
[3] Orange Labs, Orange, Rennes, France
`foued.bouchnak@orange.com`

Abstract. In this technology report we present how to design functional prototypes of smart home systems, based on Augmented Reality (AR) and Brain-Computer Interfaces (BCI). A prototype was designed and integrated into a home automation platform, aiming to illustrate the potential of combining EEG-based interaction with Augmented Reality interfaces for operating home appliances. Our proposed solution enables users to interact with different types of appliances from "on-off"-based objects like lamps, to multiple command objects like televisions. This technology report presents the different steps of the design and implementation of the system, and proposes general guidelines regarding the future development of such solutions. These guidelines start with the description of the functional and technical specifications that should be met, before the introduction of a generic and modular software architecture that can be maintained and adapted for different types of BCI, AR displays and connected objects. Overall this technology report paves the way to the development of a new generation of smart home systems, exploiting brain activity and Augmented Reality for direct interaction with multiple home appliances.

Keywords: Brain-Computer Interface (BCI) · Augmented Reality (AR) · Home automation · Smart home · Steady-State Visual Evoked Potentials (SSVEP)

1 Introduction

The developments in the fields of the Internet of Things and smart homes [8] are pushing towards the design of new interaction mechanisms in order to seamlessly operate the multitude of available connected objects. These new interaction

G. Zachmann et al. (Eds.): EuroXR 2022, LNCS 13484, pp. 3–21, 2022.
https://doi.org/10.1007/978-3-031-16234-3_1

mechanisms largely rely on Natural User Interfaces (NUI) involving speech or gesture recognition [10] to enable users to operate the appliances with reduced efforts. Following this trend, a promising way to interact with smart homes and connected objects would be based on Brain-Computer Interfaces (BCIs).

BCIs enable users to interact with computer systems by the sole mean of their brain activity [35,40]. Historically, the first prototypes [38] of BCIs were mainly designed as means to assist people with disabilities, by providing them with systems exploiting brain activity instead of potentially damaged, traditional muscle outputs [41]. Although this purpose still represents one of the main objectives of the BCI community, a new trend can be observed in recent literature, with a number of works targeting the design and development of BCIs that can be used as interaction media for the general public, with applications in Human-Computer Interaction (HCI), entertainment [18,23], or robotics.

Unfortunately, it is currently difficult to argue that Brain-Computer Interfaces are ready for large scale exploitation. Current BCIs suffer from severe limitations in terms of reliability [24], speed and user friendliness [17]. These limitations prevent BCIs from being competitive options with regards to available alternatives for healthy users. Consequently, careful design and realistic specifications are necessary in order to integrate them in any high-end interactive system. As a first step, and in order to pave the way for future systems using BCIs to interact with smart homes, this technology report introduces a prototype combining a BCI and an Augmented Reality (AR) system, in order to integrate them in a home automation system.

In general, BCI and AR are two technologies that can largely benefit each other [14,34] either through providing user interfaces that are integrated in the environment, or by enabling hands-free interaction. The case of smart-homes is particularly conducive for the development of these technologies, as the increasing number and the heterogeneity of the connected objects and appliances offer a wide variety of use cases adapted to the diversity of BCI systems. Combining AR and BCI for home automation also holds the promise of a higher degree of adaptation to the users mental states, as well as the possibility, on the longer term, to seamlessly interact with their homes.

One of the earliest systems using a BCI to interact with house appliances was proposed by [13]. Their prototype enabled to change TV channels and to turn appliances ON or OFF using the users' brain activity. These appliances were controlled using binary hierarchical menus, in which users navigated by modulating levels of alpha rhythm [3].

In 2009, Edlinger et al. developed a P300[1] [29] prototype to control home appliances [6]. Their prototype relied on a virtual representation of a house, displayed in a CAVE [5] system. Their interface relied on displaying grids of icons representing commands associated to the manipulated objects. The icons were randomly highlighted following the oddball paradigm for P300. Similarly, [1] proposed a P300-speller based system to operate different appliances. Their

---

[1] P300 is an Event Related Potential (ERP) usually measured through EEG and that is elicited when a rare and/or attended stimulus is displayed.

interface consisted in grids of icons representing the achievable actions, displayed on a computer screen. More recently, Sahal et al. [33] used a custom P300 selection matrix displayed in AR to enable users to control their environment, specifically aiming at assisting patients with Amyotrophic Lateral Schlerosis.

Following a different approach, [22] used passive BCIs in order to automatically adjust the house environment (night lamps and air conditioner) based on the users cognitive states (drowsiness and alertness), associated with α (8–13 Hz) and θ (4–7 Hz) rhythms.

Using an AR Head-Mounted Display, [12] proposed a system enabling users to operate a distant robot, navigating in a house environment, using brain activity. The robot was equipped with a camera displaying a video feed of its environment where appliances were tagged with fiducial markers. When an object entered the robot's field of view, a control panel that the users could interact with using P300 was displayed. Later on, [37] developed a P300-based AR-BCI system to control multiple house appliances based on the same system described earlier, but through a monocular Optical See-Through AR display instead of the robot.

Using a BCI to control home appliances has also been explored through several prototypes and reviews [15, 16, 19]. Overall, the scope of these previous work differed on the component they put emphasis on. Some of them focused on the EEG analysis while others highlighted the assistance benefits for people with disabilities [43]. For example, [30] proposed a prototype integrating a Steady-State Visual Evoked Potentials (SSVEP) based BCI, an eye-tracker and an Augmented Reality display to operate a smart home environment. They presented users with flickering AR icons depending on where the users gaze, and enabled the control of different appliances. The developed prototype mainly relied on two components: (1) the Head-Mounted Display (HMD) handling the graphical interfaces and the feedback, and (2) a server responsible for the classification of the EEG and gaze data into issued commands. Later, this study was followed by a usability assessment [39]. A similar prototype was designed by Park et al. [27], using an AR-based SSVEP interface for controlling home appliances.

Most of the so-far developed prototypes were realized for lab-controlled experimentation and never exceeded the state of feasibility studies. Up to now, no developed system was able to cross the borders of the laboratories. Hence the questions: What are the requirements and specifications that an AR-BCI home automation system should meet before we can foresee a broadly available system? How to develop such a system to make it operational and useful to the end-users?

To these days, the best performing type of BCIs in terms of ITR (Information Transfer Rate) and reliability [4] are the reactive BCIs (e.g. Steady State Visual Evoked Potentials [44], P300 [28]) which require the users to focus on specific stimulation in order to send commands. Thanks to Augmented Reality, it becomes possible to integrate these sensory (mostly visual) simulations directly into the user's environment, instead of their traditional display on a computer screen.

In this paper, our goal is to introduce a prototype of combining an SSVEP-based BCI with Augmented Reality in order to interact in a smart home environment. We also propose general guidelines towards the development of AR-BCI smart-home systems, in a way that they would be operational and possible to upgrade with future technological and scientific improvements. The guidelines presented hereafter, are introduced following a top-down approach. We start by discussing the general, functional and technical specifications: What are the technical requirement and the features the system should provide? Then we present a generic system architecture, describing its different components and their interaction and finally, we illustrate the implementation of the prototype by describing a specific operational system that was developed with *Orange SA*, in an industrial context.

The contributions of this technology report are the following:

- Generic guidelines for the development of smart homes based on BCIs and AR.
- An operational smart home system integrated to a smart home platform.

The remainder of this paper is structured as follows: Section 2 discusses the system requirements and specifications of the prototype, introducing in the meantime higher level guidelines regarding the features of such a system. Section 3 describes the implemented prototype in terms of software and hardware architecture while Sect. 4 discusses the potential impact and presents use cases and future work, while Sect. 5 concludes the paper.

2   System Specifications and Guidelines

A smart home is "*a dwelling incorporating a communication network that connects the key electrical appliances and services, and allows them to be remotely controlled, monitored or accessed*" [20].

When it comes to the specifications of a system combining AR and BCI for home automation, six (6) requirements or features were identified as prominent. These specifications were related to both of the BCI and the AR component of the system and are namely: *operability, asynchronicity, modularity, generalisability, contextuality* and *hardware-independence*. These feature are hereafter described in terms of functional and technical requirement of the design system.

2.1   Operability

The first requirement of the system, is that it should offer the main features of a smart home and enable the operation of multiple devices. The underlying requirement is that the system has to enable the user to select which object s/he wishes to interact with. In addition to the selection mechanism, the system has to allow the user to send the desired command. It is possible to identify two categories of objects: (1) Binary state objects, that can only be switched

ON or *OFF* (e.g. a lamp, a smart plug, etc.), and (2) Multiple commands/states objects, which can receive more that one command or have more than two states (e.g. a television).

In order to meet this specification, a selection and operation strategy has to be provided for both types of objects. For example, *binary state* objects can be automatically switched between possible states upon selection while *multiple command objects* can toggle the display of a hierarchical menu leading to the possible commands.

The operation system should also take into account the possibility to include objects that may require continuous commands instead of discrete ones, even though this type of input is harder to achieve through BCIs.

2.2 Asynchronicity

Interactive systems depend on unpredictable inputs provided by the users [7]. This unpredictability originates both from the fact that users can issue different commands, and that these commands can be issued at any time. Hence, it is important for an AR-BCI based home-automation system to be asynchronous (also referred to as self-paced) in order to enable users to operate the system at their own pace. In other words, this specification means that the system should to be able to detect idle or rest states, where users do not intend to operate the system, thus, avoiding as much false positives as possible.

In terms of BCIs, the difficulty raised by this specification originates from the difficulty to detect rest states from the users' brain activity due to the constant background noise from unrelated activity. While several algorithms and signal processing methods have been proposed to detect these states, in several BCI paradigms, it remains generally more difficult to design asynchronous BCIs.

2.3 Generalisability

In most of the cases, BCIs are conceived as a mean to rehabilitate or assist people with disabilities [40]. The first reason for this has to do with the nature of the interaction using a BCI which does not rely on muscle activity. Another reason, is the fact that BCIs are usually cumbersome and tedious to apprehend [11], further associated with lower performance than other User Interfaces (UIs). Given this statement, and the fact that some BCI paradigms are easier to apprehend and operate than others (P300 being easier than Motor Imagery for example), it is important that the system addresses a large group of users, and is not solely dedicated to people with disabilities. In terms of BCI design, this specification implies that the designed system should require as little training as possible, and ideally that it can be operated by naive users. In addition to the choice of BCI paradigm, this may also require the design of robust signal processing and classification methods that are resilient to inter-subject variability.

2.4 Contextuality

One of the main advantages of AR systems is their ability to provide and use information regarding the user context thanks to tracking mechanisms [2]. This information allows to provide users with the relevant inputs and feedback, depending on their current location in the environment as well as their orientation (gaze direction). In the particular case of smart home systems where the number of interactable objects is typically large, information regarding the user's context allows to limit the presented inputs to the ones related to the objects which are most likely to be interacted with (at close distance, in the field of view, etc.). Moreover, as the performance of most visual-based BCIs are impacted by the amount of information provided at once, it is important that the system takes the user's context into account, both to maximize the system accuracy and reduce the potential confusion arising from too many inputs to process. In shorter terms, the system should adapt its AR interface and only display commands related to the objects in the field of view of the user, or the ones that are close enough to him/her.

2.5 Hardware Independence

The combination of multiple technologies (AR, BCI and IoT) brings several layers of complexity to the designed system. On the hardware level, multiple choices can be made in terms of hardware components for the AR interface (Head-Mounted Displays, Tablet screens, Optical See-Through Displays, etc.), for the BCI (different EEG headsets are possible) and for the connected objects (several appliances and manufacturers). In order to deal with all these possibilities, it is important for the system to be hardware-independent, i.e. abstract its features from hardware considerations. It should, for example, easily integrate new connected objects added to the environment, switch the display of the AR interface from one display to another or work with different EEG electrode configurations. In practice, this can be achieved by adding an abstraction layer to the system to handle the communication between the system's components.

2.6 Modularity

Given the heterogeneity of home appliances and the different natures of their commands, as well as the rapid developments in the fields of AR and BCIs, it is important for the system to be highly modular. It is for example difficult to conceive a single BCI paradigm that would fit all the use cases met in home-automation scenarios. Moreover, given the current state of the art of BCIs, it is important that the system also enables the easy integration with other input modalities in addition or in replacement of BCIs (e.g. speech and gesture). For these reasons, it is important that the system architecture is composed of independent components that are able to be upgraded or replaced without impairing the overall function of the system.

3   Generic Architecture

In order to meet the previously described specifications, we propose a generic architecture based on four (4) main components: (1) The BCI, (2) the AR system, (3) the Home-Automation platform, and (4) the Middleware. The main advantage of this architecture is to maintain a high level of independence between the components as the middleware handles all the communication pathways in the system (see Fig. 1). As such, changing the BCI paradigm or headset, the AR display or the home-automation platform should not impact the proper functioning of the system. Our proposed architecture is similar to but extends the one which was succesfully used in [27], and which uncouples the BCI from the rest of the system and using a middleware for communication.

3.1   The BCI

One of the specificities of this proposed architecture is not to consider the overall system as a BCI, but rather to include the BCI as one of its components. In fact, the role of the BCI is to measure and translate the brain activity of the users and to transmit the corresponding mental state to the interactive system, through the middleware. The internal structure of this component is based on the traditional BCI processing pipeline introduced by [25]. All the signal processing and classification aspects should be handled by this component, and the result of this analysis is transmitted to the middleware.

In an operational mode, this component should be able to detect changes in the user's mental state, and send the corresponding information to the middleware in real-time, meeting the *asynchronicity* requirement.

Encapsulating the BCI in a separate block enables to easily update the specific processing pipeline by using with new signal processing methods, changing the BCI-related hardware or the classification methods, without inducing changes in the rest of the components. As long as the detected mental state is transmitted to the middleware, the whole system should be able to operate.

However, some parts of the component, notably the choice of the BCI paradigm cannot be completely uncorrelated from the *AR system* for example.

In particular, reactive paradigms rely, by definition, on the nature and strategy of the stimuli provided by the system which is handled by the AR system display.

3.2   The AR System

The role of this component is twofold. First, it provides the users with information and feedback about the state of the system, as well as the possible commands to send depending on their context (location, objects in field of view, etc.). When developing a system combining BCI and AR, a particular care should be given to the display strategy so that the system is intuitive and easy to apprehend [36]. Second, in addition to the feedback and information, this component is also

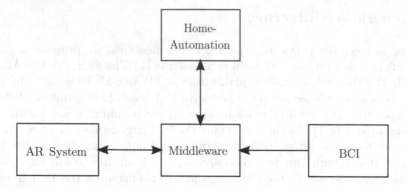

Fig. 1. Illustration of the components of a generic architecture of a home automation system using BCI and AR. The communication between the elements is done solely through the Middleware.

responsible of providing the visual stimulation (at least in the case of reactive visual BCI paradigms) for modulating the mental state.

Decoupling this component from the rest of the system allows the designer to change/upgrade the hardware, i.e. the AR display and the AR interface without altering the functioning of the other components.

3.3   The Home-Automation Platform

This component is the interface between the system and the connected appliances. Its role is to translate the commands obtained from the interpretation of the user mental state determined by the BCI and the context given by the AR system. The nature of this component depends on the specifications and features of the smart objects present in the house, i.e. their network protocol, their API[2] and should eventually allow the interaction with heterogeneous objects. If the available smart objects do not share the same protocols, it should be the role of the Home-Automation platform to adapt the commands accordingly.

3.4   The Middleware

All the components described above have the specificity of being independent from each other. In order to be able to interact, the system architecture has to provide a communication component. Essentially, the role of the middleware is to determine, from the context of the users and their mental state, the corresponding command to carry to the home automation platform.

The general interaction scenario is described as follows: At all time, the AR system provides the user context to the middleware (the location and the appliances detected in the field of view), based on which, the middleware responds with the available commands to provide and display to the user.

---

[2] Application Programming Interface.

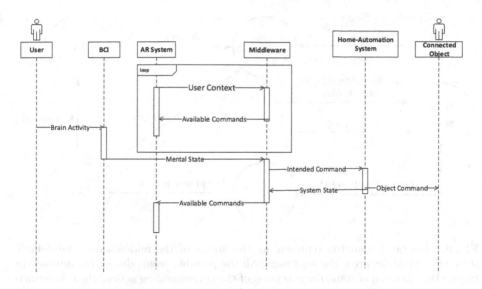

Fig. 2. Sequence diagram [9] of the system, representing the interactions and the communications between the different system components.

Whenever the BCI detects a significant mental state (corresponding to a valid command), it sends the corresponding label to the middleware which, based on the user context, transmits the corresponding command to the home automation platform. As stated before, the home automation platform operated the connected object accordingly, and sends the updated system state to the middleware which in turn, requests the AR system to update the displayed information. This interaction sequence is summarized in Fig. 2.

In this type of interaction sequence, it is the middleware that embeds the "intelligence" of the system as it is responsible for aggregating the information originating from the other components, in order to determine the appropriate command. It can also be assimilated to a finite-state automaton as described in Fig. 3.

The initial state of the automaton corresponds to the *Wait State* where the middleware is expecting a system event to proceed. Each time a new object is added to the system, the middleware moves to the state *S1*, which corresponds to the update state, in which the middleware updates the available objects and commands and sends them to the AR system, and gets back to the *Wait State*.

Whenever, a mental state is provided by the BCI component, the middleware moves to *S2* which corresponds to the BCI-handling state. In the case of SSVEP for example, the received message is under the form of a detected occipital frequency. If this frequency is not matched to any valid command, the middleware ignores the message and gets back to the *Wait State*. If the received frequency matches a command, the middleware moves to the *S3* state, which corresponds to the decoding state, in which it determines the type of the received command. If it corresponds to an object selection, the middleware switches to the *S1* state,

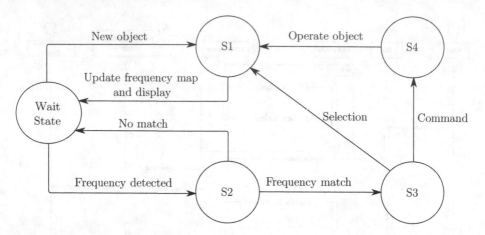

Fig. 3. General Automaton representing the states of the middleware. The default state of the middleware is the *wait state*. All the possible events during the interaction trigger the changing of state, the execution of the corresponding action, then the return to the wait state. S1: Update state, S2: BCI-handling state, S3: Decoding state, S4: Operation state

to update the available commands and the system state. If the command corresponds to an object operation, the middleware switches to the *S4* state in which the middleware transmits the command to the home automation platform, and switches to the *S1* state, where it updates the available commands.

4   Implemented Prototype

As a demonstration of the previously described concepts, specifications and architecture, we designed a prototype of a functional AR and BCI-based Home Automation system (see Fig. 4). This prototype was built in the scope of an industrial partnership project, with Orange SA, one of the main Internet Service Provider in France. The aim was to build an operational AR-BCI based home-automation system that would be integrated to their home-automation platform *Home'in*.

In this Section, we describe the conceptual and technical choices that were made in order to meet the requirements mentioned in Sect. 2.

In the scope of the project, the specific objectives of the project were as follows:

1. **The system had to enable the control of at least 3 types of objects:** The first requirement was that the developed prototype would enable the online operation of at least 3 objects present in a given environment: a fan (connected to a smart plug), a connected light and a Television. This objective was inline with the *Operability* specification.

Fig. 4. Illustration of the final prototype. The user can interact online with the three objects in front of him.

2. **The system had to integrate with an existing home automation system:**
   As a collaborative project, the objective was to integrate the global system with the home automation platform provided by Orange. In other words, the outputs of the BCI system had to be issued to the connected objects using the *Home'In* protocol.
3. **Commands should require at most 2 s to be issued:**
   The requirement in terms of performance, was that the system had to be able to issue commands in around 2 s. This requirement was particularly prominent for the choice of the BCI paradigm, as well as the employed signal processing methods.
4. **The system has to be validated online:**
   Finally, in order to showcase the functionality of the system, and to validate the results, the demonstration had to be performed online.

In the following parts, we describe the implementation of each component of the generic architecture, with regards to the previously introduced requirements, and how our proposed methodology was particularly suited for the design of this prototype.

4.1   The BCI

Considering the number of interactable objects and the possible number of commands offered by the system, and also for its low requirement in terms of user training and its relative reliability, we have opted for the *Steady State Visual Evoked Potentials* (SSVEP) paradigm.

In practice, the possible commands that the user could issue at a given moment were represented by targets flickering at different frequencies. Thus, the goal of the BCI component was to determine online, the flickering stimula-

Fig. 5. Illustration of the apparatus used in the developed prototype. (Left) A Microsoft HoloLens AR headset and (Right) an mbt Smarting EEG headset.

tion frequency that the user was attending and transmit this information to the middleware.

The different possible flickering stimulations and their corresponding commands were stored in a configuration file, namely the *frequency map* and managed by the Middleware. This way, it was easy to upgrade the system by adding more frequencies to the frequency map, or by reutilizing frequencies for different commands. For example, a target flickering 10 Hz could designate a specific command when the user was in a particular room, while this same frequency could designate another command in a different room or context, simply by updating the command associated with the given frequency in the frequency map.

Electroencephalographic (EEG) signals were recorded using a SMARTING amplifier (mBrainTrain, Serbia) with a sampling frequency 500 Hz and using 5 scalp electrodes: O1, O2, POz, Pz and CPz referenced to Cz and grounded to AFz (see Fig. 5).

Before being able to use the system online, multi-class (Common Spatial Pattern) and LDA (Linear Discriminant Analysis) classifiers were calibrated to recognize 5 classes: 4 stimulation frequencies (10 Hz, 12 Hz, 15 Hz 17 Hz) and the idle state, meeting the system's requirement of asynchronicity.

The signal acquired online was sliced into 4 s long epochs every 2 s, meaning that a decision from the classifier was issued every 2 s. The power of the signal at the neighbourhood (± 0.25 Hz) of each stimulation frequency was estimated and combined to form a feature vector. The trained CSPs were applied to spatially filter the data and LDA was used for classification. All implementation was done using OpenViBE [31].

4.2   The AR System

Given the employed BCI paradigm (SSVEP), the first objective of this component was to provide the AR interface displaying the flickering SSVEP targets, and to provide the user information about the system state. Its second objec-

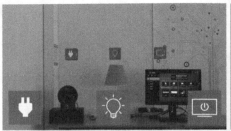

Fig. 6. Illustration of the implemented AR interface. The default view of the system (Left) represents the different objects in the field of view, with associated flickering icons. The fan and the light could be switched ON or OFF with a single command. The interaction with television was conducted through a hierarchical menu. After selecting the TV, the possible commands to issue appeared on the interface (Right).

tive was to provide the contextual information about the objects detected in the user's field of view.

Targets were represented in the form of squared-shape overlays displaying icons representing the associated command. The icon could either represent the state the represented object, in the case of on-off objects, or the commands to navigate into the hierarchical menus for multiple command objects.

Regarding the user's context, in the scope of this prototype, the spatial positions of the interactable objects were hard-coded in the AR application, meaning that every time one of these positions entered the *fov* (field of view) of the user, the command associated with the object at this position was displayed. Another alternative would have been the use of fiducial markers in order to detect the objects in the *fov* of the user, regardless of their positions.

The AR interface was displayed on a Microsoft Hololens (see Fig. 5) using a *frontal ego-centered user-anchored* display strategy [36] implemented using Unity (see Fig. 6).

4.3   The Home Automation Platform

The commands carried out from the middleware were transmitted to the *Home'In* smart home platform[3].

The commands were generated by the *Middleware* and carried to the home-automation platform through TCP using the *MQTT* protocol [21]. The selected objects for the prototype were: a Phillips Hue connected lamp and a connected plug on which a fan was plugged, to illustrate the interaction with binary state objects. And a smart television was used to illustrate the interaction with multi-commands objects.

---

[3] A Home-Automation platform from Orange SA.

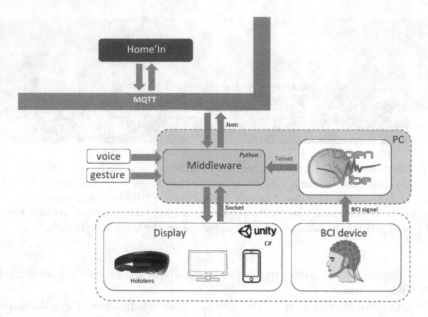

Fig. 7. Illustration of the final prototype architecture. The components are the same as proposed in the generic architecture, and all communications were done through the middleware.

4.4   The Middleware

The middleware was developed as a finite-state automaton using Python. It consisted in several listeners awaiting messages from the BCI component and the AR system, and relaying the appropriate messages to the components.

The implemented architecture of the developed system is summarized in Fig. 7.

All binary states objects were considered as switches. A single SSVEP selection switches between their 2 states. In the case of multiple commands objects, the interaction was done through a hierarchical menu. First selecting the object, then selecting the available commands (spec N Sect. 2.1).

Depending on the number of available commands at a certain time, and the context provided by the AR display, the middleware associates a flickering frequency to each object's icon and informs the AR system to display the flickering targets. When the BCI notifies the Middleware that a SSVEP command has been recognized, the Middleware notifies the AR system to update the display with the new objects states and change presented icons. The middleware also determines to what object and/or command, the SSVEP stimulation is associated and notifies the smart home platform.

The middleware allows to meet the specifications Sects. 2.5, 2.6. Regardless of the EEG system, as long as the BCI provides a detected frequency, the middleware can perform the required action and update the display regardless of its hardware type. In addition, as its role is to receive, interpret then retransmit commands, the middleware can also potentially enable to interact using other modalities (hand gestures, voice etc.) as long as they are simply used to determine the user's intent.

All in all, the BCI system was developed using OpenViBE. The middleware was developed in Python, and the AR system was developed using Unity. All the communications between the BCI, the AR system and the middleware were achieved using TCP (Transfer Communication Protocol) sockets.

5   Discussion

The contributions presented in this technology report are two-fold. First, we provided generic guidelines regarding the development of prototypes combining AR and BCI for home automation purposes. Following these guidelines in terms of functional and technical specifications namely *operability, asynchronicity, modularity, hardware independence, contextuality* and *generalisability* we proposed a new and reusable architecture decoupling each component of the system, and relying on a highly configurable middleware to operate the system.

Secondly, we illustrated how these guidelines can be implemented into a functional prototype integrated in a home-automation platform. This prototype, designed and implemented in collaboration with an industrial partner, is part of the global trend which aims at bringing BCIs out of laboratories.

Although the guidelines provided in this technology report are specifically targeting the specifications related to AR and BCI integration in the context of home automation, the field of smart home by itself also represents a challenge in many regards. Selecting the right communication protocol (Zigbee [32] or Zwave [42] to name a few) or the appropriate architecture in terms of software and hardware [26] requires a thorough analysis of the considered application.

In terms of AR and BCI, despite undeniable progress in these technologies, our prototype suffers from several limitations:

- **Performance:** The main limitation of our prototype, similar to many systems involving BCIs, lies in its poor performance when compared to existing alternatives for automation (handheld devices, voice commands) particularly for healthy users. Even though no formal study was conducted to evaluate the objective performance of our prototype, the informal testings showed a high variability in the subjects' performance, and generally remained below the accuracy of more traditional input systems.
- **Cumbersomeness:** Combining a BCI and a AR system, independently from the application, requires the association of cumbersome and bulky headsets which severely limits the use of these technologies over long period of times. A potential improvement may lie in the development all-in-one headsets, integrating easy-to-install EEG electrodes directly into the AR headsets.
- **Environment configuration:** One of the limitations regarding the AR configuration of our prototype was that the positions of the connected devices were hard set in the system. Meaning that moving the appliances from

their positions would result in the system not being able to detect them. A workaround solution would be to add fiducial markers to the appliances so that the AR system can detect them regardless of the position. Unfortunately, this solution still presents the drawback of not enabling the users to remotely operate an appliance that is not in his field of view.

– **Field of view:** Another limitation of the AR system was regarding the width of augmented field of view, i.e. the area of the field of view where virtual content can be displayed. Given the employed AR headset (Hololens), the augmented area of the *fov* represented a rectangle of 34° of visual angle. The size of this augmented *fov* plays a particularly important role with visual evoked potentials, as it may limit the number of displayable visual stimulations at once.

Moreover, associating a BCI with an AR system implies several technical challenges and difficulties to be dealt with. It is for example necessary to ensure the proposer setup of the headsets to prevent noise on the recorded signal, as well as to limit head movements to avoid muscle artefacts. It is also important to reduce the load on the AR core system in order to limit latency and jitter in displaying the stimulation (e.g. ensuring a stable flickering to elicit proper SSVEP responses), and to maximise the sycnhronization between the components (e.g. to accurately date the events in the case of event-related potentials).

Despite all these limitation, the strength of our approach lies in its high scalability that we believe can take benefit from any advancement in the BCI, the AR or the home-automation components of the overall system. The modularity of the proposed architecture can, for example, easily include any future improvement in the signal processing methods to improve the overall performance or the system. It could also easily benefit from the development of new hardware that can be easily replaced, to improve the user-friendliness of the system.

6   Conclusion

The aim of this technology report was to introduce a new architecture and methodology in building smart home systems based on BCIs and AR. It provided generic guidelines regarding the specifications and requirements that such systems should meet as well as a modular architecture enabling to meet these requirements. It also reported the result of a technological development aiming at integrating such an AR-BCI system in a home-automation platform that was showcased online. Despite the current limits of the system, the proposed prototype paves the way to the upcoming development and democratization of AR and BCI for non-medical, non-rehabilitation purposes.

References

1. Aloise, F., et al.: P300-based brain-computer interface for environmental control: an asynchronous approach. J. Neural Eng. **8**(2), 025025 (2011)
2. Azuma, R., Baillot, Y., Behringer, R., Feiner, S., Julier, S., MacIntyre, B.: Recent advances in augmented reality. IEEE Comput. Graphics Appl. **21**(6), 34–47 (2001)
3. Bazanova, O., Vernon, D.: Interpreting EEG alpha activity. Neurosci. Biobehav. Rev. **44**, 94–110 (2014)
4. Chen, X., Chen, Z., Gao, S., Gao, X.: A high-ITR SSVEP-based BCI speller. Brain Comput. Interfaces **1**(3–4), 181–191 (2014)
5. Cruz-Neira, C., Sandin, D.J., DeFanti, T.A.: Surround-screen projection-based virtual reality: the design and implementation of the CAVE. In: Proceedings of the 20th Annual Conference on Computer Graphics and Interactive Techniques, pp. 135–142 (1993)
6. Edlinger, G., Holzner, C., Guger, C., Groenegress, C., Slater, M.: Brain-computer interfaces for goal orientated control of a virtual smart home environment. In: 2009 4th International IEEE/EMBS Conference on Neural Engineering, pp. 463–465. IEEE (2009)
7. Évain, A., Argelaguet, F., Casiez, G., Roussel, N., Lécuyer, A.: Design and evaluation of fusion approach for combining brain and gaze inputs for target selection. Front. Neurosci. **10**, 454 (2016)
8. Gaikwad, P.P., Gabhane, J.P., Golait, S.S.: A survey based on smart homes system using internet-of-things. In: 2015 International Conference on Computation of Power, Energy, Information and Communication (ICCPEIC), pp. 0330–0335. IEEE (2015)
9. Garousi, V., Briand, L.C., Labiche, Y.: Control flow analysis of UML 2.0 sequence diagrams. In: Hartman, A., Kreische, D. (eds.) ECMDA-FA 2005. LNCS, vol. 3748, pp. 160–174. Springer, Heidelberg (2005). https://doi.org/10.1007/11581741_13
10. Jain, J., Lund, A., Wixon, D.: The future of natural user interfaces. In: CHI 2011 Extended Abstracts on Human Factors in Computing Systems, pp. 211–214 (2011)
11. Jeunet, C., Jahanpour, E., Lotte, F.: Why standard brain-computer interface (BCI) training protocols should be changed: an experimental study. J. Neural Eng. **13**(3), 036024 (2016)
12. Kansaku, K., Hata, N., Takano, K.: My thoughts through a robot's eyes: an augmented reality-brain-machine interface. Neurosci. Res. **66**(2), 219–222 (2010)
13. Karmali, F., Polak, M., Kostov, A.: Environmental control by a brain-computer interface. In: Proceedings of the 22nd Annual International Conference of the IEEE Engineering in Medicine and Biology Society (Cat. No. 00CH37143), vol. 4, pp. 2990–2992. IEEE (2000)
14. Kohli, V., Tripathi, U., Chamola, V., Rout, B.K., Kanhere, S.S.: A review on virtual reality and augmented reality use-cases of brain computer interface based applications for smart cities. Microprocess. Microsyst. **88**, 104392 (2022)
15. Kosmyna, N., Lécuyer, A.: A conceptual space for EEG-based brain-computer interfaces. PLoS ONE **14**(1), e0210145 (2019)
16. Kosmyna, N., Tarpin-Bernard, F., Bonnefond, N., Rivet, B.: Feasibility of BCI control in a realistic smart home environment. Front. Hum. Neurosci. **10**, 416 (2016)
17. Kübler, A., et al.: The user-centered design as novel perspective for evaluating the usability of BCI-controlled applications. PLoS ONE **9**(12), e112392 (2014)

18. Lécuyer, A., Lotte, F., Reilly, R.B., Leeb, R., Hirose, M., Slater, M.: Brain-computer interfaces, virtual reality, and videogames. Computer **41**(10), 66–72 (2008)
19. Lee, W.T., Nisar, H., Malik, A.S., Yeap, K.H.: A brain computer interface for smart home control. In: 2013 IEEE International Symposium on Consumer Electronics (ISCE), pp. 35–36. IEEE (2013)
20. Jiang, L., Liu, D.-Y., Yang, B.: Smart home research. In: Proceedings of 2004 International Conference on Machine Learning and Cybernetics (IEEE Cat. No.04EX826), vol. 2, pp. 659–663, August 2004. https://doi.org/10.1109/ICMLC.2004.1382266
21. Light, R.A.: Mosquitto: server and client implementation of the MQTT protocol. J. Open Source Softw. **2**(13), 265 (2017)
22. Lin, C.T., Lin, B.S., Lin, F.C., Chang, C.J.: Brain computer interface-based smart living environmental auto-adjustment control system in UPNP home networking. IEEE Syst. J. **8**(2), 363–370 (2012)
23. Lotte, F., et al.: Combining BCI with virtual reality: towards new applications and improved BCI. In: Towards Practical Brain-Computer Interfaces, pp. 197–220. Springer, Heidelberg (2012). https://doi.org/10.1007/978-3-642-29746-5_10
24. Lotte, F., Jeunet, C.: Towards improved BCI based on human learning principles. In: The 3rd International Winter Conference on Brain-Computer Interface, pp. 1–4. IEEE (2015)
25. Mason, S.G., Birch, G.E.: A general framework for brain-computer interface design. IEEE Trans. Neural Syst. Rehabil. Eng. **11**(1), 70–85 (2003)
26. Mocrii, D., Chen, Y., Musilek, P.: IoT-based smart homes: a review of system architecture, software, communications, privacy and security. Internet Things **1**, 81–98 (2018)
27. Park, S., Cha, H.S., Kwon, J., Kim, H., Im, C.H.: Development of an online home appliance control system using augmented reality and an SSVEP-based brain-computer interface. In: 2020 8th International Winter Conference on Brain-Computer Interface (BCI), pp. 1–2. IEEE (2020)
28. Picton, T.W.: The P300 wave of the human event-related potential. J. Clin. Neurophysiol. **9**(4), 456–479 (1992)
29. Polich, J., Margala, C.: P300 and probability: comparison of oddball and single-stimulus paradigms. Int. J. Psychophysiol. **25**(2), 169–176 (1997)
30. Putze, F., Weiß, D., Vortmann, L.M., Schultz, T.: Augmented reality interface for smart home control using SSVEP-BCI and eye gaze (2019)
31. Renard, Y., et al.: OpenViBE: an open-source software platform to design, test, and use brain-computer interfaces in real and virtual environments. Presence Teleoperators Virtual Environ. **19**(1), 35–53 (2010)
32. Safaric, S., Malaric, K.: Zigbee wireless standard. In: Proceedings ELMAR 2006, pp. 259–262. IEEE (2006)
33. Sahal, M., Dryden, E., Halac, M., Feldman, S., Heiman-Patterson, T., Ayaz, H.: Augmented reality integrated brain computer interface for smart home control. In: Ayaz, H., Asgher, U., Paletta, L. (eds.) AHFE 2021. LNNS, vol. 259, pp. 89–97. Springer, Cham (2021). https://doi.org/10.1007/978-3-030-80285-1_11
34. Si-Mohammed, H., Argelaguet, F., Casiez, G., Roussel, N., Lécuyer, A.: Brain-computer interfaces and augmented reality: a state of the art. In: 7th International Brain-Computer Interface Conference (2017)
35. Si-Mohammed, H., Casiez, G., Sanz, F.A., Roussel, N., Lécuyer, A.: Defining brain-computer interfaces: a human-computer interaction perspective (2019)

36. Si-Mohammed, H., et al.: Towards BCI-based interfaces for augmented reality: feasibility, design and evaluation. IEEE Trans. Vis. Comput. Graph. **26**, 1608–1621 (2018)
37. Takano, K., Hata, N., Kansaku, K.: Towards intelligent environments: an augmented reality brain machine interface operated with a see-through head-mount display. Frontiers Neurosci. **5**, 60 (2011). https://doi.org/10.3389/fnins.2011.00060. http://journal.frontiersin.org/article/10.3389/fnins.2011.00060
38. Vidal, J.J.: Toward direct brain-computer communication. Annu. Rev. Biophys. Bioeng. **2**(1), 157–180 (1973)
39. Vortmann, L.M., Putze, F.: Attention-aware brain computer interface to avoid distractions in augmented reality. In: Extended Abstracts of the 2020 CHI Conference on Human Factors in Computing Systems, pp. 1–8 (2020)
40. Wolpaw, J.R., Birbaumer, N., McFarland, D.J., Pfurtscheller, G., Vaughan, T.M.: Brain-computer interfaces for communication and control. Clin. Neurophysiol. **113**(6), 767–791 (2002)
41. Wolpaw, J.R., Wolpaw, E.W.: Brain-computer interfaces: something new under the sun. In: Brain-Computer Interfaces: Principles and Practice, pp. 3–12 (2012)
42. Yassein, M.B., Mardini, W., Khalil, A.: Smart homes automation using Z-wave protocol. In: 2016 International Conference on Engineering & MIS (ICEMIS), pp. 1–6. IEEE (2016)
43. Zhang, R., et al.: A BCI-based environmental control system for patients with severe spinal cord injuries. IEEE Trans. Biomed. Eng. **64**(8), 1959–1971 (2017)
44. Zhu, D., Bieger, J., Molina, G.G., Aarts, R.M.: A survey of stimulation methods used in SSVEP-based BCIS. Comput. Intell. Neurosci. **2010**, 1 (2010)

SightX: A 3D Selection Technique for XR

Chao Mei[1,2(✉)], Yifan Yang[2], and Yi Xu[2]

[1] Kennesaw State University, Marietta, GA 30060, USA
meichaomc@gmail.com
[2] OPPO US Research Center, InnoPeak Technology, Inc., Palo Alto, CA 94303, USA

Abstract. Many 3D Interaction techniques use virtual ray-casting for general selection and manipulation tasks. Some virtual ray-casting techniques are equipped with gadgets to fit specific interaction scenarios, such as selecting an object with special shapes, or a part of an object. These techniques are intuitive and largely successful. However, there are still some common situations under which the capabilities of virtual ray-casting are limited. When a user needs to select an object that is far away and small, the movement of the ray on the far end greatly amplifies hand movement of the user, which in turn results in inefficient and inaccurate selection operations. Moreover, in an Extended Reality (XR) space, especially in an Augmented Reality (AR) space, where a user's ability of performing teleportation or shifting to another view is limited, selecting an object that is occluded or from a cluster of objects with high density would be less flexible. We developed and evaluated SightX, a virtual ray-casting mechanism augmented with a remote anchor and a sight view with see-through capability for XR interactions. Our user studies suggested this design can significantly improve the performances and user experiences over the standard virtual ray-casting for 3D objects selection tasks.

Keywords: Human-centered computing · 3D user interfaces

1 Introduction

Virtual ray-casting is a common strategy of 3D interactions [15]. Joined by virtual hand, they are the two default techniques available on many recent XR devices. With the virtual ray-casting technique, a user can manipulate a 6-DoF or a 3-DoF input device as the origin of a ray and move the ray in XR spaces to indicate the selection of an object that the ray casts on. User can easily understand this technique through the metaphor of pointing with a real laser pointer or a flash light.

Despite being an intuitive interaction technique, using a standard virtual ray-casting for 3D selection tasks faces several challenges: 1) when selecting objects that are far away from the user, a small movement of the origin (e.g., controller) will be greatly amplified at the other end of the ray. This posts great demand for user's fine operation and cognitive load; 2) when selecting occluded objects

G. Zachmann et al. (Eds.): EuroXR 2022, LNCS 13484, pp. 22–35, 2022.
https://doi.org/10.1007/978-3-031-16234-3_2

(e.g., a book in a cabinet), it is impossible for the user to cast the virtual ray on the target object; 3) when selecting among cluttered objects (e.g., objects that are in close proximity to each other, even not fully occluded), it is difficult to accurately indicate an object from the rest by casting a virtual ray. High mis-operation rate and long time-consumption are two main issues under such scenarios. There are many works that tried to overcome these limitations of standard virtual rays, such as added dimensions of control like the buttons on the HTC Vive controllers and improved pointing techniques [17,18]. However, most of these designs have to balance between accuracy and efficiency, due to the increased complexity.

In this work, we developed and evaluated SightX, a virtual ray-casting mechanism augmented with a remote anchor and a sight view with see-through capability for XR interactions. The user studies suggested that our design can significantly improve the performances over plain rays for 3D objects selection.

2 Related Work

To design a 3D selection technique for head-mounted XR environments, there are three primary problems that must be addressed to support precise 3D target acquisition and manipulation: the target disambiguation, occlusion, and the "Heisenberg effect" [6].

Argelaguet and Andujar provide a taxonomy of different disambiguation techniques designed to improve virtual rays associated with a volume [2]. They categorize disambiguation into three groups: manual, heuristic, and behavioral. The manual approaches require additional steps to manually select a target among those highlighted. For example, in the Flower Ray, Grossman et al. display the objects intersected by the ray through a pie menu in a flowered out manner. Then the user can select the target on the pie menu with a 2D cursor [14]. The menu cone technique also displays the targets to disambiguate in a menu, and then the user performs gestures to select the target of interest [19]. With a smartphone to control the ray direction, Lop-cursor used a touch-screen to control the fine-grained cursor movement to distinguish the targets selections [11]. The heuristic approaches apply some heuristics to determine the target the user wants to select. The Flashlight technique, for example, highlights the object that is the closest to the central axis of the selection cone [16]. The "Sticky-Ray" is also based on the ray-casting technique [20]. In this technique the last object intersected remains selectable until another one is hit. The behavioral approaches look at the users operations and actions, which may reflect their intention of selection. For instances, IntenSelect [10] uses the time that an object stays in a selection volume to score the object, and the highest scored object will be selected. However, doing so can be inefficient.

In many cases a target is obstructed by another object or set of objects from the viewpoint of a user. For example, a molecule hidden in a cluster of molecules, or a table behind a wall. These will influence the efficiency of 3D interactions. Many previous works tried to address this issue. Elmqvist and Taigas [12] specified that there are four object interaction scenarios that will cause the occlusion:

proximity, intersection, enclosure, and containment. Some common strategies to the problem are to change the viewport, to hide and/or remove occluding objects, to distort the interaction space [7], or virtual X-Ray tools such as [3,23]. In cases when a target is partially occluded, most techniques allow for selection.

The "Heisenberg Effect" [6] is the error that resulted from a user's physical interactions with a controller during selection (e.g., when they press a button or rotate the controller). It affects the ray cursor position or ray orientation. Ray-casting is prone to this effect. Even a small perturbation at the origin of the ray will be magnified along the ray distance especially when the distance is long or the target object is small [4]. To reduce the Heisenberg effect, previous works, such as [5,21], use asymmetric bi-manual interaction. A user can point at the target with the dominant hand and activate selection with the non-dominant one. Research showed that bi-manual pointing may not affect user performance [9]. However, when the distance is very long, a small vibration of a unstable hand will still make the pointing very hard. Bi-manual interactions may also face the problem of reduced accessibility.

All these existing mechanisms are successful in addressing some of the problems. However, these techniques typically suffer from speed-accuracy trade-offs, and few techniques have explored the issue of a target being completely occluded from the user's viewpoint. SightX, on the other hand, was motivated to improve the efficiency of selection tasks, as well as addressing the Heisenberg effect.

3   System Design

In order to address the above-mentioned drawbacks of current ray-casting based methodologies, there are two main innovative features in this design: a remote anchor and a sight view enhanced by a virtual X-ray metaphor. The remote anchor is designed to address the Heisenberg effect, while the X-ray sight view is designed to address the disambiguation problem and the occlusion problem.

3.1   Remote Anchor

If an object is too far away, a small rotation at the controller end will result in a large-scale swing at the other end of the ray. This is because the controller's movements are amplified by the distance of the ray. We designed a "remote anchor" for the controller which can be placed at a location near the object. This can be understood through the metaphor that the remote anchor acts as the agent of the controller. Instead of the controller, the ray now originates from an anchor point, but its orientation is still controlled by the original controller. In such a scenario, the distance between the origin of the ray to the object of interest can be significantly reduced; thus mitigating the movement amplification effect. Figure 1 (left) shows a user uses a controller to control a ray, originating from the remote anchor, to select the black triangle. In Fig. 1 (right), the user rotates a controller to change the direction of the ray to select a red triangle. In cases when the object is very far away, both the object and the ray appear very small in the view; limiting the user's ability to select the object. We augment the remote anchor with a sight view. An extra virtual camera will render an amplified view of the remote objects as shown in Fig. 1 and 2. When sight view is enabled, the user uses the controller to control the ray, originating from the remote anchor, in a similar manner of playing a third-person view game. In the current implementation of the remote anchor, the anchor and the sight view are enabled at the same time by the swipe gesture on the controller touchscreen. The position of the anchor is co-located at the position of the sight view. However, asynchronous activation and physical separation of remote anchor and sight view are also possible. The sight view can be further enhanced by the *X-Ray* design described in the following section.

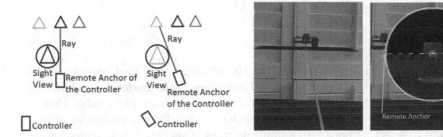

Fig. 1. Selecting a black/red object with a remote anchor (Color figure online)

Fig. 2. Selection of a cup without and with a remote anchor (Color figure online)

3.2   X-Ray Sight View

When interacting in an XR space with standard ray-casting, there are situations where 3D objects might block the view of the target object a user tries to interact with. For example, in Fig. 6, the book on the second-row shelf is hidden behind the first-row shelf. To complete the selection task on the second-row shelf, user needs to move or walk around the first-row shelf. This action is achievable with a standard ray-casting, but potentially inefficient.

When a sight view (as described in the previous section) is enabled, an extra virtual camera will render a close-up view and display it on top of all the objects (i.e., on the top most layer in the graphics pipeline). This effectively achieves an "X-ray" effect and provides users see-through capability because the objects in between the view and the user are not rendered (similar to a near clip plane of a virtual camera). Figure 6 is an example of using the X-ray sight view to see through the first row of book shelves to select a book on the second row of book shelves. User can control the depth of the X-ray sight view along the ray. Pushing forward or pulling backward operations are implemented through swiping up or down on the touchscreen respectively.

We call our remote anchor and X-ray sight view design SightX. SightX only requires a 3-DoF controller to carry out the 3D selection tasks. The reason to design for a 3-DoF controller instead of a 6-DoF one is two-fold: 1) it demands less input from the user, and 2) smartphone tethered AR glasses are becoming popular, such as commercially available nReal Light AR Glasses and Lenovo ThinkReality A3. In these designs, smartphones are used to provide power, rendering, and working as a hand-held controller paired with the glasses. It is easier to track the orientation than the position of a smartphone as the controller. We implemented the SightX using OPPO AR Glasses 2021. Remote anchor and X-ray sight view can be switched on and off through the touchscreen of the phone. SightX can also be potentially implemented with a 6-DoF controller. The efficiency difference between a 3-DoF controller with SightX and a 6-DoF one with SightX is beyond the scope of the current research.

4   User Study

A user study was conducted to evaluate the efficiency and user experiences of the SightX system. Users conducted 3D selection tasks under three different Augmented Reality (AR) environments: 1) selecting cups on a table that is far away from the user, 2) selecting molecular models from a molecular cluster model, and 3) selecting books from multiple rows of shelves. These scenarios are set to simulate the drawbacks of a standard ray-casting interface to evaluate the possible improved performance of the SightX.

4.1   Remote Selection

In the remote selection session, the participants are asked to complete the task of selecting cups from a table that is very far from the user. Selecting objects from a long distance is difficult when using standard ray. The users can only control the orientation of the ray with their hand movements. However, the movement at the far end of the ray can be greatly amplified by the distance between the user and the target object, making it difficult to control. Moreover, the distance makes the target object appears to be small. According to the Fitt's Law [13], it takes users longer to point to the target on a screen if the objects are smaller in size or farther away from the home position. This scenario is designed to evaluate whether the remote anchor design plus sight view can effectively mitigate this limitation of the standard ray-casting interaction.

In the scene, 9 regular-sized cups are located on top of a regular-sized table which is 45 m away from the participant. The table top is 1.1 m from the ground, the cups are 0.25 m away from each other. The participant first starts by selecting a white cup to initiate the task. Then by selecting a red cup, the participant successfully completes the task. As shown in Fig. 2, all other cups are rendered as blue and worked as distracting objects in the task. A selection of a distracting object at any time will mark the task as failed. The position of the white and red target cup are randomly determined, but the distance between the white and red cups remains the same in each trial (4 blue cups in between). Figure 2 (right) shows the same task with a remote anchor toggled on. The anchor is placed on the vector from the user to the center cup, and is 5 m away from the center cup.

4.2 Molecular Models

The target selection task of molecular models is derived from the work of Vanacken [22]. In the virtual environment, there is a cluster of molecular models placed on a table. A white molecule and a red molecule are hidden within several blue ones. With standard ray-casting, in each round of trial, the participant first observes and finds the white molecule from the cluster and uses the ray to point at the molecule and touches the smartphone screen to make the selection. Then they are required to observe and select the red molecule to complete the task of that round. Under the condition of SightX, a user can move the sight view forward and backward to locate and select the target object. Participants are also allowed to walk around in the room to observe the cluster from different perspectives to locate targets that are heavily occluded. Figure 3 and Fig. 4 show examples of standard ray-casting, and a sight view pushed into the cluster respectively. Remote anchor is not enabled in this molecule selection task.

Each round consists of an initial target (white), a destination target (red), and 140 distracting objects (blue). The positions are all randomly generated, with the following rules: 1) the distance between white and red molecules is consistent across all the rounds, 2) the volume of the cluster is 20 cm × 20 cm × 28 cm, 3) the radii of the blue molecules are generated between 2 cm to 4 cm following a random distribution for each round, and 4) five distracting objects are placed around the goal target in a cube-shaped Voronoi region. These rules are set to control the difficulty level of each round to be similar and avoid the learning effects which may compound the task performances.

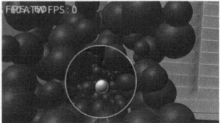

Fig. 3. A standard ray-casting aiming at a white molecular model. (Color figure online)

Fig. 4. A sight view has been pushed into the molecule cluster. (Color figure online)

4.3   Book Shelves

In the book shelves task, the participants are asked to complete the task of selecting books from several book shelves. The book shelves are positioned in two rows. The view of the second row is initially blocked by the first row. The participant first starts by selecting a book with a white cover from the first row to initiate the task. Then by selecting a red book from the second row, the participant successfully completes the task. As shown in Fig. 5, all the non-red and non-blue books are distracting objects in the task. A selection of a distracting object at any time will mark the task as failed. Figure 6 shows the same task with the X-ray sight view selecting the red book from the second row. The sight view helps see through the first row of book shelf.

The distance between the first and second row is fixed at 2 m. But the location of the white book and the red book are randomly generated with the following resections: 1) the white book is always on the first row, while the red book is always on the second row; 2) the distance between the white and red book in each round are generated from a range of 2–3 m following a random distribution. The distances are set to be close to real world scenarios and are used to control the difficulty of the tasks.

Fig. 5. A white-cover book on the first row. (Color figure online)

Fig. 6. Selection with a see-through sight view. (Color figure online)

4.4   Study Participants

We randomly recruited 15 males and 15 females participants for this user study. The age of the participants ranged from 20 to 50. 24 participants out of the 30 completed the study. 5 out of the 30 participants had previous experiences with AR/VR HMDs. None of them is a daily user of any XR HMDs. The study was conducted in an indoor lab. Two experimenters and a single participant were allowed to be present in the room. Social distancing and masks were required to mitigate the risks of COVID-19. The total duration of the study was about 100 min for each subject, including training, performing the task, and post-task interview. A set of back-up device would be used during the study, in case the main device was running out of battery during the study.

4.5   Study Procedure

The study is a within subject counter-balanced design. The subject repeated each of the three tasks 20 times, half of them with regular ray-casting and the other half with the SightX ray-casting, in a randomized order. In the Molecular Models task and the Book Shelf task, the X-ray sight view was enabled. In the remote selection task, the remote anchor and X-ray view were both enabled. After each trial, the participant was requested to respond to questionnaires.

4.6   Apparatus

The device we used in the user study was OPPO AR Glass 2021. It is an pair of AR Glasses that are tethered to a smartphone via a USB 3 cable. The smartphone not only provides power, computing, and graphics rendering for the glasses, but also serves as a primary input device.

4.7   Hypotheses and Measurements

The purpose of this research is to verify the effectiveness of the SightX design in terms of task performance and user experiences, compared with the regular ray-casting design. We made and tested several null hypotheses as below:

Hypothesis 1 (H1) - *There is no difference in time spent on the selection tasks between the standard ray-casting and SightX interface.*

Hypothesis 2 (H2) - *There is no difference in the success rate of the selection tasks between the standard ray-casting and SightX interface.*

Hypothesis 3 (H3) - *There is no difference in the user experiences between the standard ray-casting and SightX interface.*

Performance Measurements: There are three performance measurements in this study.

Time to Finish a Selection: This is the time elapsed from a participant completing the white target selection to completing the red target selection. The participant repeated this white-red selection pattern across all the three scenarios (molecular models, book shelves, and remote selection).

Task Success Rate: Each task was repeated 10 times. If the participant selected any of the distracting objects, that trial would end and the participant proceeded to the next trial. The Task Success Rate was calculated by dividing the number of times the red target has been successfully selected by 10.

Aiming Error: Between the white target and the red target selection, the participant needs to aim at the red target to make the correct selection. The Aiming Error is measured by how many times the participant aims at a distracting object before they can make the correct selection.

User Experiences Measurements. In between each session, when a participant switched between the standard ray and the SightX, we employed System Usability Scale (SUS) and NASA Task Load Index (TLX) questionnaires to investigate user's subject experience with these two interfaces. The SUS provides a "quick and dirty" but reliable tool for measuring the usability with 10 questions [8], while the NASA-TLX is a subjective workload assessment tool which allows subjective workload assessments on operator(s) working with various human-machine interface systems [1].

After the study, we also conducted one on one interviews to understand the participant's experiences with the two interfaces and tried to find out more optimization options for future work.

5   Study Results

We performed paired t-tests on normally distributed data (numerical data, such as the time), Wilcoxon signed rank tests on data that did not have a normal distribution (ordinal data, such as the questionnaires), and applied Bonferroni correction where appropriate. Significant differences are reported in this section.

5.1   Quantitative Results

Our first Hypothesis is - there is no difference in time spent on the selection tasks between the standard ray-casting and SightX interface. To test it, *Time to finish a selection* was compared across the regular ray-casting interface and the SightX interfaces. In the remote selection task, we found participants used significantly less time with SightX to finish the task (MeanX = 3.53, SD = 2.1, MeanRay = 5.15, SD = 2.61, t = −3.013, Two-Sided p = 0.003, One-Sided p = 0.006). In the tasks of selecting from Molecular Models, the trend is that users spend less time using the SightX interface at the p-value of 0.1 level (MeanX = 7.19, SD = 2.6 MeanRay = 8.86, SD = 3.21, t = −1.81, Two-Sided p = 0.086, One-Sided p = 0.043). However, in the book selection task we did not find any statistical significance.

The *Aiming Errors* were measured to triangulate with the time measurement results. The results reflected the similar trends with the time measurements. In the remote selection task, we found participants aimed at distracting objects for a significant less amount of times with SightX (MeanX = 14.57, SD = 7.95, MeanRay = 26.39, SD = 9.43, t = −5.532, Two-Sided p < 0.001, One-Sided p < 0.001). In the tasks of selecting from Molecular Models, the trend is that participants aimed at the distracting objects less often while using the SightX interface, at the p-value of 0.1 level (MeanX = 53.48, SD = 40.48 MeanRay = 70.87, SD = 33.63, t = −1.956, Two-Sided p = 0.063, One-Sided p = 0.031). And surprisingly, in the book selection task, which we did not find difference in completing time, we found participants aimed at distracting objects for a significant less amount of times with SightX (MeanX = 69.88, SD = 37.11,

MeanRay $= 115.01$, SD $= 76.39$, t $= -3.011$, Two-Sided p $= 0.003$, One-Sided p $= 0.006$).

Our second Hypothesis is - there is no difference in the success rate of the selection tasks between the standard ray-casting and SightX interface. *Task success rates* were measured in all three tasks. However, we did not find any difference between the SightX group and the standard ray group.

Our third Hypothesis is - there is no difference in the user experiences between the standard ray-casting and SightX interface. To investigate participants' subject experiences, we performed Wilcoxon test for the SUS and NASA-TLX questionnaires. Those questionnaires were taken after the participants finished each type of the tasks. We found in the NASA-TLX, in respond to the Physical Demand investigation question - "How physically demanding was the task?", the standard ray-casting interface (Mean $= 12.43$, STD $= 4.28$) was rated significant higher (z $= -2.518$ p $= 0.012$) than the SightX interface (Mean $= 9.9$, STD $= 5.82$). Moreover, in SUS question - "I found the system very cumbersome to use", we found a trend at 0.01 significant level, that the standard ray-casting interface (Mean $= 2.43$, STD $= 1.0$) was rated higher (z $= -1.875$ p $= 0.061$) than the SightX interface (Mean $= 1.96$, STD $= 1.12$).

5.2 Qualitative Results

One on one interviews were conducted with each of the participants. We identified several themes from the interview:

Remote Selection: Almost all of the participants think the remote selection task with the standard ray is "extremely difficult". They describe it as "hard to aim", "the ray is unstable", and "need some luck to make it". With the remote anchor of the SightX interface, they think it is "way more efficient", "sight view made the target more clear", and "less pressured and fun to play with the sight view".

Physical Demand: An agreement reached by almost all of the participant is that a big difference between these two interfaces is the demand of walking in the AR environment. When interacting using the standard ray, the participants needed to walk in the environment to select the target objects. Moreover, the participants mention that they had to move their heads to adjust the viewpoint, otherwise they could not see the target. While using the SightX interface, participants can just stay in place and complete the task. Even though the standard ray has higher physical demand, a small amount (4/30) of participants mentioned that they think it is fun to be able to walk in the environment.

Metaphor and Presence: Most of the participants think it is initially easier to adopt the standard ray, since it is simpler and the ray metaphor is easy to understand. They think it as a laser light or a flashlight. The SightX view will take more efforts to grasp initially, and the metaphor of remote anchor and sight view is not as straightforward. After adopting them, they feel the SightX is more efficient. The metaphor has also influenced on participants' feeling of presence. When discussing about the sight view metaphor, 6 participants think it is not as immersive. One participant commented: "I feel it is a video game instead of a real environment around me".

6   Discussion

The user studies have provided rich insights into understanding the performance and the user experiences of the SightX interface. In testing the first hypothesis regarding time efficiency, the data showed that under two of the three testing scenarios, there were statistical significance at the p-value of 0.05 or 0.1 level. SightX has constantly outperformed the standard ray in terms of time efficiency. The possible reason based on interview is that users do not need to walk around nor adjust viewpoint with SightX interface. Moreover, the remote anchor has solved the problem of unstable ray at the far end during the remote selection task. Participants do not have to aim with a unstable ray with the help of the remote anchor. In the book selection task, we did not find any significant difference. Based on our observation, we found that after the participants first found a location at which they could see both rows of book shelves, they will *stay at that location* for the rest of the book selection tasks. This behavior eliminated the occlusion condition we set in this environment, thus these two methods performed similarly in this environment. With these evidences, we can reject the first null hypothesis.

The Aiming Errors may have also contributed to the differences of time performances. In the measurement of Aiming Error, the results also triangulated with the time measurement. Differences were found in all three tasks. Participants had to aim/touch more distracting objects when they were completing the tasks with the standard ray interface. Especially in the remote selection task, the participants hit 1.8 times more distracting objects with the standard ray with a strong p-value less than 0.001. Even in the book selection task, which the time measure failed to show difference, participants had to aim at detracting objects more often with the standard ray.

In testing of the second hypothesis regarding success rate, surprisingly we did not find any significant difference in any of the tasks. A possible explanation is that since all tasks have no time limit, they will try their best to complete the task, even though they may take longer time. Therefore, the success rates are all very high across the tasks and interaction interfaces. We could not reject the second hypothesis based on the current data.

In testing of the third hypothesis regarding the user experiences, significant differences were found on both NASA-TLX and the SUS questionnaires. It is clear that interacting with the standard ray has a higher physical demand. This is proved both from the questionnaire data and the one-on-one interviews. Moving around the room, adjusting the viewpoint, as well as stabilizing the far end of ray contributed to both time difference and subject experience feedback. Moreover, this high physical demand was further converted as the user experience of "cumbersome". Even though the SightX interface requires more efforts to grasp initially, it is still rated as less "cumbersome". It is clear that we can safely reject the third null hypothesis regarding the user experiences.

Compared with the standard ray, the SightX design is more efficient and provides better user experiences. However, there are still some potential problems revealed from the interviews. First, the metaphor of SightX is complex. One can easily understand a ray or a laser pointer, but the combination of remote anchor, sight view, and X-ray will take more initial efforts to understand. The standard ray seems to have a better initial learning curve, but after the participants get use to the SightX, it still brings better efficiency and experiences. Secondly, the view of the SightX may make the XR environment less immersive and break the feeling of presence. This was found through the interview but was not initially expected, so we did not include the presence questionnaires in the current study. Without further research, we think it is better to cautiously apply SightX design in an XR environment where the presence is among the top priorities.

7   Conclusion

The standard ray-casting interface for 3D interactions has many potential inefficiencies under certain scenarios such as selecting virtual objects that are very far away from the users, heavily occluded, or blocked. We proposed and evaluated SightX, a virtual ray-casting mechanism augmented with a remote anchor and a sight view with see-through capability for XR interactions. The user study results suggested that, under the above-mentioned scenarios, compared with the standard ray interface, SightX can effectively increase the interaction efficiency, reduce the errors made during the interaction, and improve the user experiences.

Although there are many positive effects applying SightX design, we also need to be aware of the downside of the design such as the complexity of initial understanding of the metaphors, and the possible influence on user's feeling of presence. As a generalizable guideline, we suggest adopting SightX under the situations where users need to select virtual objects that are very far away, heavily occluded, or blocked. Moreover, providing the options to switch it on and off to combine with the standard ray could be an optimal design decision.

References

1. NASA TLX task load index. https://humansystems.arc.nasa.gov/groups/tlx/. Accessed 26 May 2021
2. Argelaguet, F., Andujar, C.: A survey of 3D object selection techniques for virtual environments. Comput. Graph. **37**(3), 121–136 (2013)

3. Bane, R., Hollerer, T.: Interactive tools for virtual X-ray vision in mobile augmented reality. In: Third IEEE and ACM International Symposium on Mixed and Augmented Reality, pp. 231–239 (2004)

4. Batmaz, A.U., Stuerzlinger, W.: The effect of rotational jitter on 3D pointing tasks. In: Extended Abstracts of the 2019 CHI Conference on Human Factors in Computing Systems, pp. 1–6 (2019)

5. Batmaz, A.U., Stuerzlinger, W.: Effects of 3D rotational jitter and selection methods on 3D pointing tasks. In: 2019 IEEE Conference on Virtual Reality and 3D User Interfaces (VR), pp. 1687–1692. IEEE (2019)

6. Bowman, D., Wingrave, C., Campbell, J., Ly, V.: Using pinch gloves (TM) for both natural and abstract interaction techniques in virtual environments (2001)

7. Bowman, D.A., Kruijff, E., Laviola, J.J., Poupyrev, I.: 3D User Interfaces: Theory and Practice. Redwood City (2004)

8. Brooke, J.: SUS: a "quick and dirty" usability scale. In: Usability Evaluation in Industry, vol. 189 (1996)

9. Brown, M.A., Stuerzlinger, W., Mendonça Filho, E.: The performance of uninstrumented in-air pointing. In: Graphics Interface 2014, pp. 59–66. AK Peters/CRC Press (2020)

10. De Haan, G., Koutek, M., Post, F.H.: IntenSelect: using dynamic object rating for assisting 3D object selection. In: IPT/EGVE, pp. 201–209. Citeseer (2005)

11. Debarba, H., Nedel, L., Maciel, A.: LOP-cursor: fast and precise interaction with tiled displays using one hand and levels of precision. In: 2012 IEEE Symposium on 3D User Interfaces (3DUI). IEEE (2012)

12. Elmqvist, N., Tsigas, P.: A taxonomy of 3D occlusion management for visualization. IEEE Trans. Visual Comput. Graph. **14**(5), 1095–1109 (2008)

13. Fitts, P.M.: The information capacity of the human motor system in controlling the amplitude of movement. J. Exp. Psychol. **47**(6), 381 (1954)

14. Grossman, T., Balakrishnan, R.: The design and evaluation of selection techniques for 3D volumetric displays. In: Proceedings of the 19th Annual ACM Symposium on User Interface Software and Technology, pp. 3–12 (2006)

15. LaViola, J.J., Jr., Kruijff, E., McMahan, R.P., Bowman, D., Poupyrev, I.P.: 3D user interfaces: theory and practice. In: 3D User Interfaces: Theory and Practice. Addison-Wesley Professional (2017)

16. Liang, J., Green, M.: JDCAD: a highly interactive 3D modeling system. Comput. Graph. **18**(4), 499–506 (1994)

17. Marc Baloup, T.P., Casiez, G.: RayCursor: a 3D pointing facilitation technique based on Raycasting. In: Proceedings of the 2019 CHI Conference on Human Factors in Computing Systems, pp. 1–12 (2019)

18. Pietroszek, K., Wallace, J.R., Lank, E.: Tiltcasting: 3D interaction on large displays using a mobile device. In: Proceedings of the 28th Annual ACM Symposium on User Interface Software & Technology, pp. 57–62 (2015)

19. Ren, G., O'Neill, E.: 3D selection with freehand gesture. Comput. Graph. **37**(3), 101–120 (2013)

20. Steinicke, F., Ropinski, T., Hinrichs, K.: Object selection in virtual environments using an improved virtual pointer metaphor. In: Wojciechowski, K., Smolka, B., Palus, H., Kozera, R., Skarbek, W., Noakes, L. (eds.) Computer Vision and Graphics, pp. 320–326. Springer, Dordrecht (2006). https://doi.org/10.1007/1-4020-4179-9_46

21. Sun, J., Stuerzlinger, W., Riecke, B.E.: Comparing input methods and cursors for 3D positioning with head-mounted displays. In: Proceedings of the 15th ACM Symposium on Applied Perception, pp. 1–8 (2018)

22. Vanacken, L., Grossman, T., Coninx, K.: Exploring the effects of environment density and target visibility on object selection in 3D virtual environments. In: 2007 IEEE Symposium on 3D User Interfaces. IEEE (2007)
23. Viega, J., Conway, M.J., Williams, G., Pausch, R.: 3D magic lenses. IN: Proceedings of the 9th Annual ACM Symposium on User Interface Software and Technology, pp. 51–58 (1996)

Design and Evaluation of Three User Interfaces for Detecting Unmanned Aerial Vehicles Using Virtual Reality

Günter Alce[1]([✉])(iD), Philip Alm[1], Rikard Tyllström[2], Anthony Smoker[2], and Diederick C. Niehorster[3](iD)

[1] Department of Design Sciences, Lund University, Lund, Sweden
gunter.alce@design.lth.se
[2] Lund University School of Aviation, Lund University, Lund, Sweden
[3] Lund University Humanities Lab and Department of Psychology, Lund University, Lund, Sweden

Abstract. Regulations restrict UAVs to fly only within direct view of the pilot, limiting their ability to support critical societal functions. One potential way to move beyond this limitation is by placing a 360-degree camera on the vehicle and using its feed to provide operators with a view that is the equivalent to being on the vehicle. This necessitates a cockpit user interface (UI) that amongst other things highlights flying objects, so that collision with these can be avoided. In this paper, virtual reality (VR) was used to build a prototype of such a system and evaluate three UIs that were designed to facilitate detecting aerial. Conclusions are drawn regarding which UI features support detection performance and a positive user experience.

Keywords: Virtual reality · Prototyping · Unmanned aerial vehicle

1 Introduction

Unmanned aerial vehicle (UAV) such as drones could be used to deliver medication, defibrillators, or to find missing people. However, due to regulations by the European Aviation Safety Agency (EASA)[1] and by the Federal Aviation Administration (FAA)[2] in the United States, a drone is limited to only fly within direct view of the pilot i.e. the pilot needs to maintain a visual line of sight (VLOS) to the drone. The risk of collisions with other aerial vehicles and objects is one reason for this. However, this limitation can be overcome if the drone operation can meet the requirements of Beyond Visual Line of Sight (BVLOS) operations according to EASA and the UK Civil Aviation Authority (CAA)[3]. These requirements are demanding in that they require drone opera-

---

[1] https://www.easa.europa.eu/newsroom-and-events/news/safe-operations-drones-europe.

[2] https://www.faa.gov/uas/recreational_fliers.

[3] https://publicapps.caa.co.uk/docs/33/CAP%201861%20-%20BVLOS%20Fundamentals%20v2.pdf.

© The Author(s), under exclusive license to Springer Nature Switzerland AG 2022
G. Zachmann et al. (Eds.): EuroXR 2022, LNCS 13484, pp. 36–49, 2022.
https://doi.org/10.1007/978-3-031-16234-3_3

tions to satisfy stringent safety requirements that protect other airspace users as well as society from the harm of collision in the air and harm caused by drones falling onto the property, people, and animals beneath the drone operation.

The see and be seen principle of collision avoidance is in many respects tried and trusted and custom practice for the fixed and rotary winged communities of airspace users, especially for those who operate in airspace that has no air traffic services that provide separation assurance. Collision avoidance is therefore an obligation for those flying the vehicles. This is accomplished through visual scanning of the sky, using trained visual scanning patterns to visually acquire conflicting traffic and through protocols such as the rules of the air, to take action to avoid collisions with proximate traffic.

A possible solution to enabling BVLOS operations while providing operators with the means of visually acquiring and avoiding other traffic could be a head-worn display (HWD) providing pilots with a first-person perspective through a 360-degree camera mounted on the drone and a virtual cockpit user interface for operating the drone. This change from a third-person to a first-person perspective when controlling the drone comes with other challenges such as how to visualize the environment to the operator to enable them to detect other aerial vehicles and objects. We believe that safe remote operation beyond the current legal limits could be possible with a combination of using existing warning systems and new interaction models. An example of such a warning system is the flight alarm (FLARM)[4] which signals the location of other nearby aerial vehicles that also have a FLARM system.

VR environments can potentially comprise a large number of virtual objects at various locations, making it difficult to understand and navigate an augmented scene. This problem is further enhanced by the fact that current HWDs still have a limited field-of-view. Therefore, only a small portion of the virtual environment is visible and many virtual objects are likely to be out-of-view. Several visualization techniques have been proposed in the past to locate and guide attention towards such out-of-view objects in both mobile and HWD-based mixed reality (MR) environments. Bork et al. [5] compared six different visual guidance techniques which were compared with respect to their potential for displaying out-of-view objects. The authors found that the type of visual guidance technique impacts the way users search for virtual objects in MR and in particular a 3D Radar was found to yield performance comparable to the best state-of-the-art techniques. Even though Bork et al. [5] did not specifically study the detection of UAVs, their concepts are relevant for our work. Moreover, according to Funk [8] who built and prototyped flying user interfaces for human-drone interaction, one must pay attention to three aspects: controlling the drone, knowing where the drone is, and providing communication between the drone and other systems. One example of a user interface providing such capabilities is provided in the work by Garcia et al. [9], who presented amongst other things an augmented reality system that helped a UAV pilot on the ground identify their UAV's position and orientation by annotating their third-person view of the scene. Related

---

[4] https://flarm.com/.

efforts to use AR to design and evaluate air traffic controllers are, for instance, Wickens et al. [17], Gorbunov and Nechaev [10], and Bagassi et al. [4].

Note that a position and orientation tracking mechanism is needed depending on the application scenario. Funk [8] distinguishes between on-board and external tracking systems. On-board tracking uses sensors that are mounted on the drone such as a GPS device keeping track of the drone's position, or a camera-based, drone-mounted tracking system that uses techniques such as SLAM (Simultaneous Localization And Mapping) for the same purpose but additionally are capable of determining the layout of the drone's surroundings. External tracking for instance uses cameras that are placed in the environment to track the drone such as OptiTrack.

The combination of VR and drones is something that has been used before, but mostly to view a 360-degree video of different places with little or no interaction. Jung et al. [11] used a drone equipped with a 360-degree camera to record video over Lake District National Park [11], to create virtual tours. We used a 360-degree camera mounted on a drone and recorded material which was used for testing. Santel et al. [15] conducted a user study to test the FLARM collision alerting system (CAS) on glider pilots. The study showed that there were systematic errors when the flight conditions were such that the FLARM display's orientation and the glider pilots' orientation did not match [15].

However, it is inherently difficult and costly to study and prototype different user interfaces for consumer electronics [1]. A similar problem exists for UAVs since building interactive user-interface prototypes involves many different devices and systems that are not open for prototyping, and restrict exploring what would be possible with future technologies such as larger field of view of the drone operator's HWD. Therefore, we decided to use Virtual reality (VR) devices such as HTC Vive[5] or as in our case Samsung Odyssey[6]. One advantage of such a virtual environment is that the 3D layout of the virtual world is known. Therefore, efficient techniques for guiding users' attention towards virtual objects can be developed and studied in a controlled environment. VR has been used as a design tool in many different domains, and it is a mature technology that can create computer-generated environments. Examples of areas in which VR has been used as a design tool are architecture, city planning, and industrial design [6]. However, the display resolution and lack of accurate tracking have traditionally been an issue. This has changed with the latest generation of commercial VR hardware (e.g. HTC Vive and Oculus Rift), which comes with tracking of headset and hand controllers with sub-millimeter precision [13] and increasingly large FOVs, providing a fertile design space for exploring user interfaces for future drone operator HWDs.

Using VR as a prototyping method is an area that has been well studied. Alce et al. [1–3] used VR for simulating of how to detect and interact with devices connected to the Internet such as TV, lamps, speakers etc. by using virtual AR glasses. This had the advantage of creating a realistic experience in terms of

---

[5] https://www.vive.com/us/.
[6] https://www.samsung.com/.

AR display resolution and tracking. Park and Kim [12,14] also used AR technology to study different information representation methods for drivers using
AR-HUD system, since it could help to reduce traffic accidents. The authors used
eye-tracking to determine the differences in the visual cognitive workload placed
on drivers. They did this in a controlled environment being able to superimpose
augmented virtual objects onto a real scene under all types of driving situations
including unfavorable weather such as rainy, foggy, overcast, and snowy conditions. Inspired by this previous work, we decided to follow a similar approach
and compare three user interfaces for UAV detection by using VR technology.

In this paper, a 360-degree camera recording was used as the background in
a VR interactive simulation to compare three different UIs for detecting other
aerial vehicles. The three UIs that are developed are inspired from previous
research and existing UIs. The first one is based on existing UI called FLARM;
the second is a circular Head-Up-Display (HUD) with the functionality of adjusting the user's head orientation inspired by Santel et al. [15]; and finally the third
is a radar-like display inspired from the gaming industry and also from Bork
et al. [5]. All three UIs were developed and evaluated with the focus to detect
other aerial objects. A user study of the three UIs were conducted in a controlled
environment with 30 participants.

The main contribution of this paper is to elucidate knowledge about how
the participants performed using the three suggested UIs to detect other aerial
objects in a controlled VR environment.

2   Building the Prototype

One of the main goals of the presented work was to design and test a set of UAV
UIs by exploiting the possibilities and technical advantages of the VR environment. Using the VR prototyping method enables relatively futuristic models to
be explored where technical obstacles (such as limitations in FOV of current
drone operator HWDs) can be avoided in favor of exploring human preferences,
natural behavior, and cognitive capacities. Consequently, the prototypes were
designed iteratively, starting with the FLARM UI since the FLARM transpon-
der is an established UI for indicating the location of other aerial vehicles, after
brainstorming within the research group, two more UIs were suggested that also
could show information indicating the location of other aerial vehicles. The three
UIs, referred to as FLARM, the Circular HUD and Radar, are discussed below.

To make the experience more realistic two more things are required. First,
a background that makes it look like you are flying. Secondly another drone in
the vicinity that the warning system can detect and show information about.
To allow for more, easier and safer testing, a pre-recorded 360-degree video was
used instead of having to fly every time a test was done. There were two possible
solutions for adding another drone to the scene: either including another drone
in the 360-degree video recordings or making a 3D model that can be added to a
scene in Unity. Having a 3D model of a drone superimposed on the video using
Unity had more advantages, for example, the model could be used to create

multiple scenarios with the same video feed and have full control of the model's flight path and velocity (see Fig. 1a).

(a)   (b)

Fig. 1. a) Drone model with 360 video background. b) The VR FLARM prototype.

2.1   FLARM

FLARM is a flight alarm system that broadcasts current and future flight paths to nearby aircraft. The system receives the same data from other aircraft around it. When a potential collision is detected, the pilot is alerted with the relative position of the aircraft that is on a potential collision course. This means that FLARM operation requires both aircraft to have a FLARM unit installed for it to work. There are a couple of different types of displays for the FLARM data, most of which divide the information into height difference and horizontal direction [7]. FLARM uses a spherical coordinate system: azimuth is displayed in twelve sectors, elevation in four sectors, and distance with a digital display (see Fig. 1b).

The prototype used a picture of the FLARM dashboard and illuminated a light to make it look like a functional dashboard (see Fig. 1b). The prototype information works the same as FLARM with the exception that it visualizes the position of the drone model. The FLARM UI was in a static position in space (like it would be in a real cockpit) and did not follow the operator's head direction.

2.2   Circular HUD

The second developed UI was the circular HUD (see Fig. 2a). Circular HUD also shows the direction of the drone but instead of the FLARM system which showed the location of the other drone with respect to the operator's drone, the circular HUD was designed to show location information with respect to the operator's current viewing direction. This means that if the other drone is in front of you and you look to the right, the system shows that there is something to the left of where you are looking. As such, the circular UI followed the operator's head direction and provided indications that were always in view of the operator. The adjustability was added since it was found in a study by Santel et al. [15]

that glider pilots misinterpreted the FLARM dashboard when their view and the dashboard were not aligned.

Height indication was provided by means of an arrow indicating whether the other drone was above or below the operator's drone. The arrow was red if the other drone was more than fourteen degrees above or below, it was orange if the other drone was between seven and fourteen degrees above or below, and no arrow was shown if the height difference was less than seven degrees. Red and orange were used since both these colors draw attention. Red was used for the bigger angle as it can be perceived as a "stronger" color than orange (see Fig. 2a).

Lastly, the position of the drone was highlighted using a clearly visible diamond-shaped marker.

(a)   (b)

Fig. 2. a) The circular HUD prototype. b) The radar prototype.

2.3 Radar

The third UI took the form of a radar system that uses icons to show a drone. The operators' drone was indicated in green and the other drone in orange. A white triangle was used to show which direction the operator is looking in (see Fig. 2b). The radar system has lines in the azimuth plane that indicate at which five-meter increments of distance the other drone is, depending on what circle it is in (first line is ten meter). When more than 25 m away the other triangle is clamped to the edge of the radar, showing which direction it is coming from. The same diamond-figure highlight designed for the circular HUD was also added to this prototype. The Radar UI was in a static position in space and did not follow the operator's head direction.

Since it was hard to read the numbers in the radar, a number was added to the top right of the radar to show an exact distance. The system had no way of displaying the height difference of the other drone. There were two main ideas for how to display height. The first one was to add a number to the top left showing the exact angle. The other was to add an arrow close to the triangle showing if it was above or below. Since none of the other systems had an exact number displayed the exact number option was implemented to test if this was something that users might desire.

3   Method

A comparative evaluation was conducted using the three proposed user interfaces (UIs): a) FLARM; b) Circular HUD; and c) Radar. Both quantitative and qualitative data were collected. The purpose of this test was mainly to explore the participants' preferences and to identify possible differences between the UIs in regard to how fast another object is detected. The task for the participants was to detect other UAVs. As dependent variables, we used detection time and individual ratings for the UIs. The two main null hypotheses were that neither the detection time nor the individual ratings would differ in regard to the type of UI. We also analyzed qualitative data concerning any stated difficulties with certain types of interaction and the comments from the semi-structured interview.

3.1   Setup

Tests were performed at Lund University School of Aviation. The setup used a Samsung Odyssey and a laptop powerful enough to run VR. The moderator controlled which user interface was tested and which scenario to activate. There were nine scenarios for each UI and they were activated by pressing "1–9". A separate laptop was used for taking notes as well as recording detection times during the test. The participants were seated to limit the risk of motion sickness. The participants only used the head-worn display, no hand controls were used.

3.2   Participants

30 participants were recruited by notifications on social media and by an instructor from Lund University School of Aviation presenting the study in aviation classes. The participants consisted of four females and twenty-six males, between 18 and 60 years old ($M = 34.3$, $SD = 12.46$) and from various backgrounds including an instructor from the aviation school, engineers working with IT, and students. One participant did not provide their age. Twenty-five of these were students at the University. Eighteen of them had previous experience of VR while twelve of them had none. Twenty of the participants have experience of being a drone operator.

3.3   Procedure

All participants were given a brief introduction to the project and its purpose. Next, all participants filled in a short questionnaire together with informed consent regarding their participation and the use of the data collected. Thereafter they were introduced to the HWD where they performed a quick familiarization session. The training session let the participant be a passenger in the drone virtually. A prerecorded 360-degree video was used as background. During the training participants could look around and familiarize themselves with the concept of virtually being in a drone without any distractions. This could continue for up to four minutes. However, when the initial reactions were over, they were asked to inform the experimenter when they felt ready to move on and reassured that they could continue enjoying the view if they wished to do so. The purpose of this exercise was for the participants to get familiarized with the fictive world.

The next part of the test was to try the different interaction models used as a warning system. For each UI, the test consisted of nine different scenarios: three easy, three medium, and three difficult where another drone was animated to fly nearby. Each UI was consistently paired with the same easy, medium and hard version scenario. To avoid sequence effects, the order in which the three UIs were presented was fully counterbalanced, i.e. each of the six possible orders was shown to equally many participants. Within each UI, the difficulty levels were always run in the order easy, medium, hard. The easy scenario lasted for 30 s, and the other drone's flight path was somewhat in front of the participants' drone. The medium scenario lasted for 15 s and started from the side. The hard scenario lasted for eight seconds and had the other drone's flight path start behind the participants' drone. In all scenarios, the endpoint was in front of the users' drone.

Each UI was tested on three scenarios, one from each difficulty. Before every UI was tested a short introduction was made describing the basics of the UI with a scenario that showed how different locations were shown with that UI. The showcase scenario introduced how height difference was shown, an example of the other drone being to the right and an example of the other drone behind the participant's drone. During the testing, the detection time for the different scenarios was recorded. Detection time was the time it took for the participant to verbally indicate they detected the drone, measured from the point at which the test moderator activated the scenario.

When the test case was concluded, a short semi-structured interview was held to record the participant's experience of the different UIs. The interview contained some open questions and questions about the importance of the user interface components and the display information. The participants rated on a Likert scale of one to five, one being it is not important and five being it is very important. Specifically, participants were asked to rate the importance of three different aspects:

1. The importance of the display showing the direction of your drone.
2. The importance of the display showing the direction of the other drone.
3. The importance of the display adjusting to the direction you are looking at.

Each session lasted about 30 min.

4   Results

4.1   Detection Time

The mean detection time for each scenario as well as in total for each system can be found in Table 1.

Table 1. Mean times rounded to one decimal in seconds. Standard deviation in parenthesis.

Mean times (SD)	FLARM	Circ. HUD	Radar
Easy scenario	4.7 (2.05)	5.1 (4.46)	4.4 (3.59)
Medium scenario	3.5 (2.10)	3.9 (2.70)	3.0 (1.49)
Hard scenario	7.1 (6.83)	5.0 (2.29)	4.0 (2.49)
Average	5.1 (4.50)	4.7 (3.30)	3.8 (2.70)

The Radar UI had the lowest average detection time of 3.8 s (see Table 1). A two-way dependent measures ANOVA revealed no significant interaction effect of user interfaces and the difficulty level of the scenarios ($F_{(4,261)} = 1.82$, $p = .13$). However, there were significant differences in detection time between the user interfaces ($F_{(2,265)} = 3.21$, $p = .04$), and a significant difference between difficulty levels ($F_{(2,265)} = 6.95$, $p = .0011$).

Post-hoc Tukey tests revealed that the detection time was significantly lower for the Radar UI than the FLARM UI ($p = .03$). There was no significant difference in detection time between the Circular HUD and the FLARM UI ($p = .65$) and between the Circular HUD and the Radar UI ($p = .24$).

Post-hoc Tukey tests revealed that the detection time for medium scenario difficulty was significantly lower than for both the easy ($p = .04$) and hard ($p = .0009$) scenarios (see Fig. 3). There was no significant difference in detection time between the easy and hard scenarios ($p = .41$).

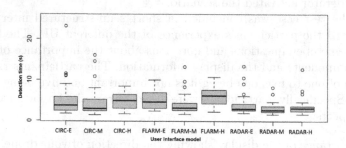

Fig. 3. Comparison of interaction models and the difficulty level of the scenarios.

4.2   Preferred Interaction Model - Questionnaire

In the questionnaire regarding the participants' opinions of the systems, the participants could report which UI model they believed best portrayed the information, fastest portrayed the information, and which UI model they overall thought worked the best for them. The result from these questions can be found in Table 2.

Table 2. Preferred UI model. The numbers in the table corresponds to how many participants selected a certain UI model.

	FLARM	Circ. HUD	Radar
Gives information best	2	16	12
Gives information fastest	4	16	10
Best system overall	2	17	11

The circular HUD was reported as the UI model which worked best for the participants. To analyze statistical differences with the UI models we used the chi-square 1-way classification test. As "overall best", showed a significant difference $\chi^2(2) = 11.4$, $p = .003$.

Chi-square 1-way classification test regarding which UI model portrayed the information best, showed a significant relation $\chi^2(2) = 10.4$, $p = .006$. Chi-square 1-way classification test regarding which UI model fastest portrayed the information, showed a significant relation $\chi^2(2) = 7.2$, $p = .03$.

4.3   User Interface Components - Questionnaire

There were dedicated questions regarding the user interface components and the display information. Participants gave a median value of four to all three UI aspects, i.e., the importance of the display (1) showing the direction of your drone and (2) the other drone, and (3) the display adjusting to the direction you are looking at, on a five-point Likert scale, with one corresponding to "it is not important" and five corresponding to "it is very important".

4.4   Semi-structured Interview

The semi-structured interview gave information consistent with that reported from the questionnaires and the detection time measurements. Common arguments in favor of the radar interaction model were that it best gave a feeling of what was forward and that it gave the most precise information of the systems. An argument for the FLARM dashboard was that it was fastest when you looked forward and it was easier to understand height than the radar system. The argument for the Circular HUD was that it was the most natural and intuitive of the systems. It was reported that it gives a good indication of where to look and then the highlight makes it easy to find the other drone. It was also reported to be chosen because it was simple and adjusts to where you are looking. All participants confirmed on having good awareness about their environment with a 360-degree view and a warning system. However, one participant added that it would take a bit more of getting used to it. More comments about each UI model are summarized in the following bullets.

FLARM

- Dashboard was cluttered and too far down.
- Hard to understand what forward is.
- It is hard to know how much you have to turn.

Circular HUD

- The entire HUD could change color to indicate how big the danger is.
- Show the other drone's direction continuously.
- Could get cluttered with multiple drones.
- Utilizes VR, whereas the other UIs do not.
- Not intuitive whether upward/downward arrows indicate other drone being forward/backward or above/below.
- The colors were misleading.

Radar

- Wish the radar was a HUD.
- Radar is harder to use since it is not a HUD and you need to turn more.
- Height (angle) was confusing and hard to utilize.
- Distance was not clear.

General Comments

- Combine angle and direction information into a 3D arrow.
- Maybe information about how big the other aircraft is or its time to contact could be displayed.

5   Discussion

As a whole, VR could be considered an interesting and valuable tool for prototyping and evaluating UAV-interaction, mainly due to the immersive user experience and the possibility of evaluating non-existing interaction technologies.

5.1   Comparative Study

Overall, the Radar UI supported the fastest detection times and the Circular HUD the second fastest times across scenarios. Since the UI is used for avoiding collisions the time it takes to discover the other drone is very important.

Moreover, differences could be observed regarding the preferred UI model. The preferred UI model was the Circular HUD, which surprisingly was not the same as the one yielding the fastest detection times i.e. Radar. Although, the Radar UI was a close second. The Circular HUD is also the most chosen system for both giving the information best and fastest. The fact that all participants believed to have a good awareness of their surroundings using a 360-degree view and a warning system is a good indication that this might be a solution to the problem that drone operators need to have a visual line of sight to their drones.

One reason for what made the Radar UI the most effective could be due to the radar interaction model providing the best feeling of what was forward and the most precise pose information of all the three suggested UIs, several participants commented on this.

Looking at the "User interface components" questionnaire we can get an idea of why the Circular HUD is popular. The most important aspect is that the system can adjust depending on where you look, i.e., the way in which it provides information about the other drone's location is adaptive to the participant's viewing direction, instead of provided in a reference frame that is fixed to the (arbitrary) orientation of the participant's drone.

5.2 Future Study

The goal of this project was not to produce a finished product but instead to explore new UI concepts to detect other aerial vehicles. Therefore, more work and research are required on this subject. The concepts presented here should be further developed. Even though the height indicators that used arrows were the preferred option, there is potential for an improved design. Using a graded number of arrows to indicate magnitude of height difference instead of color coding may, for example, be a better option, since also color-blinded drone pilots would be able to use it. A solution that allows the radar to be a HUD instead of being stationary could be a better alternative to the Circular HUD. The solution should have a way to adjust to the viewing direction of the user since this was found to be the most appreciated aspect of the UI. A risk with having the Radar as a HUD could be that it takes up a lot of the field of view. A further design space to explore is to use displays of 3D information as afforded by XR technology for designing the user interface, as suggested by some of our participants and done in air traffic control interfaces [10]. Careful evaluation is however needed to examine the depth range across which such information is usable by the operator, especially in light of depth misperception in current generation VR displays [16]. It would be important to explore in future tests the impact of a secondary task such as counting markers placed in the surrounding area or actual piloting of the drone, as it allows evaluating how well the UI design support the task of obstacle detection during more real operating conditions. In summary, the current test has revealed which aspects of the tested UIs were found valuable by the test participants, and new designs combining these value aspects should be explored, both in terms of user experience and detection performance, but also situational awareness and ultimately safety of UAV operation they afford in both lab and real-world situations.

6 Conclusion

This paper used VR to prototype remote UAV operation interfaces for detecting other aerial vehicles or objects. Three user interfaces were compared in a controlled experiment. The results showed that the Radar UI supported the fastest detection times and the Circular HUD the second fastest times across scenarios. However, the participants preferred the Circular HUD UI while the Radar UI was a close runner up. Additionally, this study implies that VR has the potential to become a useful prototyping tool to explore UAV interaction.

Acknowledgment. The authors would like to thank all participants who did the tests.

References

1. Alce, G., Hermodsson, K., Wallergård, M., Thern, L., Hadzovic, T.: A prototyping method to simulate wearable augmented reality interaction in a virtual environment-a pilot study. Int. J. Virtual Worlds Hum. Comput. Interact. **3**, 18–28 (2015)
2. Alce, G., Roszko, M., Edlund, H., Olsson, S., Svedberg, J., Wallergård, M.: [poster] ar as a user interface for the internet of things-comparing three interaction models. In: 2017 IEEE International Symposium on Mixed and Augmented Reality (ISMAR-Adjunct), pp. 81–86. IEEE (2017)
3. Alce, G., Ternblad, E.-M., Wallergård, M.: Design and evaluation of three interaction models for manipulating Internet of Things (IoT) devices in virtual reality. In: Lamas, D., Loizides, F., Nacke, L., Petrie, H., Winckler, M., Zaphiris, P. (eds.) INTERACT 2019. LNCS, vol. 11749, pp. 267–286. Springer, Cham (2019). https://doi.org/10.1007/978-3-030-29390-1_15
4. Bagassi, S., De Crescenzio, F., Piastra, S.: Augmented reality technology selection based on integrated QFD-AHP model. Int. J. Interact. Des. Manuf. (IJIDeM) **14**(1), 285–294 (2019). https://doi.org/10.1007/s12008-019-00583-6
5. Bork, F., Schnelzer, C., Eck, U., Navab, N.: Towards efficient visual guidance in limited field-of-view head-mounted displays. IEEE Trans. Vis. Comput. Graph. **24**(11), 2983–2992 (2018)
6. Davies, R.: Applications of systems design using virtual environments. In: The Handbook of Virtual Environments, pp. 1079–1100 (2002)
7. FLARM: The affordable collision avoidance technology for general aviation and UAV (2017). https://flarm.com/wp-content/uploads/man/FLARM-General-EN.pdf
8. Funk, M.: Human-drone interaction: let's get ready for flying user interfaces!. Interactions **25**(3), 78–81 (2018)
9. Garcia, J., et al.: Designing human-drone interactions with the paparazzi UAV system. In: 1st International Workshop on Human-Drone Interaction (2019)
10. Gorbunov, A.L., Nechaev, E.E.: Augmented reality technologies in air transport control systems. In: 2022 Systems of Signals Generating and Processing in the Field of on Board Communications, pp. 1–5 (2022). https://doi.org/10.1109/IEEECONF53456.2022.9744399

11. Jung, T., tom Dieck, M.C., Moorhouse, N., tom Dieck, D.: Tourists' experience of virtual reality applications. In: 2017 IEEE International Conference on Consumer Electronics (ICCE), pp. 208–210. IEEE (2017)
12. Kim, H., Gabbard, J.L., Anon, A.M., Misu, T.: Driver behavior and performance with augmented reality pedestrian collision warning: an outdoor user study. IEEE Trans. Vis. Comput. Graph. **24**(4), 1515–1524 (2018)
13. Niehorster, D.C., Li, L., Lappe, M.: The accuracy and precision of position and orientation tracking in the HTC vive virtual reality system for scientific research. i-Perception **8**(3), 2041669517708205 (2017)
14. Park, H., Kim, K.: Efficient information representation method for driver-centered AR-HUD system. In: Marcus, A. (ed.) DUXU 2013. LNCS, vol. 8014, pp. 393–400. Springer, Heidelberg (2013). https://doi.org/10.1007/978-3-642-39238-2_43
15. Santel, C.G., Gerber, P., Mehringskoetter, S., Schochlow, V., Vogt, J., Klingauf, U.: How glider pilots misread the flarm collision alerting display. Aviat. Psychol. Appl. Hum. Factors **4**(2), 86 (2014)
16. Vienne, C., Masfrand, S., Bourdin, C., Vercher, J.L.: Depth perception in virtual reality systems: effect of screen distance, environment richness and display factors. IEEE Access **8**, 29099–29110 (2020). https://doi.org/10.1109/ACCESS.2020.2972122
17. Wickens, C.D., Dempsey, G., Pringle, A., Kazansky, L., Hutka, S.: The joint tactical air controller: cognitive modeling and augmented reality HMD design. In: 20th International Symposium on Aviation Psychology, p. 163 (2019)

XR and Neurodevelopmental Disorders

Evaluating the Acceptability and Usability of a Head-Mounted Augmented Reality Approach for Autistic Children with High Support Needs

Valentin Bauer[1]($\boxtimes$), Tifanie Bouchara[1], Olivier Duris[2], Charlotte Labossière[2], Marie-Noëlle Clément[2], and Patrick Bourdot[1]

[1] Université Paris Saclay, CNRS, LISN, VENISE Team, Orsay, France
valentin.bauer@limsi.fr
[2] Association CEREP-PHYMENTIN, Day Hospital André Boulloche, Paris, France

Abstract. Virtual and Augmented Reality (VR and AR) are promising to complement practitioners' interventions with autistic children, but they mainly target the socio-emotional abilities of children with low support needs. For autistic children with high support needs, sensory-based and mediation approaches are advised with AR headsets, to keep contact with their familiar environment and their real practitioner, while VR presents risks of isolation. Yet, the acceptability and usability of AR headsets for these children remains unknown. Thus, this paper investigates the possibility to use AR headsets with Magic Bubbles, a multisensory environment designed for autistic children with high support needs, to reassure them while reinforcing the dyadic relationship with their practitioner. Drawing upon a previous design validation with 11 practitioners, acceptability and usability testings were conducted at a day hospital with 10 children with neurodevelopmental disorders and associated intellectual disability. Findings confirm a positive acceptability and usability for these children, thus validating the possibility to use Magic Bubbles with autistic children with high support needs. At last, future directions regarding the use of AR in clinical settings are outlined.

Keywords: Augmented reality · User experience · Multisensory · Autism Spectrum Disorder · Acceptability · Usability · Well-being · Children

1   Introduction

Autism Spectrum Disorder (ASD) is a neurodevelopmental condition which concerns 1% of people worldwide [23]. It is mainly characterized by social communication and interaction difficulties, restricted interests, and repetitive behaviours [1,23]. Autistic people[1] display these traits in various proportions. Some individuals have low support needs (LS) (e.g., to perform academic tasks), and

---

[1] This paper uses autism stakeholders' preferences in terms of terminology, e.g., identity first-language, with terms such as "autistic individual" [8].

others have high support needs (HS) (e.g., to perform daily tasks), being minimally verbal and with associated Intellectual Disability (ID) [23]. Recent research has largely overlooked children with HS [16], being absent from 94% of autism research published in 2016 [34]. This paper proposes to complement practitioners' interventions for children with HS through a technology-based approach.

Interventions for children with HS largely consist in reassuring the child and reinforcing the dyadic child-practitioner relationship, prior to work on other abilities (e.g., social abilities) [6,35]. To that end, mediation sensory-based interventions are common, such as *Sensory Integration Therapy* [3,37] or *Snoezelen* [21,30]. Sensory Integration Therapy seeks to train multisensory interactive processes to gradually enhance developmental abilities, with various playful sensory objects (e.g., sensory balls). Snoezelen aims at reassuring and relaxing children to gradually reinforce the dyadic relationship, with multisensory spaces often including bubble columns. It is particularly promising for children with HS [30]. Yet, practitioners can struggle to conduct such interventions, especially with children with HS [20]. Difficulties can come from a lack of resources, of flexibility of the tools and environments, time constraints, or expensive cost [20].

Practitioners often use digital tools to complement their interventions, as being individualizable, controllable [6,35], and often appealing [22]. They mainly target socio-developmental abilities through various mediums (e.g., tablet, computer, robot). Yet, such interventions lack of multisensory capabilities that are needed to work with autistic children with HS [6].

Some digitally-augmented multisensory spaces have been designed for autistic children, with successful outcomes over their well-being and the dyadic relationship [4,14,26,31,33]. Various settings were used: large spaces where physical items are augmented to trigger stimuli based on users' actions [4,14,31], a projected floor [26], or a projected screen and a Kinect camera [33]. Yet, equipment is often bespoke, bulky, or too expensive for clinical structures.

Virtual (VR) and Augmented (AR) Reality could overcome the limits of autism interventions with or without digital tools, by offering secure multisensory capabilities [12,18,25] through affordable Head-Mounted Displays (HMDs). Moreover, they allow to include all autistic children including those with HS [16]. Yet, children with HS are under-represented, as most studies focus on training socio-emotional abilities [17,25,27] which can be too advanced for them [6,9].

A previous study revealed that autism stakeholders would prefer to use AR for children with HS, in order to augment their familiar surroundings while still seeing their real practitioner, whereas VR could isolate them [6]. In particular, AR use cases should focus on reassurance and reinforcing the dyadic child-practitioner relationship [6]. Such an AR environment called *Magic Bubbles* was designed and validated in collaboration with practitioners working on a daily basis with children with HS [5].

Unknowns remain about HMD's acceptability for autistic children with HS, as their positive acceptability was mainly suggested for children with LS [7,10, 24,36]. To our knowledge, only three studies suggested a positive acceptability for individuals with HS: for twelve adults in VR [29], for five children with neurodevelopmental disorders and ID in VR [15], and for twenty children with neurodevelopmental disorders and ID in AR [2]. To complement them, this paper addresses three research questions:

1. Could autistic children with HS accept and use *Magic Bubbles* AR environment?
2. Could autistic children with HS get engaged with *Magic Bubbles* AR environment while still communicating with others?
3. Could autistic children with HS get secure when using *Magic Bubbles* AR environment?

To examine these three research questions, our team of researchers, coming both from the human-computer interaction field and the clinical field (two psychologists and one psychiatrist) conducted a study with 10 autistic children with HS, or similar traits, i.e., neurodevelopmental disorders and associated ID. Thus, this study extends a previous study that was only conducted with 11 practitioners as part of the design process of *Magic Bubbles* AR environment to ensure its acceptability among the clinical team [5]. After presenting the methodology that was used, the findings will be outlined, and then discussed.

2 Method

2.1 Participants

Two psychologists from our research team recruited 10 children with neurodevelopmental disorders and associated ID among the patients of the day hospital André Boulloche, in agreement with the clinical team. They include six boys and four girls, from 11 to 14 (MA:12.5, SD:0.98). Eight were minimally verbal and two were non-verbal. All children displayed significant intellectual disability, their Intellectual Quotient (IQ) ranging from 50 to 70. Four children had already experienced VR during cultural outings. None had experienced AR. The low number of children is imposed by the following inclusion criteria: children had to display a neurodevelopmental condition according to the ICD-10 [43], an associated ID, not display risks of epilepsy, and be at least 11 years old for using HMDs in line with recent AR/VR studies [2,15,24,28]. As this low number is common in AR/VR studies for autism, mainly because this population is hard-to-reach [18,25], it was deemed suitable to investigate our research questions. Moreover, according to the psychologists, the 3:2 male to female ratio among the recruited children would not influence the findings. Children's profiles are detailed in Table 1.

2.2 HMD-Based AR Environment Tested with Children

Magic Bubbles is a multisensory HMD-based AR environment which aims at complementing common practitioners' interventions for autistic children with HS, such as Snoezelen or Sensory Integration Therapy. The design process was

Table 1. Profiles of the children who participated to the study. M/F stands for Male/Female. IQ stands for intellectual quotient.

ID	M/F	Age	Condition (ICD-10)	IQ
1	M	13	Atypical autism (F841)	50< IQ<70
4	F	11	Other childhood disintegrative disorder (F843)	50< IQ<70
5	M	13	Other pervasive developmental disorders (F84.8)	50< IQ<70
6	M	13	Pervasive developmental disorder, unspecified (F849)	50< IQ<70
7	M	13	Pervasive developmental disorder, unspecified (F849)	50< IQ<70
8	M	14	Pervasive developmental disorder, unspecified (F849)	50< IQ<70
9	F	12	Mixed disorder of conduct and emotions, unspecified (F929)	50< IQ<70
14	F	12	Mixed specific developmental disorders (F83)	50< IQ<70
16	F	13	Atypical autism (F841)	50< IQ<70
17	M	11	Autistic disorder (F840)	50< IQ<70

first informed by 34 interviews with autism stakeholders [6], as suggested by Parsons et al. [32]'s research agenda. The design was then adapted for a day hospital context in collaboration with two psychologists, and validated through testings with 11 practitioners [5]. This subsection only summarizes the main features of *Magic Bubbles*, as a previous paper presents its full description [5].

Children can explore an augmented interaction space, while perceiving their practitioner, and interacting with audio, visuals, and controllers' vibrations. Stimuli are presented through common appealing objects (e.g., bubble columns) drawing upon common interventions. Stimuli are generic (e.g., bubbles) or individualized (e.g., music). Practitioners can prompt exploration and shared play by standing physically close to the child while perceiving what they see and hear through a screen monitor. The design is presented on Fig. 1.

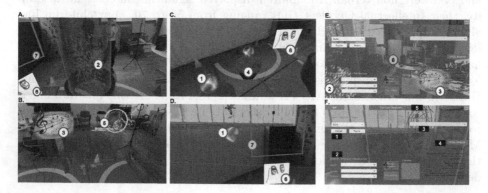

Fig. 1. Design of *Magic Bubbles* – Content: 1 Bubble; 2 Bubble column; 3 Panel; 4 Water pond; 5 Music bubble; 6 Image panel; 7 Drawing panel; 8 Recording bubble – Practitioner's UI (E, F): 1 Add/Remove objects; 2 Trigger stimuli; 3 Add/Remove feedback; 4 Show contextual information; 5 Show the UI (these images come from [5]).

Two conditions exist: spectator and actor. When spectator, the child can move in space without interacting with objects, but the practitioner can trigger all stimuli. When actor, the child can move and interact with everything.

Augmentation is presented through an AR see-through setup, by using a Zed-Mini camera plugged onto a HTC Vive Pro HMD, that "captures a live feed of the real environment, and then makes it visible inside the HMD, supplemented by virtual objects" [5]. Two HTC Vive controllers are used, as well as four Vive lighthouse outside-in tracking systems.

2.3 Development of the Semi-structured Questionnaire

To assess the experience of autistic children who cannot complete self-report questionnaires according to the psychologists, we had to build a new questionnaire that could be filled by their respective practitioners, as in Aruanno et al. [2]'s study. Hence, a two-part semi-directed questionnaire was devised to be filled by the practitioner in 5 to 10 min at the end of every child's AR session. Most questions use 1–5 likert scales, apart from questions addressing agency and engagement that use 1–7 likert scales, as drawing upon questionnaires with such scales [38,42]. Practitioners can write additional details if necessary.

In the first part, six questions address the child's state, drawing upon stakeholders' interviews [6]. Question 1 (Q1) and Q2 ask if the child was anxious and tired prior to start, and Q3 and Q4 ask the same questions about the end. Q5 asks if the child got resourced and Q6 if they could start another activity at the end. As the questionnaire has to be filled in 10 min maximum so that practitioners can complete it, these questions intend to be quickly answered, and to only provide an overall picture of the child's state. Yet, they seek to collect key elements by relying on psychologists' expertise in autism and their knowledge of these children to integrate multiple aspects in order to provide a representative answer for each question.

In the second part, nineteen questions address the acceptability, usability, control, presence, engagement, and social interaction, inspired from questionnaires [11,19,38,42], studies investigating the use of digital tools for autism [2,14,15], and interviews with stakeholders [6]. First, three questions focus on acceptability [2,15], about: the easiness to wear the HMD (Q7), the annoyance due to wearing/removing it (Q8), and cybersickness' symptoms (e.g., nausea, oculomotor symptoms, disorientation)(Q9). Then six questions address usability [6,11,42], about: the platform's complexity (Q10), the amount of information (Q11), the need for support (Q12), the confidence (Q13) and easiness (Q14) when using the system, and the ability to interact and to move at the end (Q15). Then, agency is questioned [42] regarding the ability to identify stimuli (Q16), anticipate reactions (Q17), or actively control the environment (Q18). After that, presence is questioned [2,38] about: the understanding of real versus virtual (Q19), the real-world awareness (Q20), the feeling of being captivated (Q21), and the consistency of the experience with respect to their usual real-world experience (Q22). Then engagement is addressed [2], about fun (Q23), and involvement (Q24). After that, the level of communication is questioned [14] (Q25), and practitioners can add something if needed (Q26).

2.4 Procedure

All procedures were approved by *Poléthis* Ethics Research Committee of Paris-Saclay University under reference 226.

Before the Experiment. A psychiatrist explained the protocol to the child's legal tutors and collected their informed consent. Indeed, children were unable to do it by themselves according to the clinical team. As this study did not assess the differences induced by the actor and spectator conditions (see Subsect. 2.2), practitioners affected children to each condition depending on their common interventions, and if they were mainly passive or active. Thus, ID4 and ID9 were affected to the spectator condition, and the others to the actor condition.

During the Experiment. The child tested the AR environment in a large room of the day hospital which is normally used for sensory-based activities. Four investigators were always present: two psychologists, one investigator being here for technical support, and one psychology intern. The child's educator could also come for reassurance or if interested, following common clinical practices. Sessions lasted between 5 min (minimum) and 20 min (maximum), depending on the child's acceptability, if they wanted to stop, or on practitioners' perception of their experience. Due to day hospital's constraints, unexpected events could impact the session (e.g., child being late as coming from the infirmary). Psychologists were used to the AR platform when starting the testings, as they participated to the AR design process beforehand [5]. Several sessions with different children were successively conducted, spaced by a 15-minute break to clean the equipment and air the room according to COVID security rules. Equipment was mounted (20 min) and dismounted (15 min) before and after all sessions.

At the session's beginning, psychologists introduced the child to the AR system and invited them to wear the HMD. Then, children experienced a free-play time, during which practitioners could interact with them (i.e., verbally or non-verbally) while monitoring what they perceived through the screen. Children were never forced to wear the HMD, and could remove/wear it at will. Session could end up in two ways: if children expressed that they wanted to stop (e.g., verbally, or by removing the HMD), or if time ran out. In this second case, practitioners warned that the session would end in one minute (verbally, and by triggering a gong sound in AR) and proposed to do one last action. After removing the HMD (by themselves or with practitioners' support), psychologists invited children to make a real drawing with a sheet of paper and pencils. Children only drew if they wanted to.

After the Experiment. After the child left, psychologists completed a semi-direction questionnaire (presented in Subsect. 2.3). Then, we took notes to summarize the session's unfolding, by paying attention to critical incidents (e.g., unusual events). After the sessions of the six first children, to elicit more insights, semi-directed focus group interviews were added and conducted by the first author with the two psychologists and the intern to debrief about the sessions. They happened right after the sessions were conducted. The interviews with the practitioners relied on three main questions, asking if the child had fun, if they seemed to be reassured, and if they were ready to start other tasks when leaving.

2.5 Data Collection

To assess children's experiences, multiple data sources were used to mitigate the bias due to each source. Data collected include: the semi-structured questionnaire, semi-directed interviews, first author's notes, and three video recordings (two cameras from different angles and the child's view). Moreover, efforts were made to get the child's perspective: by collecting their drawings, as suggested by Spiel et al. [40]'s study about autistic children's experiences with technology, and by filling the questionnaire while asking questions to the child, as in Aruanno et al. [2]'s study. Yet, only ID16 accepted to draw and only ID7 could answer questions. Thus, data collected mainly accounted for practitioners' perspective. In addition to that, we measured the time during which children wore the HMD. Collecting physiological data was also considered (e.g., heart rate) but abandoned, as the biosensors could hinder children's experience according to the psychologists. All data were anonymized by affecting identifiers to the children (see Table 1).

2.6 Data Analysis

The first author transcribed the data collected. This process allowed to familiarize with it, to ask the psychologists for clarifications, or to check their ratings when not matching their comments. To do so, psychologists looked at the videos and made corrections when appropriate. Then, two main analytic stages were conducted in parallel, by different researchers, and with different methods, to mitigate potential biases. First, questionnaire's answers were analysed quantitatively by the first author, while considering practitioners' comments. Second, the interviews, notes, and videos were analyzed qualitatively. The first author analyzed the notes and interviews, and two other authors who are also clinical psychologists analyzed the videos. To do so, deductive content analysis was mainly used, complemented by inductive content analysis [13]. The two main analytic stages are detailed below.

Analyzing the Semi-directed Questionnaire. Descriptive statistics were used to analyze the questionnaire's answers, as more advanced statistics were not meaningful with respect to the low number of participants. Figures 2 and 3 respectively display the findings related to the user experience's categories (e.g., acceptability, usability), and to the evolution of the child's state between the beginning and the end of sessions. Findings are presented with respect to practitioners' comments, through different paragraphs accounting for the different categories (see Subsect. 3.1). Moreover, an additional paragraph accounts for critical incidents that appeared from practitioners' comments. Questions about the feeling of presence were not analyzed, as not related to the current research objectives. They will be evaluated in a future paper.

Analyzing the Notes, Interviews and Videos. Deductive content analysis was mainly used to analyze the data with respect to the questionnaires' categories. The goal was to confirm and draw comparisons with the questionnaires' findings, as well as to gather further insights about the categories being assessed. To complement this approach, inductive content analysis was used, by constructing new categories from the data.

The first author analyzed the interviews and notes by doing open coding, with the data analysis software called $MaxQDA^2$ To mitigate potential biases, constant comparison techniques were used to compare the initial data with the phrasings and categories that were gradually constructed. The psychologists analyzed the videos, based on their clinical expertise, as in previous studies [15]. The qualitative analysis process stopped when reaching data saturation. Findings were finally compared, and presented together in Subsect. 3.2.

3 Findings

Findings are presented in two subsections, accounting for the two main analytic stages that were used. First, questionnaires' answers are presented. Then, findings from the video observations, notes and interviews are presented. The times during which children wore the HMD are not presented as they happened to be unusable. Indeed, practitioners often wore the headset during sessions to support children's acceptability, and children often worn and removed the HMD multiple times, making it impossible to collect precise data.

3.1 Findings from the Semi-directed Questionnaire

Answers about the child's experience are first presented (Q7–Q16, Q23–25) (see Fig. 2), and followed by answers about the child's state (Q1–Q6) (see Fig. 3). Q17 and Q18 were removed as unanswered for most children. Indeed, practitioners deemed them too advanced for this discovery session, and thus impossible to answer. At last, critical incidents are presented.

---

[2] MaxQDA software: https://www.maxqda.com/.

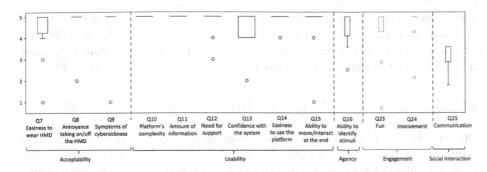

Fig. 2. Questionnaire's answers regarding the acceptability, usability, agency, engagement, and social interaction, for the 10 children with neurodevelopmental disorders and intellectual disability who tested *Magic Bubbles*. Q16, Q23, Q24 were displayed on 1–5 scales rather than 1–7 scales for enhanced readability. Bars represent the median, rectangles represent the interquartile range (IQR) (50% of the sample's values), and circles represent outliers.

Acceptability. Most children easily accepted the HMD (Q7): seven very easily (5/5) and ID9 easily (4/5). Among them, ID8 wore it nearly alone, ID4 played to wear/remove it, and ID16 expressed a slight discomfort that was not precisely identified. Yet, ID6 had some difficulties (3/5), requiring support and preferring the HMD to be a bit unscrewed. ID17 wore it for a very short time (1/5), which is normal as he usually needs time to get used to new elements. Seven children had no discomfort (Q8–5/5), contrary to ID6 and ID8 (4/5). Indeed, ID16 removed the HMD after six minutes, and ID8 was frustrated to spend so much time to adjust it. Seven children did not experience cybersickness (Q9–5/5), but ID5 said that the image was "blurry" at the start. While no answer was given for ID6, he did not have a negative experience but looked surprised after removing the HMD. ID9 had cybersickness (1/5) and said that the image was blurry. Blurry images could be perceived due to the HMD not being screwed enough, and point at the difficulty to correctly adjust the HMD with such children.

Usability. *Magic Bubbles*' complexity (Q10) was adapted to all children (5/5), and not mentioned for ID17 as he only wore it for a very short time. The psychologists advised using more complexity for three children, to not induce boredom over time (ID1), and for the spectator condition: "if actor, ID4 would have stayed longer". The amount of information (Q11) suited all children (5/5), but adding features was suggested for two of them. Most children required little practitioners' support (Q12): none for seven (5/5), some verbal reassurance for ID14 (4/5), and moderate for ID16 (3/5). Most children were confident (Q12): five entirely (5/5) and two nearly entirely (4/5). ID6 easily explored but no rating was given. Yet, ID9 was scared (1/5), but practitioners said that she expected to be scared when entering. Moreover, she may have been distressed due to feeling watched, and to not controlling the environment due to the spectator condition. Eight children very easily used the system (Q13-5/5), and ID16 easily used it (4/5). Moreover, ID1 was "immersed and discovered everything alone", and ID8 "did not move but everything was at arm length". At the end, apart from ID9, most children interacted well (Q14): totally for seven (5/5), or well for ID7 (4/5).

Agency. Most children who wore the HMD could identify the stimuli (Q16): five with great ease (7/7), and ID1 (6/7) and ID16 (5/7) with ease. In particular, ID6 actively switch off the music when wanting to. Though, practitioners were unsure about ID4's ability to identify stimuli (3.5/7), as focusing a lot on the music and not exploring much. No answer was provided for ID9 who got worried.

Engagement. Apart from the ID9 who got worried, most children had fun (Q23): seven a lot (7/7) and ID4 nearly a lot (6/7). ID1 was not amused but relaxed (4/7). About involvement (Q24), apart from ID9 (3/7), most children were involved, whether entirely for seven (7/7) or nearly entirely (6/7).

Social Interaction. Most children communicated with the adults (Q25): five a lot (5/5) (including ID17 who wore the HMD for a short time), and three moderately (4/5). In particular, ID4 interacted more than usual with people around (e.g., practitioners were struck when she asked them to dance together). ID14 also initiated shared play by giving the HMD to the practitioners. Moreover, ID17 communicated through the monitor while the practitioner was wearing the HMD. At last, ID1 (3/5) and ID6 (2.5/5) also communicated but non-verbally, maybe because not hearing well what practitioners said with the HMD.

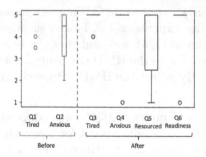

Fig. 3. Questionnaires' answers about children's state. Bars represent the median, rectangles represent the interquartile range (IQR) (50% of the sample's values), and circles represent outliers. (**A**). Evolution of tiredness and anxiousness between the beginning and the end., (**B**) Being resourced at the end and ready to start another activity.

Evolution of the Child's State. When starting, all children were in a good physical state, apart from ID17 who was tired (Q1–4/5) and ID9 (Q1–2.5/5). Six children were not anxious (Q2): five not at all (5/5) and ID17 slightly (4/5). Yet, four children were a bit worried: ID16 asked what would happen (3.5/5), ID6 if "it was a trap" (3/5), ID14 displayed apprehension (2.5/5), and ID9 asked if practitioners would "frighten her" (2/5). At the end, no child was tired (Q3–5/5), and nine children were not anxious (Q4–5/5). Hence, four children got secure (ID6, ID14, ID16, ID17). Yet, ID9 got scared (1/5) due to acceptability issues: running out of the room and throwing the HMD. Six children got resourced (Q5–5/5), and two were as before (2.5/5). Practitioners highlighted that ID7 got calmer even if anxious the day before. At last, apart from ID9 (1/5), most children were ready to start another activity when leaving (Q6): seven entirely (5/5), and two with no answer (indicating no detrimental effects).

Critical Incidents. Psychologists mitigated the fact that ID9 ran out by evoking her condition and impulsiveness. Although ID6 was slightly worried when starting, he asked to come back every week. This request is uncommon for him and accounts for his engagement. ID7 could "unload" when playing while being in control (see Fig. 5B), which is uncommon for him. ID7, ID14 and ID17, socially interacted more than usual: ID7 kept eye contact with the adults, ID14 initiated shared play by giving them the HMD (see Fig. 5E), and ID17 interacted threw the screen. At last, ID14 went on the floor when first wearing the HMD, and ID5 stepped over the column's border to go inside it (see Fig. 5D).

3.2 Findings from the Interviews, Notes, and Observations

Findings coming from the deductive content analysis are first presented. Then, three categories that were built through the inductive content analysis are presented: *Real vs. Virtual*, *Exploration of the Body and Space*, and *New Hypothesis*.

Acceptability. All children could wear the HMD with practitioners' support. Only ID9 got very anxious, and quickly asked to stop. However, she was already anxious when entering the room. Four children perceived a slight discomfort, due to the HMD being too tight, heavy, or to feeling hot. Half of the children emphasized the institutional aspect, asking questions about the other children who participated. Five children described their experience as "weird" but pleasant. Yet, some children displayed some apprehension: three children only interacted "at arm length", not daring to move too much, and two children asked the practitioners to wear the HMD before them for reassurance. Doing so, they observed the practitioners while looking at what they saw through the monitor.

Usability. Eight children easily used the equipment. For instance, ID1 was "immersed and discovered everything alone". Yet, ID14 and ID16 required a lot of guidance. As psychologists said: "We proposed her [ID14] to stand up [...]. Then she held Olivier's arm [one practitioner] to move in space, with still some difficulties", or "I made her [ID16] try things". ID16 verbally confirmed that she preferred to explore with Olivier, and even drew herself next to him (see Fig. 4). Children were not bothered by some bugs that happened, even if possibly slowing down their discovery process. The microphone bubble was hard to use, as requiring to perform two actions (touch then speak). Eight children respected the limits of the AR space, and two went beyond to observe the limits of the real room. Five children understood that the vibrations came from the controllers. ID4 could explore alone although she is usually very passive.

Fig. 4. Drawing that ID16 made, representing herself next to the practitioner.

Agency. While three children enjoyed the controllers' vibrations, other children were more interested in the audiovisual stimuli. Three children particularly enjoyed one stimulus: the bubble column (ID1), the music (ID4), and the music panel (ID7). They seemed to use it to: get secure, and/or to refocus on their body experiences after exploring. All children looked at their bodies (mainly their hands) and eight children went through virtual elements with their head and hands to see them disappear.

Engagement. Eight children were involved and enjoyed the experience. For instance, ID7 sang, laughed, or danced while touching the virtual panels, although being in a bad state the day before according to the practitioners. These children focused on their inner experiences (little social interaction), which is a significant clinical finding according to practitioners. Seven children verbally expressed their joy, asking to come back the week after. Surprisingly, ID1 said that he had fun, but that he did not want to come back the week after. ID9 expressed anxiety.

Social Interaction. All children interacted with the adults, but eight had inner experiences. Indeed, these eight children mainly asked questions when requiring support or answered practitioners' questions. Yet, some of them included practitioners in their experience: ID1 pointed at them with the controllers, or ID8 described everything aloud. At last, two children were more interested in the other rather than in technology (ID4, ID17). In particular, ID17 interacted with practitioners through the screen, and ID14 interacted "without disappearing in the relationship with the adult", which is uncommon for her.

Evolution of the Child's State. Practitioners did not comment on this evolution, except for ID9 who got worried. Yet, they highlighted that the setting was *holding* for four children. This clinical concept is used to describe a supportive environment for generating and supporting interactions between the child and the practitioner [41]. Indeed, these four children got more secure than usual: ID1 got very calm, ID4 got calm even if several adults surrounded her, ID7 kept in control while being excited, and ID14 could socially interact.

Real Versus Virtual. Five children questioned the differences between real and virtual. They asked if the physical elements in the room were real, and if the virtual elements could have an impact on the adults being in the room. Three children also experienced a possible feeling of presence, i.e., feeling of being here. Indeed, ID8 asked if the water from the column could go over the floor, ID6 hit the ponds with his feet (see Fig. 5A), and ID5 stepped over the border of the column (see Fig. 5D).

Exploration of the Body and Space. Seven children performed gentler gestures than usual, and three children mainly focused on one stimulus. Children focused on their body image: all looked at their hands, ID4 asked to look at herself in the mirror, ID5 asked to be photographed, and ID16 drew herself with the practitioner on her side. Five children made uncommon movements: softer, more hesitant, or, conversely, dancing more for ID16. Four children adopted a different gait. Indeed, three of them lied on the floor: ID4 possibly due to anxiety, while the two others may have done it to calmly explore their body and the AR space. Moreover, ID5 behaved like a robot when entering and leaving.

New Hypothesis. Practitioners raised four new hypothesis about using AR for children with neurodevelopmental disorders and associated ID. First, HMD could help to make longer eye contacts. This was raised after ID6 made long eye contacts. Second, AR could help to better understand the others' mental states, by perceiving through the monitor the practitioner's AR view. Indeed, ID17 could understand that the screen represented the practitioner' view. Third, AR could enhance body awareness. Indeed, ID14 and ID16 socially interacted without "disappearing", although uncommon for them. At that, adjusting the proportion between virtual and real elements could prompt reassurance, especially regarding the body presence of the others. This was raised after ID7 kept in control while being excited, although uncommon for him.

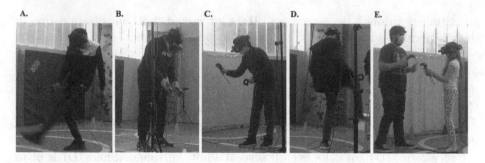

Fig. 5. Photographs of critical incidents for four children, (A) ID6 hitting a pond with his foot, (B) ID7 unloading on the music panel while keeping in control, (C) ID8 trying . to write his name on the drawing panel, (D) ID5 stepping over the border of the column, (E) ID14 giving the controller to the practitioner after proposing him to test the HMD.

4   Discussion

This paper explored the use of the HMD-based AR environment *Magic Bubbles* in a day hospital setting with ten children with autism and HS, or neurodevelopmental disorders and associated ID. As little was known so far about how these children would react when exposed to HMD-based VR/AR [7,10,24,36], the paper has four main contributions. Three correspond to the three research questions, about acceptability and usability (RQ1), engagement (RQ2), and reassurance (RQ3), and one appeared from the data analysis process. First, most children displayed positive acceptability and usability (RQ1). The inductive analysis process also showed that children explored two aspects in addition to the virtual interactions: the difference between real and virtual elements and the shift in their self perception. Second, children were engaged with an inner experience, but still communicated (RQ2). Third, apart from ID9 who experienced cybersickness, four children got more secure, and the others were in the same state after than before the experience (RQ3). At last, four new hypothesis emerged in relation to practitioners' concerns which deserve future investigation. The validation of the three research questions prompt to conduct future testings with *Magic Bubbles* during a longer period with autistic children with HS. After presenting the findings related to the three research questions, limitations and future perspectives are drawn, which include the new hypothesis that emerged.

4.1   Accepting and Using *Magic Bubbles*

All children accepted to wear the HMD, as in previous VR [15,29] and AR [2] studies. To that end, they required practitioners' support. For instance, two children asked practitioners to wear the HMD before them for reassurance, as in Garzotto et al. [15]'s study where two out of five children made the same request. In our study, three children experienced discomfort, including cybersickness for one of them. This finding echoes Newbutt et al. [29]'s findings, where four out of twenty-nine participants felt unwell and had to stop. In our study, despite their ID and limited verbal abilities, most children could express when feeling unwell. Though, they could hardly express if the HMD was correctly adjusted. This finding calls for devising future protocols to minimize potential adverse affects with HMDs for autistic children with HS, thus complementing Schmidt et al. [36]'s process-model that was mainly designed for autism with LS. At last, the methods for measuring acceptability through caregivers vary between previous studies [2,15], and between our study and previous studies, thus making definitions of acceptability to vary. To make sure that we actually measured acceptability features and not other features (e.g., engagement), future research should focus on designing new standardized acceptability and usability measures for children with neurodevelopmental disorders and ID that would allow to collect their views.

Most children easily used *Magic Bubbles*, apart from ID9 due to acceptability issues and ID17 who wore the HMD for a very short time. *Magic Bubbles* was well adapted with respect to children's sensorimotor and understanding abilities. For instance, despite understanding difficulties, ID7 could explore and have fun. Then, practitioners supported children during their discovery, as in [2,15]. Guidance was individualized, and ranged from low levels (e.g., for ID1) to moderate levels (e.g., ID16 needed physical guidance). Our positive acceptability and usability findings complement the findings from previous HMD-based studies conducted with autistic individuals with HS [2,15,29].

Children explored three main aspects: virtual interactions, real versus virtual elements, and self perception. First, they explored the virtual interactions alone or with practitioners' support. To do so, they often displayed uncommon behaviours: seven used gentler gestures than usual, and three mainly focused on one stimulus. This insight calls for more research to better understand these behaviours. In particular, focusing on one stimulus may be linked with self-regulation strategies during the discovery process (to not get overwhelmed by too many information). Hence, parallels could be drawn with VR/AR derivatives of repetitive behaviours that children often use to get resourced, that previous research already suggested to investigate [6]. Gentler behaviours may also be linked with a shift in their self perception. Second, children used various strategies to understand the difference between real and virtual elements. Future research should examine their understanding of real versus virtual, with respect to these various strategies and children's profiles. At last, children were highly interested in their self perception (e.g., looking at their hands). This unexpected insight accounts for a shift in self perception that deserves more investigation.

4.2 Communicating with Practitioners

All children socially interacted with the adults. Yet, most of them displayed inner experiences. For instance, ID1 and ID6 mainly communicated non-verbally, possibly to remain in the virtual environment (ID1, ID6), or "to benefit from the effect of immersion", as practitioners said (ID1). Moreover, three children displayed unusual social interaction behaviors. First, ID4 and ID17 were more interested in the other than in technology (e.g., ID4 communicated more than usual). Then, ID14 socially interacted without "disappearing" and drew herself next to a practitioner (see Fig. 4). These experiences highlight the social interaction potential of *Magic Bubbles*, when used with practitioners in a clinical setting. This finding contradicts potential AR risks of isolation [7], that practitioners can be afraid of when working with autistic children with HS [5].

4.3 Getting Resourced

All children who wore the HMD were engaged, apart from ID9 due to acceptability issues. Most children had fun, and ID1 got relaxed. These findings confirm the positive results that were observed in previous HMD-based VR [29] and AR [2] studies. In our study, seven children also asked to come back the week after. Two children displayed unexpected behaviours accounting for their engagement: ID14 drew the shared experience and ID16 danced a lot. Moreover, *Magic Bubbles* enabled ID4 to be resourced enough to communicate. Furthermore, children who were engaged were still in control of their actions. In particular, ID7 could "unload" without being over-aroused, which is unusual for him. Hence, practitioners said that *Magic Bubbles* was *holding* [41], i.e., a supportive environment for generating and supporting interactions between the child and the practitioner. Indeed, four children got more secure. Thus, such HMD-based AR approaches are promising to complement clinical interventions for children with HS. At last, since some children felt immersed, future studies should examine if reinforcing the feeling of immersion could also reinforce this *holding* potential.

4.4 Limitations and Future Perspectives

As this field study was conducted in a clinical setting, the environment could not be entirely controlled which limits the generalization of the findings. For instance, children's behaviours may have been influenced by external noise (children shouting in the corridors). Yet, conducting the same experience in a laboratory setting would be impossible, as changing children's environment could disturb them and induce anxiety [6]. Hence, new methods must be devised to guarantee the ecological validity of AR autism research, by conducting field studies in clinical settings while precisely controlling specific environmental aspects. To that end, some implicit measures could be used if relevant for the study and the children (e.g., number of interactions). Moreover, physiological data could also be used (e.g., skin conductance) if the clinical team and/or children's relatives deemed that biosensors could be well accepted, even if in our study the psychologists thought that they would not have been accepted by these children. In that case, analyzing physiological data would require to compare it with psychologists' insights, so that to understand the parameters being representative of children's behaviours. Although this approach remains under-used in AR/VR studies [18], it represents promising research avenues [39]. The second limitation is due to the fact that the results mainly account for practitioners' perspective. Indeed, children's limited verbal abilities prevented from directly getting their views, despite efforts that were made (e.g., using drawings). Future research should further investigate how to collect the perspective of autistic children with HS, by devising methodologies as previously proposed by Spiel et al. [40].

Four hypothesis emerged that deserve more investigation. First, HMD could allow children with neurodevelopmental disorders and associated ID to make longer eye contacts, as not direct but mediated through AR. Second, AR could prompt the understanding of the others' mental states for autistic children with HS, by perceiving through the monitor the practitioner's AR view. Third, AR could enhance body awareness for children with neurodevelopmental and associated ID. Fourth, adjusting and individualizing the proportion between virtual and real elements, in particular regarding the body presence of others, could prompt reassurance for these children. This fourth hypothesis extends the findings from previous studies, suggesting to first work in VR and then go to AR, so that to gradually fade prompts while encouraging the generalization of the skills learned [6]. Moreover, creating use cases as proposed in the last hypothesis could also help to test the other hypothesis.

Acknowledgements. The authors would like to thank the children who participated to this research and their families, as well as the clinical team of the day hospital André Boulloche for their support. This work is part of the AudioXR4TSA project, funded by the DIM RFSI Ile de France. This work was also supported by French government funding managed by the National Research Agency under the Investments for the Future program (PIA) under grant ANR-21-ESRE-0030/CONTINUUM.

References

1. American psychiatric association: diagnostic and statistical manual of mental disorders. American Psychiatric Association, Arlington, 5th edn. (2013). https://doi.org/10.1176/appi.books.9780890425596
2. Aruanno, B., Garzotto, F., Torelli, E., Vona, F.: HoloLearn: wearable mixed reality for people with neurodevelopmental disorders (NDD). In: Proceedings of the 20th International ACM SIGACCESS Conference on Computers and Accessibility, pp. 40–51. ACM, Galway, Ireland, October 2018. https://doi.org/10.1145/3234695.3236351
3. Ayres, A.J.: Sensory Integration and Learning Disorders. Western Psychological Services, Los Angeles (1972)
4. Basadonne, I., Cristofolini, M., Mucchi, I., Recla, F., Bentenuto, A., Zanella, N.: Working on cognitive functions in a fully digitalized multisensory interactive room: a new approach for intervention in autism spectrum disorders. Brain Sci. **11**(11), 1459 (2021). https://doi.org/10.3390/brainsci11111459
5. Bauer, V., Bouchara, T., Bourdot, P.: Designing an extended reality application to expand clinic-based sensory strategies for autistic children requiring substantial support: participation of practitioners. In: IEEE International Symposium on Mixed and Augmented Reality Adjunct (ISMAR-Adjunct), vol. 1, pp. 254–259 (2021). https://doi.org/10.1109/ISMAR-Adjunct54149.2021.00059
6. Bauer, V., Bouchara, T., Bourdot, P.: Extended reality guidelines for supporting autism interventions based on stakeholders' needs. J. Autism Dev. Disord. (2022). https://doi.org/10.1007/s10803-022-05447-9

7. Berenguer, C., Baixauli, I., Gómez, S., Andrés, M.D.E.P., De Stasio, S.: Exploring the impact of augmented reality in children and adolescents with autism spectrum disorder: a systematic review. Int. J. Environ. Res. Public Health **17**(17), 6143 (2020). https://doi.org/10.3390/ijerph17176143

8. Bottema-Beutel, K., Kapp, S.K., Lester, J.N., Sasson, N.J., Hand, B.N.: Avoiding Ableist language: suggestions for autism researchers. Autism Adulthood **3**(1), 18–29 (2021). https://doi.org/10.1089/aut.2020.0014

9. Bozgeyikli, L., Raij, A., Katkoori, S., Alqasemi, R.: A survey on virtual reality for individuals with autism spectrum disorder: design considerations. IEEE Trans. Learn. Technol. **11**(2), 133–151 (2018). https://doi.org/10.1109/TLT.2017.2739747

10. Bradley, R., Newbutt, N.: Autism and virtual reality head-mounted displays: a state of the art systematic review. J. Enabling Technol. **12**(3), 101–113 (2018). https://doi.org/10.1108/JET-01-2018-0004

11. Brooke, J.: SUS-A Quick and Dirty Usability Scale. Usability evaluation in industry. CRC Press, Boca Raton, June 1996. ISBN: 9780748404605

12. Dechsling, A., et al.: Virtual reality and naturalistic developmental behavioral interventions for children with autism spectrum disorder. Res. Dev. Disabil. **111**, 103885 (2021). https://doi.org/10.1016/j.ridd.2021.103885

13. Elo, S., Kyngäs, H.: The qualitative content analysis process. J. Adv. Nurs. **62**(1), 107–115 (2008). https://doi.org/10.1111/j.1365-2648.2007.04569.x

14. Garzotto, F., Gelsomini, M.: Magic room: a smart space for children with neurodevelopmental disorder. IEEE Pervasive Comput. **17**(1), 38–48 (2018). https://doi.org/10.1109/MPRV.2018.011591060

15. Garzotto, F., Gelsomini, M., Occhiuto, D., Matarazzo, V., Messina, N.: Wearable immersive virtual reality for children with disability: a case study. In: Proceedings of the 2017 Conference on Interaction Design and Children - IDC 2017, pp. 478–483. ACM, Stanford, CA, USA, June 2017. https://doi.org/10.1145/3078072.3084312

16. Happé, F., Frith, U.: Annual research review: looking back to look forward - changes in the concept of autism and implications for future research. J. Child Psychol. Psychiatry **61**(3), 218–232 (2020). https://doi.org/10.1111/jcpp.13176

17. Herrero, J.F., Lorenzo, G.: An immersive virtual reality educational intervention on people with autism spectrum disorders (ASD) for the development of communication skills and problem solving. Educ. Inf. Technol. **25**(3), 1689–1722 (2019). https://doi.org/10.1007/s10639-019-10050-0

18. Karami, B., Koushki, R., Arabgol, F., Rahmani, M., Vahabie, A.H.: Effectiveness of virtual/Augmented reality-based therapeutic interventions on individuals with autism spectrum disorder: a comprehensive meta-analysis. Front. Psychiatry **12**, 665326 (2021). https://doi.org/10.3389/fpsyt.2021.665326

19. Kennedy, R.S., Lane, N.E., Berbaum, K.S., Lilienthal, M.G.: Simulator sickness questionnaire: an enhanced method for quantifying simulator sickness. Int. J. Aviat. Psychol. **3**(3), 203–220 (1993). https://doi.org/10.1207/s15327108ijap0303_3

20. Kouo, J.L., Kouo, T.S.: A scoping review of targeted interventions and training to facilitate medical encounters for school-aged patients with an autism spectrum disorder. J. Autism Dev. Disord. **51**(8), 2829–2851 (2020). https://doi.org/10.1007/s10803-020-04716-9

21. Lancioni, G.E., Cuvo, A.J., O'Reilly, M.F.: Snoezelen: an overview of research with people with developmental disabilities and dementia. Disabil. Rehabil. **24**(4), 175–184 (2002). https://doi.org/10.1080/09638280110074911

22. Laurie, M.H., Warreyn, P., Uriarte, B.V., Boonen, C., Fletcher-Watson, S.: An international survey of parental attitudes to technology use by their autistic children at home. J. Autism Dev. Disord. **49**(4), 1517–1530 (2018). https://doi.org/10.1007/s10803-018-3798-0

23. Lord, C., et al.: Autism spectrum disorder. Nat. Rev. Dis. Prim. **6**(1), 5 (2020). https://doi.org/10.1038/s41572-019-0138-4

24. Malihi, M., Nguyen, J., Cardy, R.E., Eldon, S., Petta, C., Kushki, A.: Short report: evaluating the safety and usability of head-mounted virtual reality compared to monitor-displayed video for children with autism spectrum disorder. Autism **24**(7) (2020). https://doi.org/10.1177/1362361320934214

25. Mesa-Gresa, P., Gil-Gómez, H., Lozano-Quilis, J.A., Gil-Gómez, J.A.: Effectiveness of virtual reality for children and adolescents with autism spectrum disorder: an evidence-based systematic review. Sensors **18**(8), 2486 (2018). https://doi.org/10.3390/s18082486

26. Mora-Guiard, J., Crowell, C., Pares, N., Heaton, P.: Sparking social initiation behaviors in children with autism through full-body interaction. Int. J. Child-Comput. Interact. **11**, 62–71 (2017). https://doi.org/10.1016/j.ijcci.2016.10.006

27. Mosher, M.A., Carreon, A.C., Craig, S.L., Ruhter, L.C.: Immersive technology to teach social skills to students with autism spectrum disorder: a literature review. Rev. J. Autism Dev. Disord. , 1–17 (2021). https://doi.org/10.1007/s40489-021-00259-6

28. Newbutt, N., Bradley, R., Conley, I.: Using virtual reality head-mounted displays in schools with autistic children: views, experiences, and future directions. Cyberpsychology Behav. Soc. Nctw. **23**(1), 23–33 (2020). https://doi.org/10.1089/cyber.2019.0206

29. Newbutt, N., Sung, C., Kuo, H.-J., Leahy, M.J., Lin, C.-C., Tong, B.: Brief report: a pilot study of the use of a virtual reality headset in autism populations. J. Autism Dev. Disord. **46**(9), 3166–3176 (2016). https://doi.org/10.1007/s10803-016-2830-5

30. Novakovic, N., Milovancevic, M.P., Dejanovic, S.D., Aleksic, B.: Effects of snoezelen-multisensory environment on CARS scale in adolescents and adults with autism spectrum disorder. Res. Dev. Disabil. **89**, 51–58 (2019). https://doi.org/10.1016/j.ridd.2019.03.007

31. Pares, N., Masri, P., van Wolferen, G., Creed, C.: Achieving dialogue with children with severe autism in an adaptive multisensory interaction: the "MEDIATE" project. IEEE Trans. Vis. Comput. Graph. **11**(6), 734–743 (2005). https://doi.org/10.1109/TVCG.2005.88

32. Parsons, S., Yuill, N., Good, J., Brosnan, M.: 'Whose agenda? Who knows best? Whose voice?' Co-creating a technology research roadmap with autism stakeholders. Disabil. Soc. **35**(2), 201–234 (2020). https://doi.org/10.1080/09687599.2019.1624152

33. Ringland, K.E., Zalapa, R., Neal, M., Escobedo, L., Tentori, M., Hayes, G.R.: SensoryPaint: a multimodal sensory intervention for children with neurodevelopmental disorders. In: Proceedings of the 2014 ACM International Joint Conference on Pervasive and Ubiquitous Computing - UbiComp 2014 Adjunct, pp. 873–884. ACM Press, Seattle, Washington (2014). https://doi.org/10.1145/2632048.2632065, sensoryPaint

34. Russell, G., Mandy, W., Elliott, D., White, R., Pittwood, T., Ford, T.: Selection bias on intellectual ability in autism research: a cross-sectional review and meta-analysis. Mol. Autism **10**(1), 9 (2019). https://doi.org/10.1186/s13229-019-0260-x

35. Sandbank, M., et al.: Project AIM: autism intervention meta-analysis for studies of young children. Psychol. Bull. **146**(1), 1–29 (2020). https://doi.org/10.1037/bul0000215
36. Schmidt, M., Newbutt, N., Schmidt, C., Glaser, N.: A process-model for minimizing adverse effects when using head mounted display-based virtual reality for individuals with autism. Front. Virtual Reality **2**, 611740 (2021). https://doi.org/10.3389/frvir.2021.611740
37. Schoen, S.A., et al.: A systematic review of Ayres sensory integration intervention for children with autism. Autism Res. **12**(1), 6–19 (2019). https://doi.org/10.1002/aur.2046
38. Schubert, T.W.: The sense of presence in virtual environments: a three-component scale measuring spatial presence, involvement, and realness. Zeitschrift für Medienpsychologie **15**(2), 69–71 (2003). https://doi.org/10.1026//1617-6383.15.2.69
39. Sharma, K., Giannakos, M.: Sensing technologies and child-computer interaction: opportunities, challenges and ethical considerations. Int. J. Child-Comput. Interact. 100331 (2021). https://doi.org/10.1016/j.ijcci.2021.100331
40. Spiel, K., Frauenberger, C., Fitzpatrick, G.: Experiences of autistic children with technologies. Int. J. Child-Comput. Interact. **11**, 50–61 (2017). https://doi.org/10.1016/j.ijcci.2016.10.007
41. Winnicott, D.W.: Playing and Reality. Tavistock Publications, London (1980)
42. Witmer, B.G., Singer, M.J.: Measuring presence in virtual environments: a presence questionnaire. Presence Teleoperators Virtual Environ. **7**(3), 225–240 (1998). https://doi.org/10.1162/105474698565686
43. World Health Organization (WHO): ICD-10: international statistical classification of diseases and related health problems : tenth revision. World Health Organization, Genève, Switzerland, 2nd edn. (2004)

Exploiting Augmented Reality in LEGO Therapy for Children with Autism Spectrum Disorder

Michele Gattullo(✉) ⓘ, Enricoandrea Laviola ⓘ, and Antonio Emmanuele Uva ⓘ

Department of Mechanics, Mathematics, and Management, Polytechnic University of Bari,
via Orabona, 4, 70125 Bari, Italy
michele.gattullo@poliba.it

Abstract. Numerous computer-based therapies have been designed for cognitive-behavioral interventions to support children with Autism Spectrum Disorder (ASD) in recent years. Among these technologies, Augmented Reality (AR) offers unique educational benefits because it provides children with direct guidance on their learning tasks. In this work, we propose "AR-brickhouse," an AR application to support ASD children during LEGO therapy. It combines the benefits derived from AR technology and the LEGO tangible user interface with caregivers' involvement. The novelty of our system concerns the improvement of ASD children's basic skills such as positioning in space; focusing on tasks; acquisition of concepts of shape, color, and size. A preliminary user study involved eight ASD children and twelve therapists from a real medical center. Our results suggest that the proposed system is easy for therapists and allows children to improve the aforementioned basic skills. In fact, they were able to accomplish LEGO assembly tasks with better accuracy and in less time than traditional LEGO therapy.

Keywords: Autism Spectrum Disorder · Play therapy · LEGO assembly · Augmented Reality

1 Introduction

Autism Spectrum Disorder (ASD) is a neurological and developmental disorder that begins early in childhood and lasts throughout a person's life. It can arise in different forms and lead to problems such as dyslexia, dysgraphia, and dyscalculia. Moreover, ASD influences social relationships because it affects how a person acts, interacts, communicates, and learns with others [1]. Children with ASD have lower motivation towards the exploration of their everyday environment, and they usually isolate themselves showing a reduction in their ability to focus on a task [2].

Therapeutic interventions for ASD children mainly rely on "play therapy" [3], a method to improve their social and communication skills while playing in their own way. Caregivers (therapists, special education teachers, parents) normally use a variety of strategies to help ASD children to focus their attention on tasks, such as using verbal and physical prompts, visual supports (e.g., images and drawings), and offering rewards

G. Zachmann et al. (Eds.): EuroXR 2022, LNCS 13484, pp. 73–85, 2022.
https://doi.org/10.1007/978-3-031-16234-3_5

[4]. For example, Alessandrini et al. [5] designed ReduCat, a tool for the therapist to engage the child in a collaborative storytelling activity. In addition, LeGoff [6] introduced LEGO building blocks for both group and individual therapies, demonstrating improved social skills of children with ASD. In particular, young patients developed a sense of collaboration with the interlocutor, creativity, and knowing how to follow social rules. Children with ASD usually like to play with LEGO constructions during the therapy session and most of them are interested in technological games on mobile devices such as smartphones and tablets [7]. Therefore, they could benefit from innovative digital games to improve their skills, particularly their willingness to explore surroundings, attention, verbal comprehension, and social interactions.

Numerous computer-based therapies have been designed for cognitive-behavioral interventions to support children with ASD in recent years. They include robotics [8, 9], Virtual Reality (VR) [10–12], and Augmented Reality (AR) [7, 13, 14]. These technologies are often complemented with tangible user interfaces to merge the digital with the physical world, improving the learning effect, especially in cognition, motivation, perception, and abstract problem solving [15].

Among these technologies, many researchers found that AR offers unique educational benefits thanks to a more intuitive tangible interface metaphor, especially for young children [16]. For example, Escobedo et al. [7] and Chen et al. [17] demonstrated that AR is effective for teaching social skills and helping focus attention on task. In addition, Lee et al. [13] stated that AR encourages children with ASD to role-play with therapists as well as increases their motivation and mental cognition. Bai et al. applied AR to visually conceptualize the representation of pretense within an open-ended play environment [18]. Finally, AR allows ASD children to directly manipulate real objects while observing augmented visual feedback. This last benefit goes well with LEGO therapy [6] that makes ASD children active learners whose experience improves through sensory awareness. In fact, using AR, children can see, at the same time, both the physical LEGO construction and its virtual preview. In this way, they can visually compare them throughout the assembly task, thus improving their sensory awareness.

Although many works have already provided evidence that it is useful to integrate AR technology into therapeutic interventions to support ASD children, as far as the authors know, there are no universally recognized therapies or standardized procedures that involve AR technology, specifically in the LEGO therapy for children with ASD. Therefore, research studies are needed to explore if AR can be well integrated into consolidated LEGO therapy protocols. Furthermore, these studies are crucial to derive best practices for designing the AR experience in terms of hardware device, therapists' involvement, and protocols to guide patients' actions [19]. Therefore, the main contribution of this preliminary study is the design and development of an AR application for LEGO therapy called "AR-brickhouse." We started from the therapist's and children's needs, derived from the observation of traditional LEGO therapy sessions. While other studies are conducted on increasing interpersonal relationships with peers [7, 13, 14, 20], AR-brickhouse mainly focuses on the development of basic skills such as positioning in space, focusing on the tasks, acquisition of concepts of shape, color, and size.

A second contribution of this work is a preliminary evaluation of the suitability of AR-brickhouse to support LEGO therapy. It was performed through a user study involving a sample of eight children with ASD and twelve therapists from a real medical center. In two separate experiments, we first evaluated the usability of AR-brickhouse for the therapists. Then we measured the difference in the children's performance in LEGO therapy respectively with and without the AR support, in terms of completion time and accuracy of the LEGO assembly task. We hypothesized that children using the AR application would have a greater focus on the task, as well as they would better understand concepts related to shape, color, size, and positioning of the LEGO bricks. These benefits would lead to shorter completion time and higher task accuracy.

2 Design of "AR-Brickhouse"

2.1 Definition of User Needs

We assisted in 2 sessions of LEGO therapy to catch user needs for the design of AR-brickhouse. We observed both children and therapists during the sessions without interfering with the therapy.

LEGO therapy traditionally consists of a game settled with a child and a therapist [6]. After an initial time spent in other activities, the child starts playing with LEGO. He/she has to reproduce a LEGO construction by selecting one of those available in the medical center. Once the construction to replicate has been identified, the child must carry out this task using his/her imagination, trying to select the right brick (in color, shape, and size). Children are provided only with the bricks needed for that construction. Without guidance, after a few minutes, the child is usually unable to understand how to continue the construction, so he/she starts to feel frustrated. As a result, he/she begins to lose focus on the task and the therapist helps him/her regain attention and find the correct brick. For example, the therapist may ask the child "which is the color of the carrot?" to help identify an orange brick. Two situations may arise: i) the child completes the construction, and he/she is rewarded; ii) the child does not complete the task and does not want to continue as he/she has lost interest in the game. The reward is important to educate children in respect of the rules [7].

After having observed how LEGO therapy is traditionally accomplished, we defined the main user needs, listed in Table 1, together with the therapists of the partner medical center. Based on the user needs, we designed the hardware setup and the graphical user interface of the AR application.

2.2 Hardware Setup Design

We presented to the therapists of the partner medical center the following AR display options: (i) an optical see-through Head-Worn Display (HWD); (ii) a handheld display; (iii) a mediating screen. The display setups were tested through a therapy simulation with one therapist and one child. Interaction with the developed application was left only to the therapists for each option. In fact, as Escobedo et al. [7] stated, it is difficult and time-consuming to teach ASD children how to interact with digital commands.

The therapists immediately discarded the HWD because it is an unfamiliar and uncomfortable instrument for children, thus not respecting UN-005 and UN-006. This

Table 1 User needs deriving from the observation of the traditional LEGO therapy session

ID	User Need	Source
UN-001	Therapists need a tool to help children in LEGO construction	Children, Therapist
UN-002	Therapists need to teach children basic skills	Children, Therapist
UN-003	Therapists need to educate children to respect roles and rules	Children, Therapist
UN-004	Therapists need a tool to keep children attention at high levels	Children, Therapist
UN-005	Children need to play in an ergonomic way	Children
UN-006	Children need to use familiar tools for playing	Children

may affect children's ability to perform the required task and lead to a total rejection of the equipment. Moreover, the display of the AR application on an HWD would also complicate the therapist's role in guidance, requiring a second device to be aware of what children are watching.

The handheld display, more specifically a 10" tablet, was initially considered and tested. The therapist has complete control over the tablet during the session while guiding the child. The tablet was placed on a small easel to leave the therapist's hands-free. We tested two different arrangements. In the first one, the tablet was placed between the child and the green LEGO Duplo plate where he/she has to reproduce the LEGO assembly during therapy. After the preliminary simulation of the therapy, this arrangement was discarded because of the discomfort caused by the hindrance of the tablet during the task both for the therapist and child, thus not respecting UN-005. Furthermore, children occluded the camera with their hands during the task, thus causing distractions, against UN-004. In a second arrangement, we placed the tablet sideways using two LEGO Duplo plates, one framed by the tablet's camera and the other used by the child to build the LEGO assembly. In this way, we solved the problems encountered with the first arrangement. However, UN-005 was not respected since a new ergonomic issue was experienced. In fact, the child had to make several twists of the torso to observe the AR application on the tablet scene and then return to the initial position to perform the task. Moreover, displaying only the virtual assembly on the tablet screen limited the advantages offered by the AR in guidance.

The use of a mediating screen, i.e., displaying the AR application on a desktop monitor placed in front of the users, reduces the possibility of interfering with the setup. It is also a familiar tool for children, then both UR-005 and UR-006 are respected. The playing area is acquired through an external camera connected to the same computer of the monitor. We tested three arrangements of the camera: top, back, and front. In the top arrangement, the camera is placed above the playing area. This arrangement was discarded because the camera point of view is different from the one of the children, thus confusing them. In the back arrangement, the camera is placed on a tripod behind users. The point of view is coherent with that of children, but there is the risk of hitting the tripod during the therapy in case of unwanted movements by the children. This situation is frequent with ASD children. Furthermore, children could occlude the camera field of view during the therapy. In the front arrangement, the camera is placed in front of the user.

The video acquired through the camera is flipped on the monitor, as in videoconferencing applications. In this way, the monitor is used as a mirror. In this arrangement, there is no risk of interference between children and the setup as well as occlusion of the camera field of view. A drawback of this arrangement is the depth perception. Real objects in the foreground are displayed in the background on the screen and vice versa. However, this setup was judged as the optimal one by the therapists.

Figure 1 shows the final setup adopted and the measures between each element. The monitor is a 32-inch SONY BRAVIA LCD television, connected to the computer using an HDMI cable and placed at the same height as the worktable to prevent the child from looking up, thus avoiding incorrect posture and unnecessary fatigue. The camera is a 1080p Jelly Comb, model H606, with autofocus.

Fig. 1. The hardware setup chosen for AR-brickhouse

2.3 Graphical User Interface

The application framework was developed with Unity 3D Engine, and the scripts were written in C#. Vuforia Engine was used for the tracking with a natural feature that guarantees ease of implementation and higher accuracy compared to marker-less solutions, as stated by Bottani et al. [21]. In our study, natural feature tracking allows to recognize a picture printed on a square cardboard (12 cm in length) which shows a 2D preview of the LEGO construction to be carried out. The 3D models of LEGO bricks were created using Autodesk Inventor Professional 3D CAD software. The other 3D models used in the application were downloaded from CAD open libraries on the internet.

The AR application displays a 3D model of the final construction on the cardboard, placed in the top left corner of the LEGO Duplo plate by the therapist (Fig. 2a). During the session, the child tries to replicate this shape following the instructions provided through the AR application. They consist of animations of each LEGO brick conveying the information on how to place it on the existing assembly (Fig. 2b). The guidance provided through these animations allows to meet both UN-001 and UN-002. The first LEGO brick is displayed on the LEGO Duplo plate at the opposite corner of the cardboard. Children were free to create the construction in whatever position of the LEGO Duplo plate. At the end of the assembly task, feedback on the success of the task is displayed together with the possibility of gathering a reward for the child. It consists of a 3D model of a cartoon character that appears on the screen, accompanied by an applause sound effect, which further gratifies the child, helping to increase his/her openness to the outside world. Therapist selects the cartoon character from a list presented to the child. The displaying of an AR reward allows to meet UN-003.

The graphical user interface is very simple and presents only five buttons. Only the therapist can press the buttons through a wireless mouse. This behavior further allows the therapist to educate children in respect of the roles (UN-003). The "next" button (Fig. 2c) allows to play the animation of the LEGO brick to be placed following the assembly sequence. The "replay" button (Fig. 2d) allows to replay the LEGO brick animation. The "help" button (Fig. 2e) allows to display an animation of an object with the same color of the LEGO piece to assemble (e.g., a carrot for an orange piece). This button is pressed by the therapist when the child either cannot pick the brick of the right color or his/her attention gets low, thus satisfying both UN-002 and UN-004. The "list" button (Fig. 2f) allows the therapist to restart the assembly from previous pieces without restarting the application. This tool is useful in the case of children breaking the LEGO assembly during the therapy due to frustration. Finally, the "home" button (Fig. 2g) allows to restart the application for a new construction.

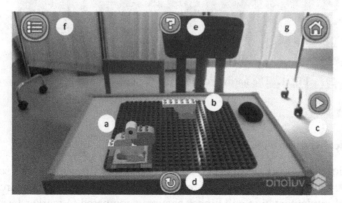

Fig. 2. The graphical user interface of AR-brickhouse: virtual preview of the target construction (a), animation of the current brick to place (b), "next" button (c), "replay" button (d), "help" button (e), "list" button (f), "home" button (g)

The AR-brickhouse application has been embellished with some sound details to catch children's attention (UN-004). In fact, when each 3D object, apart from the LEGO bricks, appears in the scene, it is associated with a characteristic sound, which recalls the link between the object and the sound itself. In addition, sound recognition has been set up every time the target is framed and recognized by the camera to increase the child's engagement.

3   Design of Experiment

We designed two experiments, one targeted to the therapists and one to the children. Before the experiments, we formalized the following hypothesis:

1. the designed application "AR-brickhouse" is easy to use for therapists.
2. "AR-brickhouse" improves children's basic skills, thus allowing them to accomplish the LEGO assembly tasks in less time and with more accuracy than traditional LEGO therapy.

To verify the first hypothesis, we asked therapists to simulate a LEGO therapy with AR-brickhouse without the presence of children. We involved in this experiment the four therapists of the partner medical center and eight other colleagues who apply the global cognitive-behavioral psycho-educational treatment. Then, the total number of participants was 12 (7 females, 35 to 54 years old, mean $= 41.8$, SD $= 5.92$). They were asked to evaluate their previous familiarity with AR applications on a 5-point Likert rating item (1: Not at all familiar – 5: Extremely familiar). They rated 1.5 on average (SD $= 0.65$, Median $= 1$, Min $= 1$, Max $= 3$). We asked therapists to explore all the functions of AR-brickhouse. Then, they filled out the System Usability Scale (SUS) questionnaire.

To verify the second hypothesis, we involved children affected by ASD disturbs. Due to the nature of this research on a special population, the number of participants was limited. The therapist proposed the study to the parents of the patients in therapy in that period. Eight families agreed to our initiative. The eight children were from 4 to 8 years old. This sample is small but well representative of the target user of AR-brickhouse.

We designed a between-subjects experiment. The eight children involved in the experiment were equally divided into two groups. One group received traditional LEGO therapy ("without-AR" - 1 female, 4 to 8 years old, mean $= 6.3$, SD $= 1.48$) while the other one was subjected to LEGO therapy using AR ("with-AR" - 2 females, 4 to 8 years old, mean $= 6.3$, SD $= 1.79$) through the developed AR-brickhouse application.

The doctor prescribed a duration of the therapy for all the children of 3 weeks with two sessions per week. The LEGO activity was performed in the final ten minutes of each session, as normally happens. At the end of the 3 weeks, the therapists provided their feedback highlighting the advantages and disadvantages of AR-brickhouse compared with the traditional LEGO therapy.

Every child assembled a different LEGO construction in each session with an increasing difficulty level from one week to the other. We selected the constructions among those usually employed by the therapists. We used the equation proposed by Richardson to initially evaluate the difficulty of each LEGO assembly:

$$diff. = 10[(0.020\,components) + (-0.117\,symmetrical\,planes) \\ +(0.047\,novel\,assemblies) + (0.028\,selections) + 1.464] \tag{1}$$

In Table 2, we reported the six constructions ranked using (1). We further asked the four therapists of the medical center to rank the constructions in terms of difficulty based on their previous experience. The ranking was the same provided by Eq. 1, except for the "pelican," which was judged harder to assemble than the "gift pack." In fact, the "pelican" has fewer components than the "gift pack," but there are more novel assemblies and a more complex shape, represented by the lower number of average symmetrical planes. Therefore, they are harder to assemble for children due to the orientation of the pieces in the construction. Furthermore, the "gift pack" components are almost similar in shape while they differ in color. It is generally easier for children affected by ASD disorders to distinguish colors than shapes. For these reasons, we decided to follow the ranking provided by the therapists.

When children could not understand where to place a LEGO brick in the "without-AR" condition, the therapist showed them where to place it with a finger and then urged them to perform the same action. In the "with-AR" condition, the therapist only used the "replay" button without providing any other help. Likewise, when children could not recognize which piece to assemble, in the "without-AR" condition, the therapist showed them a book with colored drawings useful to encourage the association of colors (e.g., lemon for yellow bricks). Again, in the "with-AR" condition, the therapist only used the "help" button.

During the therapy sessions, an experimenter observed how children carried out the experiment, particularly their interaction with AR-brickhouse. She also reported the errors accomplished by children as well as the time spent for the assembly. However, to not distract children, the experimenter's presence in the room was concealed through a medical screen.

Table 2. Difficulty of the construction used in the experiment evaluated using (1).

Construction	Duck	House	Boat	Pelican	Gift pack	Penguin
Components	6	7	7	7	9	10
Symmetrical planes	1,7	2	1,4	1,6	1,8	1,4
Novel assemblies	6	6	5	6	5	8
Selections	6	7	7	7	9	10
Difficulty	69,0	70,5	73,8	79,1	83,8	143,3

4   Results and Discussion

The experiment carried out only with the therapists provided a mean SUS score of 87.5 (SD 10.3, max 100.0, min 65.0) over a maximum of 100. Therefore, using the rating scale provided by Bangor et al. [22], we can define the usability of our application as "excellent." This result allowed us to confirm the first hypothesis of our study, validating the suitability of the design of the setup and the GUI of AR-brickhouse. In this way, we could proceed with the second evaluation involving ASD children affected by ASD disturbs.

The data gathered during the experiment with ASD children are: (i) overall time spent to accomplish the assembly task and (ii) number of errors made. Figure 3 and 4 summarizes all data collected. The results confirmed the second hypothesis of our study. Both for time and errors, we observed better performance for children using AR-brickhouse than for children carrying out traditional LEGO therapy. This result was obtained for all the construction, but we did not find any correlation between the difficulty of the task and the improvement of the performance. Both for the time and the errors, the "gift pack" was the construction that registered the greater improvement. It requires a great number of simple bricks. Therefore, in the traditional LEGO therapy, the duration of the task gets longer, and the child tends to distract more and make errors. Using AR-brickhouse, instead, the child may be more focused on the task, thus reducing the overall time and the possibility of making mistakes.

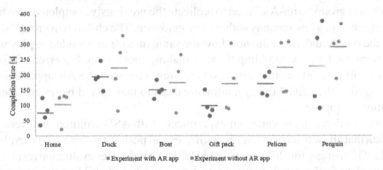

Fig. 3. Task completion time for each ASD child and for each LEGO construction with and without the AR application (horizontal lines represent group means)

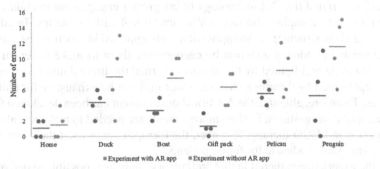

Fig. 4. Total errors made by each ASD child for each LEGO construction with and without the AR application (horizontal lines represent group means)

The improved children's performance demonstrates the purpose of the AR application regarding the development of basic skills such as positioning in space; focusing on tasks; acquisition of concepts of shape, color, and size. The main motivation for the results obtained in favor of AR-brickhouse may derive from a greater involvement and attention of the ASD child who observes the virtual information seamlessly with the real LEGO bricks thanks to the AR technology. In fact, based on their professional experience, therapists reported to us that AR-brickhouse allowed ASD children to learn the proper social behaviors more efficiently than the traditional LEGO therapy. For example, one aspect supporting this assessment is that patients waited correctly for the therapist to interact with the application to continue with the task. Moreover, caregivers stated that the visual feedback of the child's movement, captured by the webcam, also influenced the outcomes. They observed that the ASD child was more likely to self-correct his/her eye-manual coordination reducing the risk of making mistakes. As for the other basic skills, the reductions in both the overall time spent to accomplish the assembly task and the number of errors made of AR-brickhouse compared to the traditional LEGO therapy show a clear improvement in children's ability to perform tasks, especially in LEGO bricks recognition and placement.

An interesting result was reported by the observation of the children after the LEGO therapy when they were left to play with LEGO for about five minutes freely. We observed that children in group "with-AR" tried to replicate the previously completed construction successfully within a few seconds without any guidance. The children in group "without-AR," on the other hand, often did not show the same interest and tended to play with the constructions randomly assembling them or making more assembly errors. This result indicates a further confirmation that ASD children who used the AR application were more engaged in the LEGO therapy, allowing them to understand better and memorize the assembly sequence.

Despite the difficulty to carry out experiments with ASD children, we were able to collect data that allow to answer our research question positively: "can AR be exploited to support LEGO therapy for children with ASD?" Even if the user evaluation results should be confirmed by further studies involving a larger number of children, we received very positive feedback from the therapists. After both the experiments, they demonstrated a good inclination to use AR-brickhouse without too much difficulty. Based on their experience, they stated that AR technology offers greater engagement to children who are more enticed to complete the task, unlike traditional LEGO therapy. In addition, they appreciated the structure of the application with animated instructions because they further stimulated children's attention by encouraging them to make fewer mistakes. The only downside highlighted by therapists concerned the limited number of rewards currently represented by 9 cartoon characters that may not be exhaustive for children's preferences. Therefore, although the AR-brickhouse content has been developed following the therapists' suggestions, further improvements are needed to make it scalable for wider adoption in LEGO therapy. However, the therapists expressed their intention to continue using AR-brickhouse for future patients.

From the experience gathered in this preliminary study, it is possible to derive some guidelines for the design of future applications to support LEGO therapy. First of all, we believe it is important to highlight that the therapists' inclusion in the application design has been critical to getting decisions even different from what the developer would have made. Regarding the choice of hardware setup, for example, the use of a mediating screen prevented the child from interacting with the application. This choice resulted in a drastic reduction of task completion time still maintaining high attention, unlike the results that would have been obtained with other more conventional tangible devices such as smartphones, as stated by Escobedo et al. [7]. Moreover, the choices regarding the AR content were also crucial for the improvement of children's performance, thanks to the advice of therapists who knew more about ASD children's needs. An example is the added value of AR with animated instructions and sounds, proposed by the caregivers themselves, which are much more engaging for patients rather than simply watching a virtual decontextualized animation on the screen.

5 Conclusion and Future Work

In this work, we exploit AR technology for LEGO therapy for ASD children developing an application called "AR-brickhouse". It has been designed following both therapists' and patients' needs. Unlike other works in the literature focused on the development of social skills, the novelty of our preliminary study concerns the improvement of ASD children's basic skills.

A first evaluation was made involving only therapists to validate the suitability of the design of the setup and the user interface of AR-brickhouse; afterward, a second evaluation was made including the ASD children. We observed better performance for patients using the AR technology during our experiment, unlike the traditional LEGO therapy. We noticed a greater ASD children's involvement and a reduction of mistakes thanks to the visual feedback provided through the AR graphics. Furthermore, we detected that AR-brickhouse allows ASD patients to understand better and memorize the assembly sequence. Positive feedback was provided by the therapists who expressed their intention to continue using our application for LEGO therapy.

The main limitation of this work is the involvement of only 8 children, further divided into two groups. These small samples did not allow us to perform a statistical analysis of the collected data. For future work, we plan to collect data on a larger sample of ASD children by introducing a study on knowledge retention to assess better the effects our application has on learning.

References

1. Fodstad, J.C., Matson, J.L., Hess, J., Neal, D.: Social and communication behaviours in infants and toddlers with autism and pervasive developmental disorder-not otherwise specified. Dev. Neurorehabil. **12**, 152–157 (2009). https://doi.org/10.1080/17518420902936748
2. Quill, K.A., Institute, A.: Instructional considerations for young children with autism: the rationale for visually cued instruction. J. Autism Dev. Disord. **27**, 697–714 (1997). https://doi.org/10.1023/A:1025806900162
3. Morgenthal, A.H.: Child-centered play therapy for children with autism: a case study. Ph.D. Diss. Clin. Psychol. Antioch Univ. New England, Keene, New Hampsh (2015)
4. Hayes, G.R., Hirano, S., Marcu, G., Monibi, M., Nguyen, D.H., Yeganyan, M.: Interactive visual supports for children with autism. Pers. Ubiquitous Comput. **14**, 663–680 (2010). https://doi.org/10.1007/s00779-010-0294-8

5. Alessandrini, A., Loux, V., Murray, C.: Designing ReduCat : audio - augmented paper drawings tangible interface in educational intervention for high - functioning autistic children (2016)
6. LeGoff, D.B.: Use of LEGO© as a therapeutic medium for improving social competence. J. Autism Dev. Disord. **34**, 557–571 (2004). https://doi.org/10.1007/s10803-004-2550-0
7. Escobedo, L., Tentori, M., Quintana, E., Favela, J., Garcia-Rosas, D.: Using augmented reality to help children with autism stay focused. IEEE Pervasive Comput. **13**, 38–46 (2014). https://doi.org/10.1109/MPRV.2014.19
8. Farr, W., Yuill, N., Raffle, H.: Collaborative benefits of a tangible interface for autistic children. In: Proceedings of CHI, pp. 1–4 (2009)
9. Kozima, H., Nakagawa, C., Yasuda, Y.: Interactive robots for communication-care: a case-study in autism therapy. In: Proceedings of - IEEE International Workshop on Robot and Human Interactive Communication 2005, pp. 341–346 (2005). https://doi.org/10.1109/ROMAN.2005.1513802.
10. Parsons, S., Cobb, S.: State-of-the-art of virtual reality technologies for children on the autism spectrum. Eur. J. Spec. Needs Educ. **26**, 355–366 (2011). https://doi.org/10.1080/08856257.2011.593831
11. Barajas, A.O., Al Osman, H., Shirmohammadi, S.: A serious game for children with autism spectrum disorder as a tool for play therapy. In: 2017 IEEE 5th International Conference on Serious Games and Applications for Health, SeGAH 2017 (2017). https://doi.org/10.1109/SeGAH.2017.7939266.
12. Nunnari, F., Magliaro, S., D'Errico, G., De Luca, V., Barba, M.C., De Paolis, L.T.: Designing and assessing interactive virtual characters for children affected by ADHD. In: Virtual Reality and Augmented Reality, pp. 285–290 (2019). https://doi.org/10.1007/978-3-030-31908-3.
13. Lee, I.J., Chen, C.H., Wang, C.P., Chung, C.H.: Augmented reality plus concept map technique to teach children with ASD to use social cues when meeting and greeting. Asia-Pacific Educ. Res. **27**, 227–243 (2018). https://doi.org/10.1007/s40299-018-0382-5
14. Soares, K.P., Burlamarqui, A.M.F., Gonçalves, L.M.G., Costa, V.F., Cunha, M.E.: To help in psycho-pedagogical tasks with children belonging to autism spectrum disorder. Ieee Lat. Am. Trans. **15**, 2017–2023 (2017)
15. Zhou, Y., Wang, M.: Tangible user interfaces in learning and education. Int. Encycl. Soc. Behav. Sci. Second Ed. 20–25 (2015). https://doi.org/10.1016/B978-0-08-097086-8.92034-8.
16. Billinghurst, M.: Augmented reality in education: current trends. New Horizons Learn. **9** (2002). https://doi.org/10.4018/jgcms.2011010108.
17. Chen, C.H., Lee, I.J., Lin, L.Y.: Augmented reality-based video-modeling storybook of nonverbal facial cues for children with autism spectrum disorder to improve their perceptions and judgments of facial expressions and emotions. Comput. Human Behav. **55**, 477–485 (2016). https://doi.org/10.1016/j.chb.2015.09.033
18. Bai, Z., Blackwell, A.F., Coulouris, G.: Using augmented reality to elicit pretend play for children with autism. IEEE Trans. Vis. Comput. Graph. **21**, 598–610 (2015). https://doi.org/10.1109/TVCG.2014.2385092
19. Wu, H.K., Lee, S.W.Y., Chang, H.Y., Liang, J.C.: Current status, opportunities and challenges of augmented reality in education. Comput. Educ. **62**, 41–49 (2013). https://doi.org/10.1016/j.compedu.2012.10.024
20. Escobedo, L., et al.: MOSOCO: A mobile assistive tool to support children with autism practicing social skills in real-life situations. Conf. Hum. Factors Comput. Syst. Proc. 2589–2598 (2012). https://doi.org/10.1145/2207676.2208649

21. Augmented reality technology in the manufacturing industry: a review of the (2019). https://doi.org/10.1080/24725854.2018.1493244

22. Bangor, A., Kortum, P.T., Miller, J.T.: An empirical evaluation of the system usabi Int. J. Hum. Comput. Interact. **24**, 574–594 (2008). https://doi.org/10.1080/104473 05776

Algorithms for XR

Evaluation of Point Cloud Streaming and Rendering for VR-Based Telepresence in the OR

Roland Fischer[1](✉), Andre Mühlenbrock[1], Farin Kulapichitr[1],
Verena Nicole Uslar[2], Dirk Weyhe[2], and Gabriel Zachmann[1]

[1] University of Bremen, Bremen, Germany
{r.fischer,muehlenb,farin1,zachmann}@uni-bremen.de
[2] University Hospital for Visceral Surgery, University of Oldenburg, PIUS-Hospital,
Oldenburg, Germany
verena.uslar@uni-oldenburg.de, Dirk.Weyhe@Pius-Hospital.de
https://cgvr.informatik.uni-bremen.de

Abstract. Immersive and high-quality VR-based telepresence systems could be of great benefit in the medical field and the operating room (OR) specifically, as they allow distant experts to interact with each other and to assist local doctors as if they were physically present. Despite recent advances in VR technology, and more telepresence systems making use of it, most of the current solutions in use in health care (if any), are just video-based and don't provide the feeling of presence or spatial awareness, which are highly important for tasks such as remote consultation, -supervision, and -teaching. Reasons still holding back VR telepresence systems are high demands regarding bandwidth and computational power, subpar visualization quality, and complicated setups. We propose an easy-to-set-up telepresence system that enables remote experts to meet in a multi-user virtual operating room, view live-streamed and 3D-visualized operations, interact with each other, and collaboratively explore medical data. Our system is based on Azure Kinect RGB-D cameras, a point cloud streaming pipeline, and fast point cloud rendering methods integrated into a state-of-the-art 3D game engine. Remote experts are visualized via personalized real-time 3D point cloud avatars. For this, we have developed a high-speed/low-latency multi-camera point cloud streaming pipeline including efficient filtering and compression. Furthermore, we have developed splatting-based and mesh-based point cloud rendering solutions and integrated them into the Unreal Engine 4. We conducted two user studies with doctors and medical students to evaluate our proposed system, compare the rendering solutions, and highlight our system's capabilities.

Keywords: Telepresence · Virtual Reality · Collaborative VR · Point cloud · Avatar · Point cloud rendering · Unreal Engine · Azure Kinect · Mesh reconstruction

G. Zachmann et al. (Eds.): EuroXR 2022, LNCS 13484, pp. 89–110, 2022.
https://doi.org/10.1007/978-3-031-16234-3_6

1 Introduction

Telemedicine plays a major role in medicine and health care and, although it is hardly a novel concept, it has received increased attention lately. The ability to provide assistance from a distance, and collaborate without the need for being physically present, exhibits a huge potential to provide patients with better care, increase efficiency, and save costs [11,19]. There is a wide range of applications for telemedicine and the more advanced telepresence systems: from telementoring and training, remote consultation and collaboration, to remote diagnosis, surgery, and rehabilitation [2,30]. One example scenario is emergency situations with traumatic injuries where fast interventions are critical. Regularly, the dilemma is to either spend valuable time transporting the patient to specialized health care facilities, or to go to the nearest hospital although the local surgeons, especially in rural areas, might be less experienced [10]. These local surgeons could benefit from consultation or even mentoring from remote experts via telepresence systems that could preemptively be integrated into the surgery rooms [20]. Another example would be to reduce health risks by limiting the physical contact with possibly contagious patients and medical staff to a minimum; novice surgeons could consider attending surgeries via telepresence instead of being physically present in the operating room [8]. Other applications could be patient visits/ward rounds in intensive care units, or tumor conferences where normally many experts from different medical areas come together to discuss the situation and the further procedure [31].

Telemedicine in the past, and to a significant degree today too, relied mostly on classical video conferencing systems and other video-based solutions [3,16]. These systems are inherently limited by the fixed point of view, lack of depth perception, and 2-dimensional screens, preventing a distinct feeling of (tele-)presence [4,34]. Continuous technological advances and the emergence of improved, affordable VR/AR devices lead researchers to focus on 3D VR/AR-based telepresence solutions. These systems are intended to deliver a more immersive experience compared to older video-based solutions, enable more natural interactions, and provide a better spatial understanding of the objects and their surroundings [29]. Many studies showed that in such systems the users' representation through personalized high-quality avatars is fundamental [7,13,39]. To create virtual 3D representations of the scene, these systems usually employ RGB-D cameras or other depth sensors, whose data then has to be streamed to the remote location to be viewed in VR. However, VR-based telepresence systems still face several challenges: high bandwidth requirements for transmission of the data, inadequate real-time 3D reconstruction and rendering quality, or hard-to-set-up systems.

Our proposed telepresence system is designed to tackle all the aforementioned challenges with a combination of an immersive multi-user VR system with a real-time RGB-D streaming pipeline and two fast, custom point cloud rendering solutions integrated into a state-of-the-art 3D game engine. Our solution enables remote doctors to meet and interact in a virtual operating room with real-time point cloud avatars as well as assist in operations that are live-streamed and visualized in the virtual room in 3D. Our proposed system is capable of handling multiple cameras per location, as our streaming pipeline includes efficient real-time compression and filtering algorithms. Furthermore, we integrated an easy-to-use registration, i.e. extrinsic calibration, method. To evaluate the benefits of VR-telepresence systems in general and ours specifically, we conducted two user studies with doctors exploring possible use cases, comparing the different rendering solutions, and investigating aspects such as spatial and social presence, realism as well as preference. To summarize, our contributions are:

- A multi-user VR-based telepresence system implemented in the state-of-the-art game engine Unreal Engine 4 (UE4) with a prototype for avatar face reconstruction.
- A modular low-latency multi-camera RGB-D streaming pipeline including filtering, denoising, and compression of RGB-D data, which is easy to extend.
- Custom splat- and mesh-based point cloud rendering solutions and a accompanying user study to compare the two methods.
- An extensive qualitative evaluation of the proposed system as well as a user study exploring clinical benefits and relevant aspects such as spatial and social presence.

2 Related Work

Many VR/AR-based telepresence systems have been proposed in the past, some still rely on video feeds that can be augmented [17,35], others do make use of real-time point clouds and 3D reconstruction [18]. For instance, Boehlen et al. [5] recently presented a real-time telepresence system intended for usage in caregiving that uses multiple RGB-D cameras as well as point cloud visualization and Anton et al. [2] proposed an augmented telemedicine platform for real-time medical consultation in which the patient is captured via an RGB-D camera, a remote expert can assist using a 3D display, and annotated feedback is sent back to the patient-side. The former system doesn't support multiple users or avatars and doesn't consider compression to reduce the required bandwidth. The latter uses only one RGB-D camera and a limited 8-bit YUV-based compression. Thoravi Kumaravel et al. [36] successfully demonstrated the benefits of immersive telepresence for remote teaching of physical tasks via a bi-directional Mixed-Reality system that combines AR and VR. In this system, point cloud hologlyphs visualize the remote scene, although only 10 Hz on the AR side. Gasques et al. [14] developed a collaborative mixed reality system based on multiple color and depth cameras for live 3D scene scanning and reconstruction, OptiTrack marker-based tracking which is used for registration and annotations, and AR and VR devices. The focus of this system lies more in tracking and interaction, as the depth images are transmitted unprocessed to the remote location. Based on the work by Gasques et al., Roth et al. [31] recently presented another mixed reality tele-consultation system that is intended for telepresence in ICUs. In their system multiple RGB-D cameras are mounted on the ceiling and, as commonly done, connected to dedicated PCs ("capture nodes"). The data is then compressed and transmitted to the remote location where the point cloud is computed but eventually rendered as surface mesh via a custom shader. One drawback they report is the high latency of 300–400 ms.

For telepresence applications, it is of high interest to constrain the required bandwidth to a reasonable level which makes real-time streaming of RGB-D sensor data and point clouds a difficult task. Therefore, one important but often still lacking aspect of such streaming systems is efficient data compression, particularly of depth data. Not only must the amount of data be reduced as much as possible but also as quickly as possible. Often this is only achieved by sacrificing the quality, which is problematic in medical contexts though. The two main approaches in which most of the previous dedicated research on RGB-D compression can be split into are 2D approaches using image- and video compression techniques that compress the individual color- and depth images [38] and 3D approaches which directly compress the point cloud. The latter often rely on hierarchical subdivision using octrees [24] and tend to be slower and less effective compared to 2D approaches if the reconstruction quality should remain high or even be lossless [22]. To achieve convincing results, the image- and video compression techniques need to be adapted to depth images and their specific characteristics though [28]. A comprehensive overview of the recent work in this department was recently provided by Cao et al. [6]. Even with the ongoing work in this field, the problem is far from solved.

Another important task is to produce high-quality 3D visualizations of the RGB-D data. One persistent obstacle is the inherently noisy output of the depth sensors, even the newest ones like the Azure Kinect suffer from temporal noise and effects such as the flying pixel and multipath effects [37]. Since the emergence of low-cost RGB-D cameras, much research was done to enhance the depth images by proposing different denoising, inpainting, and filtering approaches [1, 12,21]. Though, the problem is still relevant today, as the proposed solutions often have difficulties with dynamic content, e.g., in form of ghosting artifacts, or take too much time for real-time application.

To eventually visualize point clouds and, specifically, point cloud and 3D reconstructed avatars, different techniques were proposed. While, in principle, very high-quality representations can be achieved via offline scanning and elaborate reconstruction techniques, these methods are not suitable for real-time telepresence applications [23]. Dou et al. [9] presented an online performance capture system with advanced volumetric 3D reconstruction achieving real-time speed, however, multiple high-end PCs were necessary to 30 Hz which leaves no room for other necessary tasks in a telepresence system such as compression, rendering of multiple users, and rendering the scene itself in VR. Similarly, Orts et al. [27] were able to stream high-quality 3D reconstructed avatars in real-time. The avatars are produced via temporal-volumetric fusion of the data of multiple RGB-D cameras, however, the proposed system is computationally highly demanding, requires a 10 Gigabit connection, and is complicated to set up. On the other hand, Gamelin et al. [13] showed that even simpler and faster point cloud visualization techniques such as splatting are sufficient to outperform pre-

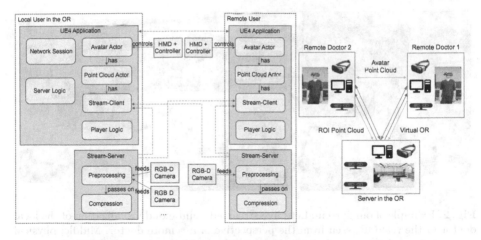

Fig. 1. Left: system architecture of our application. Right: system setup and communication channels between the server in the OR and the remote users.

constructed animated avatars in collaborative spatial tasks. Yu et al. [39], too, compared point cloud avatars with tracked mesh avatars in their telepresence prototype and found the point cloud avatars to be superior regarding perceived co-presence and social presence.

3   System Overview

In this section we present our telepresence system for remote consultation and collaboration in healthcare. In our system, the doctors and the patient in the physical operating room as well as the remote experts in VR are visualized via accurately registered live-streamed point cloud-based 3D representations. To provide high-quality graphics and robust network components, we decided to use the Unreal Engine 4 as a basis. This also has the benefit that a lot of basic aspects such as collision handling and different Virtual Reality Headsets (HMDs) are supported out-of-the-box. A core pillar in our system architecture is the RGB-D streaming pipeline that we realized not with the Unreal Engine, as the engine and its network components specifically are not suited for low-latency transmission of huge data loads. Instead, the RGB-D data is streamed via custom client-server connections that we implemented using C++ and CUDA; we integrated these into our Unreal Engine application. This is illustrated by the system diagram on the left side of Fig. 1 which shows our system's components in more detail.

The image on the right side of Fig. 1 illustrates the general setup and the communication channels between the participants: The server, which acts as a client too, is located in the operating room, has multiple RGB-D cameras connected to it, and hosts the virtual operating room scene. Remote doctors connect to the server and receive the point cloud visualization of the physical scene – the region of interest (ROI) of the OR – from the server. If the users have an RGB-D camera for a personalized point cloud avatar themselves, they

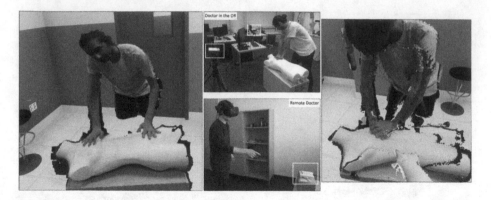

Fig. 2. Example of our system. Left: live-streamed point cloud visualization of the local doctor in the real OR, seen from the perspective of a remote doctor. Middle: physical environments of the local (top) and remote (bottom) doctors with RGB-D cameras (see white rectangles). Right: point cloud visualization of the local doctor using two cameras to minimize occlusions, and part of the remote doctor's self-avatar.

directly broadcast the corresponding data to all participants. The application's network traffic, apart from the RGB-D data, however, is always routed via the server.

An example of our telepresence system in action can be seen in Fig. 2. The left image shows the doctor in the real OR as a live-streamed point cloud visualization in the virtual OR, seen from the viewpoint of a remotely connected doctor. The right image shows the same doctor rendered with the point clouds from two cameras which helps to minimize occlusions. The middle images illustrate the physical environments of the local and remote doctors with their respective RGB-D cameras.

3.1   Multi-user VR Environment

The central part of our system is a virtual operating room in which all the RGB-D data gets streamed and rendered, and in which the remote doctors can meet using HMDs, see Fig. 3 (left). The network architecture is based on Unreal's session system. After starting the application, the users arrive in a lobby where they can start a session or join an existing one. The focus of our system lies in users making use of HMDs to have an immersive VR experience and having real-time personalized point cloud avatars. However, for the case that the required technology is not available, we made sure the system is usable with a mouse and keyboard, too, and integrated flying mesh avatars as a fallback. For VR locomotion the room scale system is used in which the users can physically walk to move. We also provide a teleport functionality for cases where the physical space runs out. Research showed that this locomotion metaphor exhibits the least risk of inducing cybersickness. Also, to not confuse other present users, a simple particle effect is shown to indicate the deliberate nature of the teleport.

Other features of our virtual operating room are a virtual monitor to show medical image data and 3D organ meshes modeled based on real patient data, in this case, livers. The fully synchronized organ models consist of separate parts for arteries, tumors, and a half-transparent outer shell and can be grabbed and inspected by the users, as can be seen in Fig. 3 (right). Also, the organ data is quickly replaceable to represent new cases.

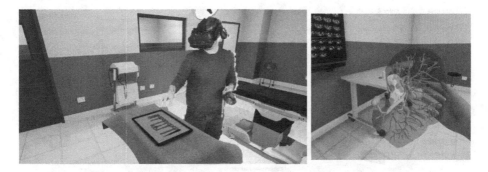

Fig. 3. Our virtual operating room with a point cloud avatar of a remote user on the left and an interactive virtual liver on the right.

3.2   Point Cloud Streaming

In this section, we describe the point cloud streaming pipeline of our telepresence system, which is one of its core parts. Instead of implementing everything from scratch, which would be tedious and time-consuming, we opted to use "Dyn-Cam: A Reactive Multithreaded Pipeline Library for 3D Telepresence in VR" by Schröder et al. [32] as a base and extended it for our needs. Generally, the Dyncam library provides a good foundation, as it has low latency streaming capabilities, which are crucial for telepresence in VR, and is easily extendable. However, we found some aspects such as compression and rendering to be lacking and decided to extend or replace them. We also adapted the architecture so that a single server-client connection can handle multiple cameras to reduce overhead and integrated functionality to record point cloud sequences and replay them later without the need for cameras to be connected. In Fig. 4 you can see an illustration of our final streaming pipeline. One or multiple RGB-D cameras are connected to the streaming server and will be processed individually. We use the new Azure Kinect RGB-D camera from Microsoft, as it has a high resolution and precision, hardware synchronization, and uses the TOF principle which is very suited for indoor use. The first step of our pipeline is the preprocessing of the color and depth images, which consists of lens correction, cropping, and filtering algorithms including background subtraction, and morphological filters for hole-filling and denoising. Then the images get compressed and transmitted to the client where they will be decompressed. We decided to compress and transmit the color- and depth images instead of point clouds, as this enables us to use more efficient image- and video-based compression algorithms. This means that the point cloud will only be computed client-side. For this, the camera's intrinsic data will be transmitted once too. Lastly, the point clouds of multiple cameras will be registered to each other and to the virtual scene and then rendered.

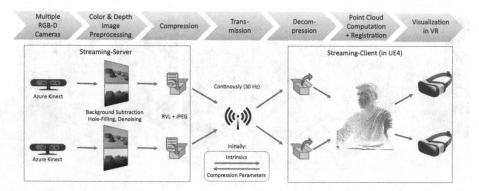

Fig. 4. Our point cloud streaming pipeline. Color and depth images of multiple cameras get individually preprocessed and compressed server-side and then transmitted to the clients where the point clouds get computed and registered before rendering.

We have implemented the filtering algorithms using CUDA to minimize latency. For background subtraction, there are two options. The first one is to set a simple depth threshold per camera to exclude points from rendering (depth set to zero). As a second option, the user can do a one-time recording of the scene, e.g., the empty operating room. In this case, the pixel-wise minimum valid value will be stored and acts as the threshold to distinguish between foreground and background. For hole-filling and depth denoising, we did extensive experiments with various filter algorithms, such as optical flow, Navier-Stokes-based inpainting, local regression, etc., but found them to be too slow, or the provided improvements were not significant enough to warrant the additional performance cost. Thus, we settled for faster solutions that achieve a good trade-off in this regard. Hole filling is done via multiple iterations of median-based morphological filtering and denoising using an adapted Kalman filter. As the Azure Kinect camera masks off the corners of the depth images with non-usable data, we added the option to do a cropped transmission and save bandwidth. Regarding the compression of the depth images, we extend the solution present in Dyncam (quantization plus LZ4) by integrating the H.264 video codec, and multiple efficient lossless algorithms, i.e., an ANS coder, RVL, and Zstandard. We found that even after compression the depth images are responsible for most network traffic while the color images are sufficiently small by just using jpeg compression. Therefore, we adapted the integrated lossless depth compression algorithms to achieve higher compression ratios by adding temporal delta compression. As with all compression and streaming systems, at some point, a trade-off has to be made between the required bandwidth and the computational speed. To allow the users to adapt this to their local capabilities, i.e., hardware power and network bandwidth, our design allows the client-side user to select the compression algorithm and parameters which will be used for their individual connection. For example, one user could choose to use RVL compression, which is fast and efficient, while another user may have a slower internet connection and opt for a different compression technique with a higher compression ratio at the cost of increased computational costs and lower speeds. The modular design of our pipeline also makes it easy to implement other and even more efficient compression algorithms in the future.

3.3 Point Cloud Registration and Rendering

To be able to have individual point cloud avatars for remote users, a registration procedure between the RGB-D camera and the VR coordinate system has to be done. When using multiple cameras, these have to be registered to each other too. For these registration tasks, we use the novel method by Mühlenbrock et al. [25]. It uses a grid-like registration target that is visible in the depth images to register multiple RGB-D cameras with each other and the VR coordinate system. This registration method proved to be very quick and easy to use. In the virtual scene, we have a hierarchy of actors in which each one is responsible for rendering one point cloud/camera. To account for the registration occasionally being slightly off, we allow the user to manually tweak the transformation in-game via sliders.

Of paramount interest is the fast and visually pleasing rendering of the point clouds. The Unreal Engine historically does not natively support point cloud rendering, however, by now, there is a publicly available point cloud rendering plugin "LiDAR Point Cloud"[1]. We experimented with the plugin but found it to be too slow with dynamic point clouds and, therefore, not suitable for our application. Our investigations indicate that the reason for the poor performance is that the plugin was designed to handle huge but static point clouds – it builds a spatial acceleration data structure intended for LOD. With dynamic point clouds, this costly operation would have to be done in each frame. The rendering solution provided in Dyncam was not convincing to us, both visually and from a performance point of view. We also considered implementing more complex volumetric reconstruction techniques similar to the ones in [27] and [9] but eventually decided against it, as they are computationally highly demanding, and we prioritized keeping the latency, which is critical in VR, to a minimum. Therefore, we have developed two different and very quick rendering solutions that we both integrated and tested in the Unreal Engine.

The first method is splatting-based but uses Unreal's new Niagara particle system. To get the point cloud positions and colors from the CPU to the GPU, we adopted Dyncam's approach of using two dynamic textures. In our case, all cameras from one user share a single texture with the size of 2048^2 which is

---

[1] https://www.unrealengine.com/marketplace/en-US/product/lidar-point-cloud.

sufficient for at least 11 cameras. Via Niagara module scripts we then calculate the UV coordinates based on the particle ID and forwarded parameters such as the point count per camera, texture size, etc., exploiting the fact that the point clouds are ordered. For point clouds meant to represent avatars of VR users, we additionally filter out all points that exceed a set distance from the center of mass which we compute dynamically via the HMD position. Also, points representing the HMD are filtered out for the local avatar's user in a similar fashion to prevent occluding the vision. When using splatting methods, the size of the points is important. To minimize holes and overlaps, we compute the diameter of each point based on the distance recorded from the sensor, as, because of the parallel projection, the density of points decreases with the distance. Another effect to consider is that surfaces perpendicular to the line of sight of the camera get sampled with a significantly lower density which results in bigger holes. To account for this fact, we also dynamically compute the local density of points, which is computationally cheaper than approximating their normals, and adjust the diameter accordingly. As blend mode in the material we use the masked mode instead of the translucent mode to circumvent the costly depth sorting.

Our second rendering method is based on a very fast mesh reconstruction and is intended to prevent visible holes between individual points altogether and instead provide continuous surfaces. Figure 5 shows a comparison of the two renderers. As can be seen, in some instances the individual points are still clearly visible with the splatting method. With our mesh reconstruction method, we can again exploit the fact that the point cloud is ordered and establish a one-to-one relation between point cloud points and the vertices of a plane mesh. At start-up, we once automatically create a plane mesh with the exact vertex dimensions and structure as the depth image on which the point cloud is based. E.g., a rectangular grid-like pattern of 640×576 vertices. At runtime, we then make the point cloud positions and colors available to the mesh's material, again, via dynamically updated textures. In the material, the vertices get transformed via Unreal's WorldPositionOffset-function according to the corresponding point cloud positions in the RGB-D camera's local space and the world-transform. We wrote custom shader nodes to exclude triangles from being rendered (alpha set to zero) if, based on the original position, the point was invalid, or one of the triangle's edges is too long. This prevents long, stretched triangles between foreground and background objects.

4   Evaluation and Results

4.1   Performance

To quantitatively evaluate our system's performance, we measured the time needed for filtering, compression, and rendering as well as the frame rate with which camera updates can be processed. All performance measurements were done using a PC with Windows 10, an Intel i7 7800x processor, 16 GB of main memory, and an Nvidia GeForce 2070 graphics card. As HMD we used the HTC

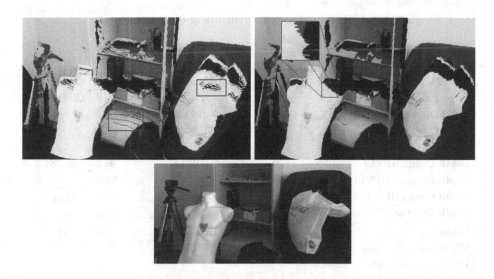

Fig. 5. Comparison of the two point cloud renderers, splatting on the left, fast mesh reconstruction on the right. Both look quite good but the splatting method still has visible holes in some areas, see the red rectangles. With the mesh however, object borders can look jagged (see highlighted region). The bottom image shows the captured scene.

Vive Pro Eye with a mounted Facial Tracker. Our application was developed using the Unreal Engine 4.26. All measurements were done without background subtraction to maintain the full worst-case workload.

First, we evaluated the speed of the filtering step of our pipeline (see the top left part of Table 1). As a whole, it took 1.34 ms to filter an un-cropped depth image (640 × 576 pixel), of which 0.59 ms were spent on hole-filling. Next, we measured the time for compression and decompression of the registered color image using JPEG: each took 1.5 ms. Using the cropped transmission (540 × 476 pixel) to discard the Azure Kinect camera's unused border areas resulted in only 1.08/1.22 ms being needed. Using H.264 (preset: ultrafast, tune: zerolatency), the computation was significantly slower: 7.72 ms for compression and 4.84 ms for decompression of the full-sized color images, and 11.04 ms and 9.4 ms for the depth images, respectively. Compression and decompression of the un-cropped depth images using the RVL method, which we found to be the most efficient, took 1.76 ms and 1.19 ms, respectively. Cropping reduced the time needed to 1.31 ms and 0.987 ms, respectively. An important detail to note is that the (de-)compression of color- and depth are done in parallel, meaning that the time won't stack on top of each other. The results show that in our pipeline, preprocessing and compression are very fast and can be accelerated even further by cropping the unused borders of the Azure Kinect's depth images, although the speed-up doesn't reach its theoretical potential (19–28% less time for 30% fewer pixels).

Table 1. Performance measurements of our application.

Task Duration	Time (ms)	
	Full	Cropped
Filtering	1.34	-
Color Comp. (jpeg)	1.5	1.08
Color Decomp. (jpeg)	1.5	1.22
Color Comp. (H.264)	7.72	-
Color Decomp. (H.264)	4.84	-
Depth Comp. (tRVL)	1.76	1.31
Depth Decomp. (tRVL)	1.19	0.987
Depth Comp. (H.264)	11.04	-
Depth Decomp. (H.264)	9.4	-
Latency		
VR Round-Trip Time	22-29	-
PC MotionToPhoton	120-150	-

Compression	Image Size (kB)	
	Full	Cropped
Color (JPEG)	21.9	18
Color (H.264)	15.85	-
Depth (RVL)	208	-
Depth (tRVL)	96.6	81.78
Depth (H.264)	59.69	-
Rendering Perf. (ms)	PC	Mesh
VR Frametime (1 Cam)	10.9	8.5
VR Frametime (2 Cam)	15	13

After these individual measurements, we evaluated the overall performance by measuring the more comprehensive metrics of the point cloud (PC) update rate that was maintainable as well as the eventual fps/frame times in VR. We measured the point cloud update rate by calculating the delta time both in our streaming server application as well as in the UE4 telepresence application that received and rendered the data. Throughout all cases, even using two cameras sending in full resolution and being in VR at the same time, our system was able to maintain a delta time of 33 ms which corresponds to the 30 fps capturing capability of the Azure Kinect cameras. The final performance in the packaged VR application was not only dependent on the number of cameras and the rendering technique but also heavily dependent on the general graphics settings the scene was rendered with ("scalability settings" in Unreal). Using the mesh rendering technique, Unreal Engine's "high" graphics preset, and the full depth resolution, we achieved a frame time of 12.5 ms with one camera and 15.5 ms with two. Setting the graphics preset to "low", we were able to reach 8.5 ms and 13 ms, see the bottom right part of Table 1. We found the splatting technique to be slower than the mesh variant, achieving only 10.9 ms and 15 ms under the "low" graphics preset. Important to note here is that the rendering resolution was held constant throughout the presets, and the graphics preset had no effect on the visualization of the point cloud rendering but only on the surrounding scene, most noticeably on reflective materials, anti-aliasing, and ambient occlusion. As can be seen from the performance measurements, our pipeline is very efficient throughout all stages and enables VR performance even with just a single PC per location. Both of the rendering techniques are very quick to compute, but especially the mesh version is highly efficient. As the performance scales with the number of cameras, at some point (e.g., 4+ cameras), more powerful hardware or a second PC would be needed to maintain the real-time VR performance, though.

4.2 Network

Regarding network performance metrics, we measured the round-trip time for interactions in VR, and the motion to photon latency of the whole pipeline, see the bottom left part of Table 1. The round-trip time – the time it takes for a client-side action to be transmitted to the server and back to a client – was between 22 ms and 29 ms., depending on the tick rate the server and client could achieve. The tests were conducted with 2 PCs in a local network. With greater distances, e.g., different cities, the time will likely be higher. The time between the camera capturing the scene and it being rendered on the display – the motion to photon latency – was measured by pointing a camera in such a way that both the physical scene and the display were recorded by an external camera. By analyzing the videos frame-by-frame, we found a latency of 4 to 5 frames which corcspondents to a 120–150 ms delay. However, roughly half of this is caused by the camera itself, as it is reported that delivery of the raw images by the Azure Kinect SDK needs ∼75 ms, depending on various parameters. We couldn't find any significant differences in delay for a varying number of cameras, between the rendering methods, or different graphics presets, which may also be because the external camera that we used for the measurement itself only captured 30 Hz. Although the measurements were not highly precise due to the limited temporal resolution of the external camera, the results show a rather low delay for such a system.

Lastly, we measured the compression efficacy and bandwidth required to transmit the RGB-D Data. The color images with an original size of 1440 kB were compressed with JPEG to 21.9 kB (on average) with a compression ratio of 66. Cropping further reduced the size to 18 kB, as can be seen in the top right part of Table 1. With H.264, the color images were compressed to 15.85 kB, and the depth images to 59.69 kB. However, the size and image accuracy are heavily dependent on the parameters; we used CRF values of 20 and 10 for the color and depth images, respectively. For depth images, we found the RVL algorithm to be a good trade-off between speed and compression ratio. Using it, depth images were losslessly compressed from the original 720 kB down to 208 kB with a compression rate of 3.46. With our temporally extended RVL, the average compressed size shrunk to 96.6 kB with a compression rate of 7.45, though the achievable compression here strongly depends on the amount of motion in the scene. With the cropped transmission, the size was further reduced to 81.78 kB. With the 30 images per second that the cameras provide, our system requires per camera 3,555 kB/s in full and 2,993 kB/s in cropped mode, which corresponds to 23.4 and 27.8 Mbps. This is a very good result considering that the depth images are transmitted losslessly and the high computational speed the compression runs on. Naturally, using lossy compression algorithms such as H.264, the bandwidth could easily be reduced further at cost of higher latency, if need be. However, we noticed visible artifacts on H.264-encoded depth images.

5   User Studies

To demonstrate the capabilities of our telepresence system and evaluate it regarding crucial aspects such as visualization quality, realism, and spatial- and social presence, we conducted two user studies with doctors and medical students in a hospital.

Fig. 6. Our telepresence system in action during the studies: on the left the remote doctor and on the right the live-captured operating room scene.

5.1   Study 1: Qualitative Feedback, Presence, and Preference

The goal of the first user study was to get general feedback from the doctors, evaluate it regarding relevant aspects like presence, and see how beneficial the telepresence system could be in clinical practice. The study was conducted with $N_1 = 12$ doctors and medical students with varying amounts of experience in the operating room and with AR/VR. The experimental setup for this study was as follows: In a room similar to an operating room, we divided the space in half. In the one half, a PC was set up that acted as the server for the streaming pipeline and host for the VR session. Connected to the PC was an RGB-D camera facing an operating table and a staff member acting as a surgeon, see Fig. 6 (right). In the second half of the room was a second PC with an HMD which the participants had to put on and join the session in the virtual operating room where they could see the operating table and staff member as a live-streamed point cloud, see Fig. 6 (left). The PCs were connected via a local network.

The task for the participants was to observe the staff member and help him with specific spatial tasks he had to perform with interlocking bricks (Lego). We did use interlocking bricks for this study, as their shape, size, and inherent ability to be combined into various more complex structures makes them suitable to recreate spatial tasks done by surgeons. First of all, the staff member did work alone so the participants could familiarize themselves with the VR experience and the scene. After roughly one minute, the staff member started asking questions and presenting problems to facilitate interaction with the participant and steer his attention to individual bricks. Questions were, for example, how many bricks of one color were used in a construction, how many studs of one color were visible, or how a specific construction could be built with a set amount of available bricks. After the VR experience, which lasted roughly 8 min, the participants had to fill out a questionnaire. The questionnaire consisted of a demographical part (age group, sex, experience in the operating room, experience with AR/VR), the Igroup Presence Questionnaire (IPQ) [33], which is split into the three subscales spatial presence, involvement, and realism, and a social-presence part taken from Nowak et al. [26]. Additionally, we added various specific questions: about cybersickness; if the participants see benefits of our system compared to more traditional video-based systems; if they would prefer it to those systems; how often they would want to use our system. For all questions, we used a 7-point Likert scale (1–7, but shifted to 0–6 for the evaluation; higher scores are better).

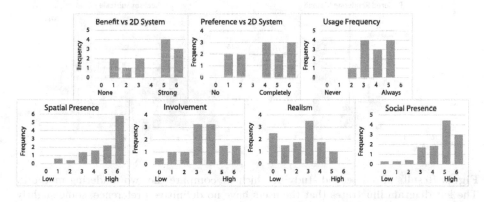

Fig. 7. Results of our first user study (in Likert scores, higher scores are better). Especially the spatial- and social presence scored very well, involvement and realism mediocre. The users see moderate to high benefits of the system and most of them would like to use it.

The results of this study can be seen in Fig. 7. Note that the scores can be fractional in some cases, as the IPQ subscales are aggregations of multiple questions. Our system scores especially high regarding both spatial- and social presence. 58% of the participants stated that they had a strong feeling of being present in the virtual world (Likert scale >= 5), the most often given score even being the maximal one. For the rest, the feeling was still moderately pronounced. Similarly, 62% stated that they had a strong feeling of actually being in the same room with the other person/having a personal meeting with another real person. Only 5% definitely had not the feeling. We also found that our system fares very well with cybersickness, as no participant had a significant occurrence of it, and 75% had nearly none to none. The results for the involvement and realism subscales of the IPQ are moderately good, most participants gave scores relating to "somewhat captivated by the virtual world" or "moderately real world", although, especially on the question "The virtual world seemed more realistic than the real world" of the IPQ, 75% gave the minimal score dragging down the subscale. One possibility for this particularly low result could be that the participants took the question too literally, and the question may be not that appropriate in our context. The other questions of the realism subscale[2] scored significantly better. In the end, 25% of the participants would attest moderate advantages and 58% even strong advantages to our system compared to more traditional videoconferencing systems. Also, 83% would prefer this system at least somewhat over teleconferencing systems, and 33% would use it on all possible occasions, while the other 77% at least sometimes. The results for the realism subscale as a whole are in-line with the comments made by some participants during and after the study – that the point cloud visualization is still somewhat grainy and low precision.

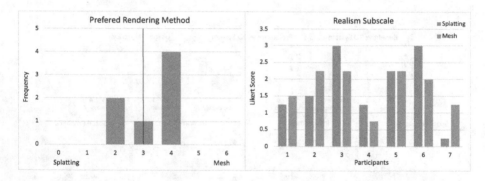

Fig. 8. Results of our second study in which we compare the two rendering methods. The left diagram illustrates that the users have no definitive preference, some slightly prefer the splatting (left side of the x-axis), others the mesh rendering (right side of the x-axis). The right diagram shows that also the realism scores fairly similar between the two rendering methods (higher scores are better).

5.2   Study 2: Comparison of Point Cloud Rendering Solutions

In a second study, we compared our two point cloud rendering methods and further investigated the specific clinical use cases in which our system could provide benefits. The experimental setup was similar to the one in the first study, but this time there were two VR phases for the participants. First, they saw the live-streamed staff member with the interlocking bricks using one rendering method, filled out a questionnaire, and then repeated the procedure with the second rendering method and a second part of the questionnaire. Which rendering method

---

[2] http://www.igroup.org/pq/ipq/download.php.

was seen first, point cloud or mesh, was randomized. The task in both phases was the same as in the first study, helping the staff member with the interlocking bricks. For this study, we discarded the social presence part from the first study and the spatial presence and involvement subscales of the IPQ, retaining only the realism one. Instead, we focused on getting more precise feedback regarding the potential benefits and use cases of the system. We also directly asked which rendering method would be preferred. The study was conducted with $N_2 = 7$ doctors and medical students in a hospital.

The results can be seen in Fig. 8. The left diagram shows the answers to the question of which rendering technique the doctors would prefer, the value of 3 meaning they found them similar, lower values meaning the splatting technique was preferred, and higher values correspond to the mesh visualization. The right diagram shows the scores of the realism subscale for the two rendering techniques. Again, scores are fractional, as the IPQ subscale is an aggregation of multiple questions. The results show that there was no absolute preference for one rendering method or the other. According to the data, the participants found them to be rather similar, some slightly preferring the splatting and others the mesh method. From the direct question and its result in the left diagram, we can see a small tendency for the mesh technique, which lines up with verbally given statements from two doctors after the study that they found the mesh rendering a bit better. The results for the realism subscale also indicate that there is no clear advantage for one or the other method. With a sample size of seven, it is hard to make statements with any significance, though. We did perform a Wilcoxon rank-sum test to test the null hypothesis of both distributions being equal and had not enough evidence to reject this hypothesis. Similar to the first study, the question about if the virtual world was more realistic than the real world scored particularly bad. Asked about it, one doctor argued that a positive answer to this would be impossible, as he obviously knew that he was in a virtual world during the experiment. The rest of the questionnaire's answers confirmed the results of the first study: most doctors would like to use such a telepresence system from time to time (57.1%), and some would even be eager to use it very often (28.5%). The more in-depth questions about the benefits and use-cases showed that most doctors see moderate benefits over video-based solutions for our proposed system in its current state and very strong benefits if, in the near future, the point cloud visualization quality and precision could be improved. The doctors stated that the system could be advantageous and helpful in emergency operations, or if an inexperienced doctor is on duty. Additional use-cases given by the doctors were educational operations, learning of the anatomy, patient anamnesis, and learning and teaching of practical skills in general.

6   Limitations

From the results of the first and particularly, the second study, we conclude that our telepresence system is a very good basis and has very high potential, but the

RGB-D cameras' sensor resolution is a main limiting factor at the moment, at least concerning tasks involving high precision or small details. Naturally, sensors with higher resolutions being released would bring the biggest relief, however, we also think about combining 3D cameras with different sensing techniques to complement each other. E.g., stereo cameras, which typically produce higher-resolution color and depth images, could be added and used to enhance the fidelity of our system. Another limitation of our current system is the lack of a dedicated point cloud/mesh fusion process. Individually rendering multiple point clouds or meshes that depict the same object leads to visible seams or artifacts, even though they are registered precisely. The flying pixel effect and internal interpolation routines in the cameras may be one of the causes. Efficient and precise real-time fusion is a challenging topic in itself though, for example, Dou. et al. [9] proposed a sophisticated but computationally demanding approach, and, thus, was not the focus of this work.

6.1   Face Reconstruction

A glaring problem with real-time reconstructed avatars in VR/AR telepresence applications is the HMD blocking the face. To be able to see the people's faces is highly important in collaborative virtual environments, though. To solve this issue, we developed a prototype combining the HMD's eye- and mouth-trackers with 3D Morphable Face Models (3DMM). A straightforward solution would be to use the deformable face model delivered with the HTC eye-tracking SDK and let the trackers drive the deformation. However, this generic model wouldn't be too realistic, as it can't be personalized. Also, we found the resulting facial expressions often do not match the actual mimic that well, sometimes even being weird-looking. Therefore, we acquired a more advanced morphable face model from "eos: A lightweight header-only 3D Morphable Face Model fitting library in modern C++11/14" [15] which can be automatically adapted to the person's facial geometry via a photo taken beforehand. Instead of directly applying the trackers' output to the morphable face, we pre-animated six facial expressions relating to basic emotions that are dynamically selected, interpolated, and applied to the face. The selection is based on a custom neural network that we pre-trained to map the trackers' output to the emotions. The six basic emotions we decided on are sadness, disgust, happiness, surprise, anger, and neutrality. To train the neural network, we created a small data set of facial expressions by asking multiple people to mimic the six emotions while we record the tracker output. To further customize the face model, we initially take six photos of the user's face, one for each of the facial expressions, and apply the most appropriate as a texture on the face at run-time. Again, the selection and interpolation is being driven by the neural network's output. The morphable face model is eventually rendered at the HMDs' 3D position while point cloud points or mesh triangles corresponding to the face are hidden. An example is illustrated in Fig. 9. To get a homogeneous avatar appearance for the point cloud rendering method, we wrote a custom shader transforming the mesh of the morphable face to look like a point cloud.

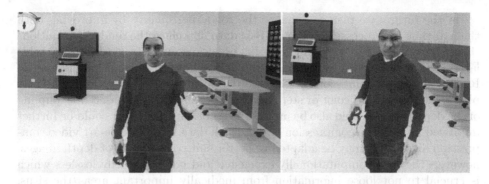

Fig. 9. Our mesh-rendered point cloud avatar with the reconstructed face, on the left with a neutral look and on the right showing disgust.

7   Conclusion and Future Work

In this paper, we have presented an immersive VR telepresence system for telementoring and remote collaboration in the operating room. Multiple Azure Kinect RGB-D cameras and point cloud avatars enable doctors to interact with each other and to view and assist in operations from a distance as if they were there. Thanks to our modular, low latency RGB-D streaming pipeline and efficient point cloud rendering and reconstruction techniques implemented in the Unreal Engine 4, we achieve very low latencies: our evaluation shows motion-to-photon latencies of only 120–150 ms, of which half of the latency is caused by the camera itself. At the same time, our pipeline handles all relevant tasks from filtering, denoising, and compression of the RGB-D data, to registration and computation of the point clouds. Using lossless compression, a bandwidth of only 23.4 Mbit/s per camera is required, although this can be further reduced by lossy compression when appropriate. In contrast to many other telepresence systems, our proposed solution is easy to set up and doesn't require multiple high-end PCs to run. We also presented a prototype to tackle the issue of occluded faces via personalized semi-real-time face reconstruction. A user study we conducted with doctors indicated that our system is capable of inducing very strong feelings of spatial and social presence. 83% of the participating doctors attested moderate to high benefits to our system compared to video-based solutions, and one-third would like to use it at every opportunity. Lastly, we compared two point cloud rendering solutions, splatting and fast mesh reconstruction, via another study. The results showed that they scored quite similar regarding the IPQ's realism subscale, and the doctors had no clear preference for one or the other method. If directly asked for a comparison, there was a slight tendency in favor of the mesh method. In general, though, the RGB-D sensors' lacking resolution seems to be a limiting factor. Accordingly, most doctors would attest medium-high benefits to the system in the current state, reaching from educational scenarios to consultation in emergency situations, and very strong benefits if the fidelity could be improved upon in the near future.

In the future, we plan to enhance the rendering quality by improving both the real-time preprocessing of the RGB-D data as well as the rendering solutions themselves. For instance, neural networks became popular in many related fields lately and may lead to improvements in hole filling, denoising, or merging of RGB-D data and point clouds, too. In order to further increase the fidelity, we plan to add dedicated color or stereo cameras. Deep-learning-based up-sampling of the depth images could also be promising. Another aspect that could be further improved upon is the compression of the depth data. State-of-the-art video compression algorithms may be adapted to better suit compression of depth images, however, they are computationally expensive and not necessarily lossless which is crucial to not loose information from medically important areas/the situs. Using different compression algorithms and a combination of lossy and lossless techniques depending on the area of the scene and the visualized object may be a valid solution to circumvent this problem. To tackle the issue of the obstructed faces, we plan to finalize the prototype of our proposed reconstruction pipeline. Point cloud/mesh fusion is also an important topic we want to explore. Lastly, integrating the option to also use AR HMDs would be a great addition, especially for the doctors in the operating room.

Acknowledgements. This work was partially funded by the German Federal Ministry of Education and Research (BMBF) under the grant 16SV8077.

References

1. Amamra, A., Aouf, N.: GPU-based real-time RGBD data filtering. J. Real-Time Image Process. **14**(2), 323–340 (2014). https://doi.org/10.1007/s11554-014-0453-7
2. Anton, D., Kurillo, G., Yang, A.Y., Bajcsy, R.: Augmented telemedicine platform for real-time remote medical consultation. In: Amsaleg, L., Guðmundsson, G.Þ, Gurrin, C., Jónsson, B.Þ, Satoh, S. (eds.) MMM 2017. LNCS, vol. 10132, pp. 77–89. Springer, Cham (2017). https://doi.org/10.1007/978-3-319-51811-4_7
3. Augestad, K., Lindsetmo, R.O.: Overcoming distance: video-conferencing as a clinical and educational tool among surgeons. World J. Surg. **33**, 1356–1365 (2009)
4. Baños, R., Botella, C., Alcañiz Raya, M., Liaño, V., Guerrero, B., Rey, B.: Immersion and emotion: their impact on the sense of presence. Cyberpsychology Behav. Impact Internet Mult. Virtual Reality Behav. Soc. **7**, 734–41 (2005)
5. Böhlen, C.F.v., Brinkmann, A., Mävers, S., Hellmers, S., Hein, A.: Virtual reality integrated multi-depth-camera-system for real-time telepresence and telemanipulation in caregiving. In: 2020 IEEE International Conference on Artificial Intelligence and Virtual Reality (AIVR), pp. 294–297 (2020)
6. Cao, C., Preda, M., Zaharia, T.: 3d point cloud compression: a survey, pp. 1–9, July 2019
7. Cho, S., Kim, S.W., Lee, J., Ahn, J., Han, J.: Effects of volumetric capture avatars on social presence in immersive virtual environments. In: 2020 IEEE Conference on Virtual Reality and 3D User Interfaces (VR), pp. 26–34 (2020)
8. Dedeilia, A., Sotiropoulos, M., Hanrahan, J., Janga, D., Dedeilias, P., Sideris, M.: Medical and surgical education challenges and innovations in the covid-19 era: a systematic review. Vivo **34**, 1603–1611 (2020)

9. Dou, M., et al.: Fusion4d: real-time performance capture of challenging scenes. ACM Trans. Graph. **35**(4), 1–13 (2016)
10. Dussault, G., Franceschini, M.: Not enough there, too many here: understanding geographical imbalances in the distribution of the health workforce. Hum. Resour. Health **4**, 12 (2006)
11. Flodgren, G., Rachas, A., Farmer, A., Inzitari, M., Shepperd, S.: Interactive telemedicine: effects on professional practice and health care outcomes. Cochrane Database Syst. Rev. **9**, CD002098 (2015)
12. Essmaeel, K., Gallo, L., Damiani, E., De Pietro, G., Dipanda, A.: Comparative evaluation of methods for filtering Kinect depth data. Multimedia Tools Appl. **74**(17), 7331–7354 (2014). https://doi.org/10.1007/s11042-014-1982-6
13. Gamelin, G., Chellali, A., Cheikh, S., Ricca, A., Dumas, C., Otmane, S.: Point-cloud avatars to improve spatial communication in immersive collaborative virtual environments. Personal Ubiquitous Comput. **25**(3), 467–484 (2020). https://doi.org/10.1007/s00779-020-01431-1
14. Gasques, D., et al.: Artemis: a collaborative mixed-reality system for immersive surgical telementoring. In: Proceedings of the 2021 CHI Conference on Human Factors in Computing Systems, CHI 2021, Association for Computing Machinery, New York (2021)
15. Huber, P., et al.: A multiresolution 3d morphable face model and fitting framework. In: Proceedings of the 11th International Joint Conference on Computer Vision, Imaging and Computer Graphics Theory and Applications, University of Surrey (2016)
16. Jang-Jaccard, J., Nepal, S., Celler, B., Yan, B.: Webrtc-based video conferencing service for telehealth. Computing **98**, 169–193 (2016)
17. Kamimura, K., Fujita, Y., Miura, T., Matsumoto, Y., Maeda, Y., Zempo, K.: Tele-clinical support system via MR-HMD displaying doctor's instructions and patient information, pp. 477–479, March 2021
18. Kolkmeier, J., Harmsen, E., Giesselink, S., Reidsma, D., Theune, M., Heylen, D.: With a little help from a holographic friend: the open impress mixed reality telepresence toolkit for remote collaboration systems, pp. 1–11, November 2018
19. Kvedar, J., Coye, M., Everett, W.: Connected health: a review of technologies and strategies to improve patient care with telemedicine and telehealth. Health affairs (Project Hope) **33**, 194–199 (2014)
20. Latifi, R., et al.: Telemedicine and telepresence for trauma and emergency management. Scand. J. Surg. **96**, 281–289 (2007)
21. Lin, B.S., Su, M.J., Cheng, P.H., Tseng, P.J., Chen, S.J.: Temporal and spatial denoising of depth maps. Sensors **15**, 18506–18525 (2015)
22. Liu, Y., et al.: Hybrid lossless-lossy compression for real-time depth-sensor streams in 3D telepresence applications. In: Ho, Y.-S., Sang, J., Ro, Y.M., Kim, J., Wu, F. (eds.) PCM 2015. LNCS, vol. 9314, pp. 442–452. Springer, Cham (2015). https://doi.org/10.1007/978-3-319-24075-6_43
23. Mao, A., Zhang, H., Liu, Y., Zheng, Y., Li, G., Han, G.: Easy and fast reconstruction of a 3d avatar with an RGB-d sensor. Sensors **17**(5), 1113 (2017)
24. Mekuria, R., Blom, K., César, P.: Design, implementation and evaluation of a point cloud codec for tele-immersive video. IEEE Trans. Circ. Syst. Video Technol. **27**, 1 (2016)
25. Mühlenbrock, A., Fischer, R., Weller, R., Zachmann, G.: Fast and robust registration of multiple depth-sensors and virtual worlds. In: 2021 International Conference on Cyberworlds (CW), pp. 41–48 (2021)

26. Nowak, K., Biocca, F.: The effect of the agency and anthropomorphism on users' sense of telepresence, copresence, and social presence in virtual environments. Presence Teleoperators Virtual Environ. **12**, 481–494 (2003)
27. Orts, S., et al.: Holoportation: virtual 3d teleportation in real-time, December 2016
28. Pece, F., Kautz, J., Weyrich, T.: Adapting standard video codecs for depth streaming, pp. 59–66, January 2011
29. Ragan, E., Kopper, R., Schuchardt, P., Bowman, D.: Studying the effects of stereo, head tracking, and field of regard on a small-scale spatial judgment task. IEEE Trans. Vis. Comput. Graph. **19**(5), 886–896 (2012)
30. Rojas, E., et al.: Telementoring in leg fasciotomies via mixed-reality: clinical evaluation of the star platform. Mil. Med. **185**, 513–520 (2020)
31. Roth, D., et al.: Real-time mixed reality teleconsultation for intensive care units in pandemic situations, pp. 693–694, March 2021
32. Schröder, C., Sharma, M., Teuber, J., Weller, R., Zachmann, G.: Dyncam: a reactive multithreaded pipeline library for 3d telepresence in VR. In: Proceedings of the 20th ACM Virtual Reality International Conference (VRIC 2018), ACM (2018)
33. Schubert, T., Friedmann, F., Regenbrecht, H.: The experience of presence: factor analytic insights. Presence Teleoperators Virtual Environ. **10**(3), 266–281 (2001)
34. Söderholm, H., Sonnenwald, D., Cairns, B., Manning, J., Welch, G., Fuchs, H.: The potential impact of 3d telepresence technology on task performance in emergency trauma care, pp. 79–88, November 2007
35. Teng, C.C., Jensen, N., Smith, T., Forbush, T., Fletcher, K., Hoover, M.: Interactive augmented live virtual reality streaming: a health care application, pp. 143–147, June 2018
36. Thoravi Kumaravel, B., Anderson, F., Fitzmaurice, G., Hartmann, B., Grossman, T.: Loki: facilitating remote instruction of physical tasks using bi-directional mixed-reality telepresence, pp. 161–174, October 2019
37. Tölgyessy, M., Dekan, M., Chovanec, L., Hubinský, P.: Evaluation of the azure Kinect and its comparison to Kinect v1 and Kinect v2. Sensors **21**, 413 (2021)
38. Wilson, A.: Fast lossless depth image compression, pp. 100–105, October 2017
39. Yu, K., Gorbachev, G., Eck, U., Pankratz, F., Navab, N., Roth, D.: Avatars for teleconsultation: effects of avatar embodiment techniques on user perception in 3d asymmetric telepresence. IEEE Trans. Vis. Comput. Graph. **27**(11), 4129–4139 (2021)

Fast Intra-Frame Video Splicing for Occlusion Removal in Diminished Reality

Chengyuan Lin$^{(\boxtimes)}$ and Voicu Popescu

Purdue University, West Lafayette, IN 47906, USA
lin553@alumni.purdue.edu, popescu@purdue.edu

Abstract. In a real world scene objects of interest might be occluded by other objects. Diminished reality (DR) aims to remove such occluders. A popular approach is to acquire the geometry of the occluded scene, and then to render it from the user's viewpoint, effectively erasing the occluder. However, the approach is ill-suited for scenes with intricate and dynamic geometry, which cannot be acquired quickly, completely, and with only minimal equipment. This paper proposes a method to erase an occluder in a primary video by splicing in pixels from a secondary video. For each frame, the method finds the region in the secondary frame that corresponds to the occluder shadow, and integrates it seamlessly into the primary frame. Precise matching of the occluder contour is achieved by a novel pipeline with a tracking, global alignment, and local alignment stages. The result is a continuous multiperspective frame, which shows most of the scene from the primary viewpoint, except for the part hidden by the occluder, which is shown from the secondary viewpoint. A high quality multiperspective transparency effect is achieved for complex scenes, without the high cost of 3D acquisition. When compared with other DR methods, the proposed method shows fewer artifacts and better continuity.

Keywords: Occluder removal · Video splicing · Multiperspective visualization · Diminished reality · Augmented reality

1 Introduction

Augmented reality improves a user's view of the real world by *adding* graphical annotations. However, improving the user's view sometimes calls for *removing* objects from the user's view. Such diminished reality visualizations are used to eliminate distracting clutter, to preview possible changes to a real world scene without actually modifying it, and to let the user see hidden parts of the scene quickly, from the current location. Removing an occluder from the user's view of the real world requires finding the footprint of the occluder, finding a visual description of what the user should see in the absence of the occluder, and transferring it to the occluder footprint. One approach is 3D scene acquisition.

© The Author(s), under exclusive license to Springer Nature Switzerland AG 2022
G. Zachmann et al. (Eds.): EuroXR 2022, LNCS 13484, pp. 111–134, 2022.
https://doi.org/10.1007/978-3-031-16234-3_7

Once the geometry of the scene is known, the scene can be rendered from the user's viewpoint, without the occluder. This works well, for example, when one wants to remove an object from a corner of a room, whose color and geometry are easy to acquire or synthesize. A challenging case for this approach is when the parts of the scene hidden by the occluder have intricate and dynamic appearance and geometry, which cannot be acquired comprehensively in real time, and with minimal equipment.

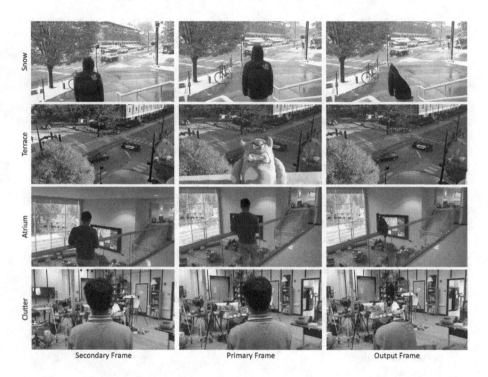

Fig. 1. Results preview. The output frame is obtained by erasing the occluder from the primary frame using pixels from the secondary frame. The result is a quality transparency effect, with good continuity at the occluder contour. Our method supports intricate dynamic scenes, and the frame rate is 75fps or better for an output resolution of 1,920 × 1,080.

In this paper we propose a method to remove an occluder in a primary video, acquired from the user viewpoint, using pixels from a secondary video, acquired from a translated viewpoint. The secondary frame pixels are integrated seamlessly into the primary frame, with good continuity across the occluder contour. The result is a multiperspective frame, which shows most of the scene from the user viewpoint, except for the part hidden by the occluder, which is shown from the secondary viewpoint. The effect is a good approximation of the transparency effect needed to remove the occluder, which comes without the high cost 3D geometry acquisition.

We have tested our method with good results on a variety of challenging scenes, with intricate and dynamic geometry (see Fig. 1 and accompanying video). We have compared our method to ground truth and to state of the art occluder inpainting techniques, both qualitatively, through visual inspection, and quantitatively, through two traditional per-pixel similarity metrics and two perceptual image similarity metrics. The comparison reveals that our results are closer to ground truth than those of the prior art methods. Furthermore, since we only compute correspondences between frames along the occluder contour, and we do not engage in full 3D reconstruction, our method is fast, running at 75 Hz in a CPU implementation.

2   Prior Work

The removal of objects that hinder the user's viewing of a region of interest is a typical diminished reality problem [42]. By covering up a real object with the image of the background it occludes, one can make the object virtually invisible by creating a "see-through" effect [23]. The effect is implemented in three main steps: acquisition of the occluder background, modification of the acquired background to fit the occluder footprint, and compositing of the modified background into the user's view.

The background can be captured by the user in advance in the form of a dataset of images [25] or a detailed 3D model [3,29]. When the hidden background objects are known, such as a specific person's face, a pre-captured dataset with angle-dependent images is sufficient [32]. An internet photo collection can also be used to delete a person in a video sequence, especially when the scene is a frequently photographed sightseeing spot [19]. Another approach is to search for the best matching disoccluded view of the target in an earlier frame [12,37]. For a moving camera, SLAM was used to reconstruct the background progressively [27,33]. These methods fail when the current background configuration has not been observed in any of the earlier frames. Both the pre-acquisition and the temporal resampling methods cannot handle highly dynamic scenes, such as a busy intersection.

A dynamic scene has to be acquired in parallel, from additional viewpoints. Using multiple cameras installed all around the scene, unstructured light fields can be acquired and used to render occluded rays [24]. Surveillance cameras have been used to see through walls [17,22]. Multiple users, each with their own handheld camera, can capture the background for each other but the approach was only demonstrated for planar backgrounds with markers [10]. The background was also acquired with a remote-controlled robot equipped with a camera [4]. Like these prior methods, we acquire the background information with a secondary camera, but without background geometry assumptions or markers.

Once acquired, the background needs to be transferred to the primary camera viewpoint. By assuming the scene only consists of large planes, homography matrices have been used to warp the background to the user view [6]. Homographies have also been used to transfer the best matching background image

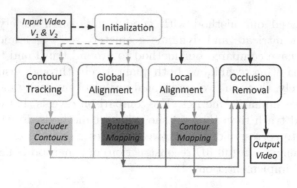

Fig. 2. System pipeline.

from an internet image collection to the user view [19]. Another approach is to extract the 3D geometry of the background. Using stereo vision, the background has been approximated with a set of small planes [42], or with a depth map [30]. The pixels missing due to disocclusion errors have to be filled in, e.g., through texture synthesis [9,34]. The background geometry has also been acquired with the help of RGB-D cameras [21]. Reconstructing an accurate model of a complex 3D scene in real time remains challenging, and inaccurate geometry leads to output image artifacts, such as holes and tears. We bypass 3D geometry acquisition by computing a two stage bijective mapping that avoids such artifacts.

Inpaiting approaches approximate the occluded background from the surrounding, visible parts of the background [8]. Patched-based inpainting methods search iteratively in the neighborhood for best fitting patches [2,5]. Prior information about the occluded part of the scene is useful for achieving a higher quality inpainting, such as of occluded human faces [16,18]. Deep-learning has also been used to find matching patches at greater distances in the frame, with improved global consistency [15,20,38]. These methods have the advantage of not requiring a second video source, but they depend on the uniformity and predictability of the disoccluded background. As such, these methods are typically used to remove the annoying visual presence of the occluder, and not to provide a detailed and accurate description of the scene visible once the occluder is removed. Their goal is to erase the occluder well enough as to *not* draw the user's attention to the disoccluded part of the image; on the other hand, our method has the more challenging goal of allowing the user to focus precisely on the part of the scene that has been disoccluded.

3   Approach

We first give an overview of our occlusion removal pipeline.

3.1   Pipeline Overview

Given a primary input video stream and a secondary input video stream, acquired from a translated viewpoint, our method removes an occluder from the primary video using pixels from the secondary video, according to the pipeline shown in Fig. 2. First, an initialization stage defines the occluder contour in the first frame of each video, and computes an approximate mapping between these two first frames. Then, pairs of primary and secondary video frames are processed in four stages: the contour of the occluder is updated in each of the two frames; an initial mapping between the pair of frames is computed as a rotation, by minimizing color differences outside the occluder; the initial mapping is locally refined at the occluder contour to enable splicing in the pixels from the secondary frame with good continuity to the surrounding primary frame pixels; finally, the occluder is removed from the primary frame by looking up its pixels in the secondary frame, using a concatenation of the global and local mappings.

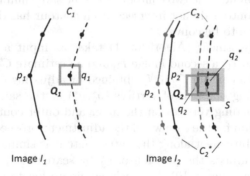

Fig. 3. Adjustment of approximate contour C_2^* to C_2 in image I_2, given the corresponding contour C_1 in image I_1 (Algorithm 1). The algorithm searches for a better position for each inner contour vertex q_2^* over its neighborhood S; a good position q_2 yields a high color similarity between I_2 at q_2 and I_1 at q_1; q_1 is the inner contour vertex of C_1 corresponding to q_2^*. Once q_2^* is adjusted, the corresponding outer contour vertex p_2^* is adjusted to p_2 with the same offset.

3.2   Contour Adjustment

Our pipeline relies several times on a contour adjustment algorithm, which we describe first. We define a *contour* as a pair of polylines that model the inner and outer boundaries of an object visible in an image. The inner contour is on the

---

Algorithm 1. Contour adjustment (also see Fig. 3)

Input: Image I_1, contour C_1 in I_1, image I_2, contour C_2^* in I_2
Output: Adjusted contour C_2

1: **for** each vertex pair (p_2^*, q_2^*) in C_2^* **do**
2:     $s_{max} = -\infty$
3:     **for** each pixel center q in neighborhood S of q_2^* **do**
4:         $Q_1 = I_1$ patch centered at q_1
5:         $Q_2 = I_2$ patch centered at q
6:         $s_q = \text{sim}(Q_1, Q_2) + \lambda e^{-|q-q_2^*|^2/(2\sigma^2)}$
7:         **if** $s_q > s_{max}$ **then**
8:             $q_2 = q$, $s_{max} = s_q$
9:         **end if**
10:    **end for**
11:    $p_2 = p_2^* + q_2 - q_2^*$
12: **end for**
13: RemoveSelfIntersections(C_2)

---

object and the outer contour is on the surrounding background. The inner and outer contours are needed to restrict color comparisons to the occluder or to its surrounding background. The two contours have the same number of 2D vertices, the segments of a contour do not intersect, each contour has disk topology, and contours do not have to be convex.

Our contour adjustment (Algorithm 1) takes as input a first image I_1, a known contour C_1 in I_1, a second image I_2, and an estimate C_2^* of C_1 in I_2. The algorithm output is a contour C_2 in I_2 obtained by adjusting C_2^*. The algorithm adjusts C_2^* by moving one pair of vertices (p_2^*, q_2^*) at the same time, where p_2^* and q_2^* are corresponding vertices on the inner and outer contours (line 1). We describe the algorithm for the case when the adjustment proceeds along the inner contour (Fig. 3). Adjustment along the outer contour is similar.

The algorithm adjusts the position of q_2^* by searching its neighborhood S for a better location (lines 3–10). For each candidate location q, the algorithm computes color similarity between I_2 at q and I_1 at q_1. Color similarity is evaluated over square image patches Q_1 and Q_2 (lines 4–6). The inner contour vertex q_2 is adjusted every time image similarity improves (lines 7–8). Once the entire neighborhood of q_2^* has been searched, the contour vertex p_2 is adjusted by the same offset $q_2 - q_2^*$ as q_2^* (line 11). Once the inner and outer contours have been adjusted, C_2 is returned after any self intersection is removed (line 13). Our algorithm checks and removes self-intersections by traversing the outer contour; if two outer contour segments (p_2^i, p_2^{i+1}) and (p_2^j, p_2^{j+1}) intersect, where $i < j$, all outer contour vertices from p_2^{i+1} to p_2^j are removed, together with their corresponding inner contour vertices.

In line 6, the similarity between image patches Q_1 and Q_2 is computed differently based on whether images I_1 and I_2 are frames of the same video, i.e. both primary or both secondary, or not, i.e. one primary and one secondary. When

Algorithm 2. Intra-frame video splicing for occlusion removal

Input: Primary video V_1, secondary video V_2
Output: Disoccluded primary video V_d

    // Initialization
  1: $B_1^0 = \text{UserInputContour}(V_1^0)$
  2: $C_1 = \text{RefineContour}(B_1^0)$
  3: $C_2^* = \text{HomographyMapping}(C_1, V_1^0, V_2^0)$
  4: $C_2 = \text{AdjustContour}(C_1, V_1^0, C_2^*, V_2^0)$
  5: $R_1^0 = I;\ R_2^0 = \text{InitializeRotation}(C_1, V_1^0, V_2^0)$
  6: **for** each frame i **do**
      // Contour tracking
  7:     $C_1 = \text{AdjustContour}(C_1, V_1^{i-1}, C_1, V_1^i)$
  8:     $C_2 = \text{AdjustContour}(C_2, V_2^{i-1}, C_2, V_2^i)$
      // Global alignment
  9:     $j = k \times \lfloor i/k \rfloor$
10:     $R_1^i = R_1^j \times \text{RotationMapping}(C_1, V_1^j, V_1^i, R_1^{i-1})$
11:     $R_2^i = R_2^j \times \text{RotationMapping}(C_2, V_2^j, V_2^i, R_2^{i-1})$
12:     $R = (R_2^i)^{-1} \times R_1^i$
      // Local alignment
13:     $A_1 = \text{SalientContourPoints}(C_1)$
14:     $A_2 = \text{AdjustContour2}(A_1, V_1^i, R \times A_1, V_2^i, R)$
      // Occlusion removal
15:     $V_d^i = V_1^i$
16:     **for** each pixel $p \in C_1$ **do**
17:         $p' = \text{LookUp}(p, R, A_1, A_2, C_2)$
18:         $V_d^i[p] = \text{Blend}(V_1^i[p], V_2^i[p'])$
19:     **end for**
20: **end for**

I_1 and I_2 are from the same video, we compute similarity using negative sum of squared per-pixel color differences:

$$sim_{intra}(Q_1, Q_2) = -\sum_p (Q_1[p] - Q_2[p])^2. \tag{1}$$

When I_1 and I_2 are from different videos, we use a cosine similarity [31], in order to compensate for any large exposure and white balance differences between the two videos. Cosine similarity is computed by treating each patch as a vector, and by computing the cosine of the angle between the two vectors:

$$sim_{inter}(Q_1, Q_2) = \frac{\sum_p Q_1[p] \cdot Q_2[p]}{\sqrt{\sum_p Q_1[p]^2}\sqrt{\sum_p Q_2[p]^2}}. \tag{2}$$

In addition to the color similarity value sim, the aggregate similarity score s_q (line 6) also includes a displacement term $\lambda e^{-|\delta p|^2/(2\sigma^2)}$, which favors small contour adjustments when sim values are similar. The displacement follows a normal distribution $\mathcal{N}(0, \sigma)$, where σ controls the distribution flatness. The weight

λ achieves the right balance between the cosine similarity term and the displacement term. Both parameters σ and λ are set empirically in the 5–10 and 0.5–1.5 ranges, respectively, and tuned for each of the scenes. The displacement term aims to avoid large adjustments for marginal color similarity improvements, e.g. to avoid that a patch on an object edge slide up and down the edge without meaningful color similarity changes.

3.3 Video Splicing for Occlusion Removal

Our pipeline implements Algorithm 2, which takes as input the primary V_1 and secondary V_2 videos and removes an occluder from V_1 using pixels from V_2.
Initialization. The algorithm first performs a once per session initialization (lines 1–5). The user selects the occluder to be removed interactively by drawing in the first frame V_1^0 of the primary video an approximate piecewise linear outer boundary B_1^0 of the occluder (line 1, red line in Fig. 4 left). An approximate boundary that overestimates the occluder is sufficient, as the occluder will be removed with safety margins. Whereas other applications of segmentation have to recover an object contour with high-fidelity, as needed to paste it inconspicuously into a destination image, our application simply has to make sure that the entire occluder is discarded.

The outer boundary B_1^0 is refined to define the initial contour C_1 in frame V_1^0 (line 2), as follows: B_1^0 is rasterized to obtain a pixel mask M_1; M_1 is eroded to pixel mask M_1'; the inner contour of C_1 is defined as a subset of the outer pixels of M_1', i.e. pixels who have at least one of their eight neighbors not part of M_1' (white dots in Fig. 4 left); every inner contour vertex is moved outwards along its normal to define its outer contour vertex pair (white line in Fig. 4 left).

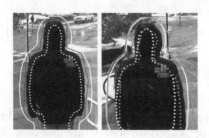 

Fig. 4. Contour initialization (left and middle), and contour tracking (right). Left: first frame of primary video, with user drawn outer contour (red), and initial inner (white dots) and outer (white line) contours. Middle: first frame of secondary video, with contour lines transferred from primary video (white), and adjusted (green). Right: old contour in blue, adjusted contour in red. (Color figure online)

C_1 is used to initialize the occluder contour C_2 in the secondary video. C_1 is transferred to V_2^0 in two steps.

First, C_1 is taken almost all the way to its correct location in V_2^0 with a homography mapping from the C_1 region of V_1^0 to V_2^0; this provides an esti-mate C_2^* of the occluder contour in V_2^0 (line 3). The homography assumes that the occluder is a 3D plane, which is imaged by the two cameras with known intrinsic parameters. The homography is computed by detecting SURF features [7] inside the occluder region C_1 in V_1^0, and over the entire frame V_2^0. Each V_1^0 feature is matched to a V_2^0 feature with similar descriptor using FLANN [26]. The homography is determined by minimizing the reprojection error of corre-sponding features, using a RANSAC approach [11], which provides robustness to outlier feature correspondences. Fig. 4, middle, shows the outer and inner contours of C_2^* with white solid and dotted lines, respectively; C_2^* does not cap-ture the occluder quite perfectly as the outer contour crosses into, and the inner contour crosses out of the occluder.

Second, C_2^* is adjusted to C_2, using our contour adjustment Algorithm 1 (line 4). Since the frames provided to Algorithm 1 belong to different videos, the cosine similarity metric is used. Figure 4, middle, shows the adjusted contour C_2 with green solid and dotted lines.

The algorithm maintains two arrays of 3D rotations, R_1 and R_2, one for each video. R_1^i rotates frame i of the primary video to frame V_1^0. R_2^i rotates frame i of the secondary video to V_1^0 as well, that the first frame of the primary video serves as a common reference. The last step of the initialization sets R_1^0 and R_2^0 (line 5). R_1^0 is the identity matrix. R_2^0 is computed by minimizing feature reprojection error, as described in Sect. 3.4. Figure 5 illustrates R_2^0 by blending the rotated V_2^0 on top of V_1^0.

Fig. 5. Initialization of rotation from the first frame of the secondary video V_2^0 (left) to the first frame of the primary video V_1^0 (middle). The rotation is visualized by blending V_1^0 with the rotated V_2^0 (right). The rotation is recovered robustly (see alignment of distant parts of the scene), despite the considerable disparity between the two frames (see ghosting of near parts of the scene).

After initialization, each pair of primary and secondary video frames is pro-cessed with the four main stages of our pipeline.

Contour Tracking. Contours C_1 and C_2 are updated in the current frames V_1^i and V_2^i, using the known contours in the previous frames V_1^{i-1} and V_2^{i-1} (lines 7–8). We use Algorithm 1 again: the frame with the known contour is the previous frame, the frame where to adjust the contour is the current frame, and the estimate of the contour in the current frame is given by the contour in the previous frame. This no-motion contour prediction is sufficient because of the high frame rate of the videos compared to camera and occluder motion and velocity, and it bypasses the expense of computing a homography to provide the initial guess [13]. The frames are part of the same video, so similarity is computed using color difference. Figure 4, right, shows the output of our contour tracking stage.

Global Alignment. The algorithm has to compute a mapping from the primary video frame V_1^i to the secondary video frame V_2^i. For this, the algorithm first computes an approximate mapping. The approximate mapping is found by computing, for each video, the rotation of the current frame i to an earlier frame j *of that same video* (lines 9–11). Once the two rotations R_1^i and R_2^i are known, the approximate mapping R from V_1^i to V_2^i is easily obtained by leveraging the common reference V_1^0 of all rotations (line 12).

Fig. 6. Global alignment of two primary video frames (left and middle). The frames differ in view direction (see light post), and in time (see turning car). The blended visualization (right) shows that the global alignment recovers the rotation robustly (see alignment of distant scene), despite the motion in the scene (e.g., turning car) and the disparity of near objects (e.g., occluder and handrail).

To find the rotation of the current frame i with respect to the earlier frames we use a more distant key frame j, and not the previous frame $i-1$, as consecutive frames would be too similar, and the alignment would drift. The key frames are spaced k frames apart (typically $k = 120$). Unlike for initial rotation computation (Sect. 3.4), here the rotation has to connect two video frames acquired by the *same* camera, from a *similar* viewpoint. Consequently, the global alignment can be computed by directly minimizing color differences, bypassing the slower feature detection and matching. However, global alignment has to avoid the inconsistencies introduced by moving or near geometry, which create frame disparity even for small camera translations. Our global alignment computation is described in Sect. 3.5. Figure 6 illustrates the accuracy and robustness of our global alignment stage.

Local Alignment. The mapping R between frames V_1^i and V_2^i will be used to replace the occluder pixels in frame V_1^i with pixels from V_2^i. The mapping is approximate when the occluded scene is near and it has to be refined. The inaccuracy of the mapping is noticeable only at the occluder contour C_1, where the V_2^i pixels are spliced into V_1^i (Fig. 7, left). The algorithm computes a local alignment that alleviates color differences on each side of the occluder contour

Fig. 7. Local mapping need (left), implementation (middle), and result (right). Left: disoccluding using only the global mapping results in discontinuities where near objects cross the occluder contour, e.g. where the sidewalk and handrail cross the red line in the left image. Middle: the local mapping connects primary frame salient contour points (red points) to their correspondence in the secondary frame (green points); the local alignment offset is larger for near objects. Right: disocclusion with continuity at occluder contour.

(lines 13–14). First, the outer contour of C_1 is sampled to gather a set of points A_1 with large color changes (line 13, and red dots in Fig. 7, middle). These points are better suited for computing the local alignment than the outer contour vertices because they do not sample wastefully regions of uniform color, and because they sample most regions with large color changes.

The newly defined outer contour A_1 is adjusted with an algorithm similar to Algorithm 1, with two differences. The first difference is that the adjustment now proceeds following the outer contour, and not the inner one. Using Fig. 3 again, adjustment based on the outer contour is not concerned with the outer contour vertices and directly moves p_2' to its better position p_2 that minimizes the color difference between I_2 at p_2 and I_1 at p_1. The second difference is that the adjustment now compares Q_1 to a rotated image patch Q_2, and not an axis aligned one (line 6 in Algorithm 1). The rotated Q_2 is computed using rotation R. This more accurate comparison is now needed because the contour adjustment for the local alignment crosses between videos, and axis aligned patches do not match. Furthermore, adjustment is performed at the output frame cut line between the two video sources, so an inaccurate alignment would be readily visible. Figure 7, middle, visualizes the displacement of the points of A_1 (red dots) to their correct locations A_2 (green dots). Figure 7, right, shows the continuity achieved at contour boundary in the disoccluded frame using our local alignment.

Occlusion Removal. Finally, the algorithm removes the occluder in the primary frame V_1^i (lines 15–19). The disoccluded frame V_d^i starts out as a copy of V_1^i (line 15), and then pixels p inside the contour are looked up in V_2^i. A pixel p is first rotated to p_r using R, and then p_r is offset with a weighted sum of offsets $a_2 - R \times a_1$, for all a_1 points in the vicinity of p (typically in a 45×45 neighborhood). We support several disocclusion visualization modes, such as cutaway, where p' completely replaces p, and transparency, where p and p' are blended together, with and without showing the contour of the occluder.

3.4   Rotation Initialization

The videos V_1 and V_2 are acquired from different viewpoints, so computing the rotation R_2^0 of frame V_2^0 to V_1^0 is challenging, as it does not benefit from frame to frame coherence. Indeed, the gap between V_1 and V_2 only has to be bridged for the first frame of V_2, as subsequent V_2^0 frames only have to be registered to their previous frame, whose rotation to V_1^0 is already known.

R_2^0 is computed by finding SURF features [7] in V_1^0, outside of C_1, and in V_2^0. V_1^0 features are matched to V_2^0 features using FLANN [26]. A pair of corresponding features is given a weight commensurate to the confidence in its correctness. The weight w_{ij} of a correspondence between a feature f_{1i} in frame V_1^0 and the most similar feature f_{2j} in frame V_2^0 is computed with:

$$w_{ij} = |f_{1i} - f_{2k}|/|f_{1i} - f_{2j}| \tag{3}$$

where f_{2k} is the feature second most similar to f_{1i}, and $|f_a - f_b|$ is the difference between the descriptors of two features f_a and f_b. The smallest possible weight is 1, when f_{1i} is equally similar to its best two matches, indicating the possibility of an ambiguous correspondence. When the second most similar feature f_{2k} is considerably less similar to f_{1i} than f_{2j} is, the correspondence is less likely to be incorrect, hence the larger weight. The reprojection error of corresponding features is minimized using a Gauss-Newton non-linear optimization [28], while also leveraging a RANSAC [11] approach to mitigate possible incorrect correspondences.

Fig. 8. Weights used in the global alignment from Fig. 6. Moving objects (e.g., car, pedestrians), and regions with high disparity (e.g., contour of near person), are assigned low weights, to reduce noise in the rotation computation.

3.5   Global Alignment

The global alignment computes the rotation of the current frame i to a previous key frame j, independently, for each of the two videos. We globally align two frames with a rotation because it provides a good approximation of the mapping between the frames without the prerequisite of scene geometry. We use the

Gauss-Newton method [28] to find the three rotational degrees of freedom that minimize color difference.

Given a current frame V^i, a key frame V^j, the camera intrinsic matrix M (from a standard camera calibration process [41]), and a candidate rotation R from V^i to V^j, the color residual r_p at pixel p is:

$$r_p(R) = V^j[p] - V^i[M^{-1}(RM) \cdot p] \tag{4}$$

In Eq. 4, p is first unprojected from V_i, then rotated, and then projected to V_j. The stacked color residual vector over the entire frame is $\vec{r} = (r_1, \ldots, r_n)^T$, and the color error $E(R)$ is the ℓ_2 norm $|\vec{r}|$ of the residual vector. We use a left-compositional formulation. Starting with an initial estimate R^* given by the rotation of V_{i-1} to V_j, we compute an increment δR for each iteration:

$$\delta R = -(J^T J)^{-1} J^T \vec{r}(R), \text{ where } J = \frac{\partial \vec{r}(\epsilon \oplus R)}{\partial \epsilon}|_{\epsilon=0} \tag{5}$$

J is the derivative of the residual vector $\vec{r}$ with respect to an increment ϵ, and $J^T J$ is the Gauss-Newton approximation of the Hessian matrix of E. We then update the rotation estimate by multiplying it with the iteration's increment:

$$R = \delta R \oplus R \tag{6}$$

To gain robustness with outliers caused by moving objects, by the disparity of near objects, and by view dependent effects (e.g. reflections), the minimization is done in an iteratively reweighted fashion [14]. The weight of a pixel p equals the inverse $1/r_p$ of its residual. The weight is capped to avoid infinite weights when a pixel residual is very small. Figure 8 visualizes the pixel weights for the global alignment from Fig. 6. The weighted rotation increment is:

$$\delta R = -(J^T W J)^{-1} J^T W \vec{r}(R), \text{ where } W = \text{diag}(1/r_1, \ldots, 1/r_n) \tag{7}$$

For speed, we perform this color residual minimization with a coarse-to-fine approach, that works at different levels of the image resolution pyramid. We start from the coarsest level of 30×17, as our frames have a 16:9 aspect ratio, and we stop at four levels deeper, i.e. at 480×270. The minimization converges at each level in between 2 and 4 iterations.

4   Results and Discussion

We have tested our occlusion removal method on several scenes, including *Snow, Terrace, Atrium,* and *Clutter* (Fig. 1), *Crossing* (video), and *Intersection* (Fig. 11). All scenes were abundantly dynamic, except for the *Clutter* scene, which was stationary. Each scene was acquired with two videos, captured with separate handheld phone and tripod mounted tablet cameras, from different viewpoints, matching the scenario described in the paper; the *Clutter* scene was acquired with a single handheld camera that revolved around the occluder, and

Table 1. Average per-frame running times for the stages of our pipeline [ms], and overall frame rate [fps].

Stage	Contour tracking	Global alignment	Local alignment	Occlusion removal	FPS
Snow	1.3	1.8	3.3	1.8	122
Terrace	1.1	1.8	4.8	5.5	76
Atrium	1.6	1.8	5.1	2.9	88
Clutter	1.9	1.8	4.5	4.6	79
Crossing	1.3	1.8	5.3	1.6	100
Intersection	1.4	1.8	3.4	2.1	114

the later frames were used to disocclude the earlier frames. The input and output videos have a $1,920 \times 1,080$ resolution. Our method worked well with all scenes, alleviating occlusions by creating a convincing transparency effect. We first report the running time of our method (Sect. 4.1), we discuss the quality of the occlusion removal achieved by our method (Sect. 4.2), we compare our method to ground truth (Sect. 4.3), and we compare our method to state of the art occlusion removal method (Sect. 4.4).

4.1   Time

We ran our disocclusion method for each pair of videos on an Intel i5-7600k workstation with a 3.8 GHz CPU clock. Our implementation uses only the CPU (and not the GPU). The videos were played back at the original frame rate (60fps for *Snow* and *Terrace* and 30fps for the other scenes), and our method comfortably processed the frames in real time, with no precomputation.

Table 1 gives the average times for each of the four stages of our pipeline, as well as the average frame rate, which is at least 75fps. Contour tracking performance depends on the number of contour vertices, global alignment performance depends on the number of pixels in the resolution pyramid level used, local alignment performance depends on the number of salient contour points, and occlusion removal depends on the number of pixels in the occluder footprint. For *Snow, Atrium, Crossing* and *Intersection*, the slowest stage is the local alignment stage, which evaluates color differences with rotated and not axis aligned patches (parameter R of line 14 in Algorithm 2). In addition to the cost of the rotation itself, comparing color between a rotated patch and an axis aligned patch introduces a bilinear interpolation per color comparison. For *Terrace* and *Clutter*, the occluder footprint is larger than for the other scenes, and occlusion removal takes slightly longer than local alignment. In all cases, our performance is sufficient even 60 Hz videos.

4.2   Quality

Our method handles well a variety of scenes, replacing the occluder pixels with pixels from the secondary video, with good continuity, as can be seen in the figures throughout the paper and in the accompanying video. The limitations of our method are discussed in the next section. Our method relies on a weak connection between the primary and the secondary frames: the frames are connected by an approximate mapping inside the occluder contour, and by a more rigorous mapping along the occluder contour. The weaker connection is faster to compute than the per-pixel correspondences used in structure from motion. Moreover, the weaker connection has the advantage of avoiding disocclusion errors.

Our method bypasses the computational expense of finding depth based on the disparity between the two video feeds, yet it avoids disocclusion errors that would plague such a depth-based approach.

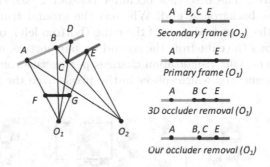

Fig. 9. Disocclusion error caused by 3D occluder removal. The secondary frame with viewpoint O_2 does not capture the green object between B and D. Even if the secondary frame has perfect depth per pixel, projecting the 3D samples of the secondary frame onto the primary frame will leave a gap between the projection of B and the projection of C. Our occluder removal method does not suffer from such a disocclusion error, as the mapping it uses does not allow B and C to separate in the primary frame.

Even if both videos are replaced with perfect RGBD streams, disocclusion errors can occur when the occluder is removed and the primary viewpoint gains line of sight to a part of the scene not visible from the secondary viewpoint. In Fig. 9, the primary viewpoint is O_1 and the secondary viewpoint is O_2. The secondary frame samples the green object from the left until B, and then the blue object from C towards the right. The primary frame is affected by the occluder FG. The primary frame sees the green object from the left until A, then the occluder, and then the blue object from E to the right. A depth-based, 3D occluder removal method leverages the perfect depth available at each secondary frame pixel to project the secondary frame pixels to their correct location in the primary frame. However, since the secondary frame does not sample the green object between B and D, the 3D occluder removal method leaves a gap, i.e. a disocclusion error, between B and C.

Our occluder removal method replaces the occluder pixels FG in the primary frame with the secondary frame pixels from A to E. Our local alignment makes sure that the primary and secondary frames are aligned at A and E. Our method does not recreate the primary view for the disoccluded part of the scene. Instead, the pixels used to fill in the occluder shadow in the primary view come from the secondary view which has a different viewpoint, i.e. a different perspective on the disoccluded scene. This different perspective is maintained because the global alignment of our method is a homography and not a 3D warp. Our method does not remove the viewpoint difference but rather transitions from one viewpoint to another at the occluder contour.

Figure 10 illustrates on a synthetic scene the multiperspective nature of the disocclusion effect achieved by our method. In the primary view (top left), the yellow rectangle occludes a cube with red, green, and blue faces. In the secondary view (top right), the cube is seen from a translated viewpoint, which reveals the blue and green faces. The first view occluder contour is shown with black in all images. On the background grid. Whereas the ground truth transparency effect only shows the front (red) face of the cube (bottom left), our visualization (bottom right) shows the cube from the secondary perspective, revealing its red, green, and blue faces. Our visualization changes perspective continuously based on the local alignment step which splices in the pixels from the secondary view.

Fig. 10. Illustration of the multiperspective effect achieved by our disocclusion method: primary view, secondary view, ground truth transparency effect, and our output.

4.3 Comparison to Ground Truth

We have also compared our method to ground truth transparency over a real world video sequence (Fig. 11). For this, we recorded primary and secondary videos with the occluder obstructing both views (a), from which we extracted the occluder from each video (b); then we recorded primary and secondary videos without the occluder (c), which serve as ground truth; then we inserted the extracted occluders in each video (d), on which we run our algorithm. Our algorithm produces results (f) that are comparable to the ground truth (e). A sliver of the occluder remains at the bottom of our frame since the secondary view direction is tilted up and it does not cover that part of the occluder. Please also refer to the accompanying video.

4.4 Comparison to State of the Art Methods

We compare our results to those obtained with a commercial image processing platform, i.e. by using the *content-aware fill* tool of Adobe PhotoShop 2020 [1].

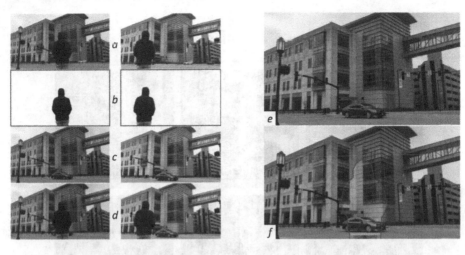

Fig. 11. Comparison of our disocclusion method to a ground truth transparency effect: (*a*) primary and secondary frames with occluder, (*b*) extracted occluder, (*c*) primary and secondary frames without occluder, (*d*) extracted occluder b inserted into frames c, (*e*) ground truth transparency effect, (*f*) output of our algorithm.

The tool is based on earlier occluder removal techniques [5,36], updated based on image correction techniques based on deep-learning [38]. The tool relies on a second image from where to select pixels to inpaint the first image. In addition to the primary and secondary view frames, we provide as input the contour of the occluder in each frame. We also compare our method to a state of the art inpainting method based on partial convolution [20], and to two state of the art inpainting methods that use deep learning with typical convolution layers, namely *DeepFill v2* [39] and *Globally and Locally Consistent Image Completion* (GLCIC) [15]. All three inpainting methods find occluder replacement pixels in the input frame, and therefore they have the advantage that they do not require acquiring the scene from a secondary viewpoint.

Figure 12 shows the results obtained by the five methods and the ground truth result, on the same frame. Our result shows significantly fewer artifacts and better continuity. We quantify the quality achieved by each method by comparing the result of each method to ground truth. We quantify the differences in terms of two per-pixel image comparison metrics, i.e. the mean ℓ_1 error and the peak signal-to-noise ratio (PSNR), as well as in terms of two perceptual image comparison metrics: the Learned Perceptual Image Patch Similarity (LPIPS) metric [40], and the Structural SIMilarity (SSIM) index [35]. Table 2 summarizes the comparisons which show that our result is closer to ground truth than that of the two other methods, even with the residual occluder sliver. Furthermore, the methods above were not designed for real-time video processing; according to our measurements, they require about one second of processing time per frame, on the same machine used to time our method. The authors of GLCIC report 0.5 s on the GPU or 8.2 s on the CPU for 1,024 × 1,024 images [15]. The authors

Fig. 12. Comparison to prior art methods: *a* ground truth, *b* our method, *c* content-aware fill [1], *d* partial convolution [20], *e* DeepFill [39], *f* GLCIC [15].

Table 2. Quality of occluder removal quantified by comparison to ground truth, for the images in Fig. 12, using two per-pixel comparison metrics, i.e. mean ℓ_1 error and PSNR, and two perceptual image comparison metrics, i.e. LPIPS, which measures image dissimilarity, so the lower the better, and SSIM, which measures image similarity, so the higher the better.

	ℓ_1 error (%)	PSNR	LPIPS	SSIM
Our method	**1.928**	**26.46**	**0.024**	**0.952**
Content-aware fill [1]	2.565	23.15	0.100	0.810
Partial convolution [20]	3.476	21.61	0.143	0.818
DeepFill v2 [39]	4.046	20.41	0.170	0.810
GLCIC [15]	4.775	20.75	0.219	0.785

of DeepFill v2 report 0.2 s on the GPU or 1.5 s on the CPU for 512×512 images [39]. We conclude that inpainting methods are better suited for the offline filling-in of small-area image holes, where they can extrapolate successfully from not too distant neighboring regions, and are less suited for filling-in in real time the large occluder footprint.

5 Conclusions. Limitations. Future Work

We have presented a method for removing an occluder from a video, by transferring pixels from a second video that captures what the first video should show if the occluder were not present. In actual use cases, the secondary viewpoint can be provided by a surveillance camera, or can be crowd-sourced, i.e., from the cameras of other people in the scene who volunteer to share their camera feed.

The pixels from the second video are spliced in with good continuity across the occluder contour. The method is based on the insight that a convincing transparency effect can be obtained without knowledge of 3D scene geometry. The method computes a mapping from the first video to the second video, which orients the second camera the same way as the first camera, but which does not attempt to translate the second camera viewpoint to the first viewpoint. The result is a multiperspective visualization, where the scene surrounding the occluder is shown from the first viewpoint, and the scene behind the occluder is shown from the second camera viewpoint. The two perspectives are connected seamlessly, with a local mapping that achieves a gradual transition from one viewpoint to the other.

The method achieves good results on a variety of scenes with intricate and dynamic geometry. We have shown that our method can produce results comparable to ground truth video obtained by recording the scene without occluder, and better results than prior occluder removal approaches. The method is fast, with a minimum frame rate of 75fps. Our method is fast because it only searches for correspondences between the two video frames along the occluder contour, and not for all the frame pixels, a fundamental advantage over traditional multi-camera computer vision pipelines. Our method is at a performance/quality point that prior art methods cannot approach, as shown in Fig. 12.

Our method does not require that any of the cameras be stationary—camera movement is accounted for by the global alignment stage. In fact, both cameras can move freely, as long as the region of interest is captured by the secondary camera. This first, rough alignment aligns well for the distant part of the scene, but it alone does not produce continuity across the contour (Fig. 7 middle). Continuity is achieved by our second step, i.e., local alignment along the contour, which is a key distinguishing feature with respect to prior methods.

Our method is interactive, allowing the user to specify the object to be removed by sketching a rough contour in the first frame, after which the contour is tracked automatically. Our pipeline is readily compatible with prior art techniques that can detect the "near" object from the first two frames of the primary and secondary feeds, which can be used to seed contour tracking automatically.

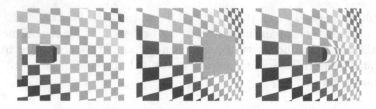

Fig. 13. Disocclusion of partially visible object: secondary view frame (left) primary view frame (middle) and our output (right).

Fig. 14. Method limitation due to near object crossing the occluder contour: (left) perspective switch deformation (A) and extrapolation discontinuity (B); (right) the local mapping achieves continuity across the occluder contour for the pavement line (A), for the moving foot (B), but fails for the backpack (C).

One limitation of our method pertains to near objects that cross the occluder contour. A near object is imaged from different directions by the two cameras, and therefore it has a different appearance in the two frames, a difference that cannot be alleviated by the global mapping rotation. This poses no problems when the near object is completely hidden behind the occluder (e.g. Fig. 10). However, when the object crosses the occluder contour, the object is distorted by the multiperspective effect, as it starts out in one perspective and ends in the other, the same way the subject is distorted in Picasso's cubist portraits that connect two views of the subject's face in a single painting. In Fig. 13, the switch from the primary to the secondary perspective occurs over the cube, distorting the cube. In Fig. 14, left, the handrail crosses the occluder contour in region A, where it switches from the primary perspective, outside the occluder, to the secondary perspective, inside the occluder. The switch is continuous, but the handrail is distorted as it is shown with two perspectives.

Another problem posed by partially occluded near objects arises when the secondary frame does not see everything the occluder hides in the primary frame. In such a case, a piece of the object is missing from both frames, and the local mapping cannot fill in the missing piece. In Fig. 14, left, the visualization appears discontinuous to a human observer in region B, who knows that the scene has one straight, uninterrupted handrail, and therefore expects that the disoccluded hand rail be aligned with the handrail reemerging to the left of the occluder. We call this an extrapolation discontinuity.

The perspective switch deformation and the extrapolation discontinuity problems are inherent to our method, in the sense that they occur even though our algorithms work as intended. The *Atrium* scene is a worst case scenario for these problems as the long, straight handrail makes them conspicuous. Future work could aim to reduce the perspective switch deformation by widening the area over which the switch between perspectives occurs; the extrapolation discontinuity could be reduced by leveraging or even pursuing a high-level understanding of the scene that maintains handrail continuity even though a handrail piece is missing from both frames.

A third problem posed by near objects that cross the occluder contour is that the local mapping fails occasionally (Fig. 14, right). For near objects, correcting the global mapping requires large offsets, and the search is less robust. The problem is exacerbated when the object moves quickly, and when the object does not have much texture, as is the case of the backpack and jacket in region C of Fig. 14, right. Using a small search neighborhood in the interest of performance reduces local mapping robustness. Future work could examine increasing the robustness of the local mapping with a strategy that leverages the image resolution pyramid to search over large distances to gain robustness without a significant performance trade-off.

Another limitation of the current implementation is that the visualization is not always perfectly stable. Presently, the set of salient points used by the local mapping is computed from scratch for every frame. Future implementations could limit the number of points replaced at every frame, in the interest of stability. Finally, the current implementation computes the global alignment with respect to a fairly recent key frame of the same video, and global alignment is computed across videos only once, for the first pair of frames. This works well for our sequences of 30 s, but for longer sequences, global alignment drift could be a concern, which will have to be addressed by occasionally recomputing the global alignment between the current frames of the two videos.

We have shown that our method runs fast enough on a workstation, using only its CPU, to keep up with prerecorded videos. Future work should deploy our pipeline to phones and tablets, leveraging their GPUs. Future work could focus on absorbing into the local adjustment algorithm the latency of transmitting the secondary video to the user device where the disocclusion effect is computed. Another possible direction of future work is to use multiple secondary video streams to handle complex occlusions.

We describe a multiperspective framework for the continuous and non-redundant integration of multiple images, which, compared to traditional structure from motion, comes at the lower cost of only having to establish $O(w)$—and not $O(wh)$—correspondences between pairs of $w \times h$ images. This framework might find other applications, in augmented reality and beyond.

References

1. Adobe photoshop. https://www.adobe.com/products/photoshop.html. Accessed 30 Apr 2020

2. Álvarez, H., Arrieta, J., Oyarzun, D.: Towards a diminished reality system that preserves structures and works in real-time. In: VISIGRAPP (4: VISAPP), pp. 334–343 (2017)
3. Andre, E., Hlavacs, H.: Diminished reality based on 3D-scanning. In: van der Spek, E., Göbel, S., Do, E.Y.-L., Clua, E., Baalsrud Hauge, J. (eds.) ICEC-JCSG 2019. LNCS, vol. 11863, pp. 3–14. Springer, Cham (2019). https://doi.org/10.1007/978-3-030-34644-7_1
4. Avery, B., Piekarski, W., Thomas, B.H.: Visualizing occluded physical objects in unfamiliar outdoor augmented reality environments. In: Proceedings of the 2007 6th IEEE and ACM International Symposium on Mixed and Augmented Reality, pp. 1–2. IEEE Computer Society (2007)
5. Barnes, C., Shechtman, E., Goldman, D.B., Finkelstein, A.: The generalized Patch-Match correspondence algorithm. In: Daniilidis, K., Maragos, P., Paragios, N. (eds.) ECCV 2010. LNCS, vol. 6313, pp. 29–43. Springer, Heidelberg (2010). https://doi.org/10.1007/978-3-642-15558-1_3
6. Barnum, P., Sheikh, Y., Datta, A., Kanade, T.: Dynamic seethroughs: synthesizing hidden views of moving objects. In: 2009 8th IEEE International Symposium on Mixed and Augmented Reality, pp. 111–114. IEEE (2009)
7. Bay, H., Tuytelaars, T., Van Gool, L.: SURF: speeded up robust features. In: Leonardis, A., Bischof, H., Pinz, A. (eds.) ECCV 2006. LNCS, vol. 3951, pp. 404–417. Springer, Heidelberg (2006). https://doi.org/10.1007/11744023_32
8. Bugeau, A., Bertalmío, M., Caselles, V., Sapiro, G.: A comprehensive framework for image inpainting. IEEE Trans. Image Process. 19(10), 2634–2645 (2010)
9. Criminisi, A., Perez, P., Toyama, K.: Object removal by exemplar-based inpainting. In: 2003 IEEE Computer Society Conference on Computer Vision and Pattern Recognition, 2003. Proceedings, vol. 2, pp. II–II. IEEE (2003)
10. Enomoto, A., Saito, H.: Diminished reality using multiple handheld cameras. In: Proceedings of ACCV, vol. 7, pp. 130–135 (2007)
11. Fischler, M.A., Bolles, R.C.: Random sample consensus: a paradigm for model fitting with applications to image analysis and automated cartography. Commun. ACM 24(6), 381–395 (1981)
12. Hasegawa, K., Saito, H.: Diminished reality for hiding a pedestrian using handheld camera. In: 2015 IEEE International Symposium on Mixed and Augmented Reality Workshops, pp. 47–52. IEEE (2015)
13. Herling, J., Broll, W.: High-quality real-time video inpaintingwith pixmix. IEEE Trans. Visual Comput. Graphics 20(6), 866–879 (2014)
14. Holland, P.W., Welsch, R.E.: Robust regression using iteratively reweighted least-squares. Commun. Stat. Theor. Methods 6(9), 813–827 (1977)
15. Iizuka, S., Simo-Serra, E., Ishikawa, H.: Globally and locally consistent image completion. ACM Trans. Graph. (ToG) 36(4), 1–14 (2017)
16. Jampour, M., Li, C., Yu, L.F., Zhou, K., Lin, S., Bischof, H.: Face inpainting based on high-level facial attributes. Comput. Vis. Image Underst. 161, 29–41 (2017)
17. Kameda, Y., Takemasa, T., Ohta, Y.: Outdoor see-through vision utilizing surveillance cameras. In: Proceedings of the 3rd IEEE/ACM International Symposium on Mixed and Augmented Reality, pp. 151–160. IEEE Computer Society (2004)
18. Li, Z., Zhu, H., Cao, L., Jiao, L., Zhong, Y., Ma, A.: Face inpainting via nested generative adversarial networks. IEEE Access 7, 155462–155471 (2019)
19. Li, Z., Wang, Y., Guo, J., Cheong, L.F., Zhou, S.Z.: Diminished reality using appearance and 3d geometry of internet photo collections. In: 2013 IEEE International Symposium on Mixed and Augmented Reality (ISMAR), pp. 11–19. IEEE (2013)

20. Liu, G., Reda, F.A., Shih, K.J., Wang, T.C., Tao, A., Catanzaro, B.: Image inpainting for irregular holes using partial convolutions. In: The European Conference on Computer Vision (ECCV) (2018)

21. Meerits, S., Saito, H.: Real-time diminished reality for dynamic scenes. In: 2015 IEEE International Symposium on Mixed and Augmented Reality Workshops, pp. 53–59. IEEE (2015)

22. Mei, C., Sommerlade, E., Sibley, G., Newman, P., Reid, I.: Hidden view synthesis using real-time visual slam for simplifying video surveillance analysis. In: 2011 IEEE International Conference on Robotics and Automation, pp. 4240–4245. IEEE (2011)

23. Mori, S., Ikeda, S., Saito, H.: A survey of diminished reality: techniques for visually concealing, eliminating, and seeing through real objects. IPSJ Trans. Comput. Vis. Appl. 9(1), 1–14 (2017). https://doi.org/10.1186/s41074-017-0028-1

24. Mori, S., Maezawa, M., Ienaga, N., Saito, H.: Diminished hand: a diminished reality-based work area visualization. In: 2017 IEEE Virtual Reality (VR), pp. 443–444. IEEE (2017)

25. Mori, S., Shibata, F., Kimura, A., Tamura, H.: Efficient use of textured 3d model for pre-observation-based diminished reality. In: 2015 IEEE International Symposium on Mixed and Augmented Reality Workshops, pp. 32–39. IEEE (2015)

26. Muja, M., Lowe, D.G.: Fast approximate nearest neighbors with automatic algorithm configuration. VISAPP (1) 2(331–340), 2 (2009)

27. Nakajima, Y., Mori, S., Saito, H.: Semantic object selection and detection for diminished reality based on slam with viewpoint class. In: 2017 IEEE International Symposium on Mixed and Augmented Reality (ISMAR-Adjunct), pp. 338–343. IEEE (2017)

28. Nocedal, J., Wright, S.: Numerical Optimization. Springer, New York (2006). https://doi.org/10.1007/978-0-387-40065-5

29. Queguiner, G., Fradet, M., Rouhani, M.: Towards mobile diminished reality. In: 2018 IEEE International Symposium on Mixed and Augmented Reality Adjunct (ISMAR-Adjunct), pp. 226–231. IEEE (2018)

30. Rameau, F., Ha, H., Joo, K., Choi, J., Park, K., Kweon, I.S.: A real-time augmented reality system to see-through cars. IEEE Trans. Visual Comput. Graphics 22(11), 2395–2404 (2016)

31. Singhal, A., et al.: Modern information retrieval: a brief overview. IEEE Data Eng. Bull. 24(4), 35–43 (2001)

32. Takemura, M., Ohta, Y.: Diminishing head-mounted display for shared mixed reality. In: Proceedings of the 1st International Symposium on Mixed and Augmented Reality, p. 149. IEEE Computer Society (2002)

33. Tiefenbacher, P., Sirch, M., Rigoll, G.: Mono camera multi-view diminished reality. In: 2016 IEEE Winter Conference on Applications of Computer Vision (WACV), pp. 1–8. IEEE (2016)

34. Wang, L., Jin, H., Yang, R., Gong, M.: Stereoscopic inpainting: joint color and depth completion from stereo images. In: 2008 IEEE Conference on Computer Vision and Pattern Recognition, pp. 1–8. IEEE (2008)

35. Wang, Z., Bovik, A.C., Sheikh, H.R., Simoncelli, E.P.: Image quality assessment: from error visibility to structural similarity. IEEE Trans. Image Process. 13(4), 600–612 (2004)

36. Wexler, Y., Shechtman, E., Irani, M.: Space-time video completion. In: Proceedings of the 2004 IEEE Computer Society Conference on Computer Vision and Pattern Recognition 2004, CVPR 2004, vol. 1, pp. I-I. IEEE (2004)

37. Wu, M.L., Popescu, V.: Rgbd temporal resampling for real-time occlusion removal. In: Proceedings of the ACM SIGGRAPH Symposium on Interactive 3D Graphics and Games, p. 7. ACM (2019)
38. Yu, J., Lin, Z., Yang, J., Shen, X., Lu, X., Huang, T.S.: Generative image inpainting with contextual attention. In: Proceedings of the IEEE Conference on Computer Vision and Pattern Recognition, pp. 5505–5514 (2018)
39. Yu, J., Lin, Z., Yang, J., Shen, X., Lu, X., Huang, T.S.: Free-form image inpainting with gated convolution. In: Proceedings of the IEEE International Conference on Computer Vision, pp. 4471–4480 (2019)
40. Zhang, R., Isola, P., Efros, A.A., Shechtman, E., Wang, O.: The unreasonable effectiveness of deep features as a perceptual metric. In: CVPR (2018)
41. Zhang, Z.: A flexible new technique for camera calibration. IEEE Trans. Pattern Anal. Mach. Intell. **22**(11), 1330–1334 (2000)
42. Zokai, S., Esteve, J., Genc, Y., Navab, N.: Multiview paraperspective projection model for diminished reality. In: Proceedings of the 2nd IEEE/ACM International Symposium on Mixed and Augmented Reality, p. 217. IEEE Computer Society (2003)

Coupling AR with Object Detection Neural Networks for End-User Engagement

Tina Katika[✉] [iD], Spyridon Nektarios Bolierakis, Emmanuel Vasilopoulos [iD],
Markos Antonopoulos, Georgios Tsimiklis, Ioannis Karaseitanidis,
and Angelos Amditis

Institute of Communication and Computer Systems, Athens, Greece
tina.katika@iccs.gr

Abstract. The mobile Augmented Reality (AR) technology offers an accessible, inexpensive, and rich user experience that has the potential to engage end-users to an immersive environment. Machine learning (ML) algorithms can be tailored and tuned to carry out a large variety of tasks pertaining to data coming from highly specific environments, thereby improving the decision-making process, and uncovering gaps and opportunities in a wide range of applied fields. High data availability and modern algorithms contribute to the changing way end-users interact with their environment to obtain information, train, and socialize. In this study, we leverage the widespread adoption of mobile phones in daily lives and their advanced features (such as connectivity and location-awareness along with powerful optical and image sensors) to design, develop and test, an AR application that offers a unique user-environment interaction through object detection functionalities. The intended use of the mobile AR application is to foster end-user engagement, enrich user experiences, improve self-efficacy and motivation, and contribute to dissemination and communication activities. Due to its technical and gamification features, and the ability to customize its content through a web-based Content Management Service, it has great potential to be exploited in a variety of contexts including education and training, touristic and cultural appreciation, art and heritage promotion, among others. This paper presents the development and testing of the mobile application and details its architecture and the pertaining implementation challenges. The design features and implementation details of our approach result in a 90% detection accuracy for common objects. Such a performance contributes to the discourse on the use of mobile AR coupled with ML functionalities as a tool stimulating end-user engagement and hands-on learning by facilitating environment exploration, and helping end-users to move from passive observation to creative interaction.

Keywords: Augmented reality · Object detection · Neural networks · User engagement

1 Introduction

Our experience of the surroundings and the environment we live in is based on simple observation rather than active exploration and participation. Such an experience limits

G. Zachmann et al. (Eds.): EuroXR 2022, LNCS 13484, pp. 135–145, 2022.
https://doi.org/10.1007/978-3-031-16234-3_8

the engagement potential and thus the motivation to understand how specific interactions and behaviors may impact our everyday lives. Augmented Reality (AR) offers an interface between reality and the perception of reality, bridging the gap between real and virtual worlds. AR provides experiences that enable the end-users to move from observation to immersion, which is often associated with the encouragement they experience in a digitally enhanced setting (Dede 2009). In addition, AR's immersive nature helps the audience perceive evolving details in action, and connect events between a virtual story and their own lives. Therefore, much effort is currently put in laying the foundation of an efficient engagement process towards actions, changes and policies aiming to improve our experience of the surroundings (Hall and Takahashi 2017). In this endeavor, AR technology appears to be an excellent tool for engagement in sustainability and environmental consciousness (Katika et al. 2021, 2022a). Engagement is a term often associated with consumers, citizens, employees, gamers, and other software end-users, encompassed and exemplified by a range of attributes, including the adoption of technologies and their usability (O'Brien and Toms 2008). An effective engagement process ensures that the voices and needs of the end-users are taken into account, facilitates knowledge acquisition of an issue or topic of interest, and encourages end-users to apply this earned knowledge to improve the quality of their life and the community they belong (Church 2020).

AR can couple the actual, real-time fulfillment of a given task with relevant information by displaying information without disturbing the user's focus. AR has proven to be an invaluable interactive medium to reduce the used amount of working memory resources (Sahu et al. 2021). While AR systems have seen immense research innovation in recent years, the current strategies utilized in mobile AR for navigation, 3D visualizations, virtual object creation, registration, and rendering are still dominated mainly by traditional non-AI approaches (Sahu et al. 2021).

Classical AR methods can be significantly improved by incorporating various AI techniques like deep learning and other ML and data-driven approaches to adapt to broader scene variations and user preferences. For a seamless and realistic integration of the real and virtual worlds through an AR-supported interface, the real and virtual environments must align. Contemporary AI techniques appear as promising tools for increasing the adaptability and versatility of AR systems. The potential of AI techniques in AR is clear from the unprecedented success of AI in image processing and related tasks. Mobile AR gets inputs from camera images and projects rendered images and other media with augmentations onto the display or interface. In this setup, AI has the potential to bring revolutionary changes in AR applications considering that AR can be adopted without modification to the environment (Sahu et al. 2021).

However good AI may be, adoption reluctance from the end-users is one of the most common issues faced by this technology. People have demonstrated attraction to new ways of interaction as they like to communicate and share information as freely as possible, but at the same time, they judge harshly projects not well-executed, with poor usability, and not interesting content (Katika et al. 2021; Duguleană et al. 2020). Privacy and security issues may also be raised, considering the vast volume of data that are processed from ML technologies integrated into AR applications (Roesner et al. 2014).

The proposed mobile AR application fosters an environment that aims at understanding and addressing the specific needs of each end-user by providing alternative representations and meta-data. It also aims at facilitating interactivity and offering personalized information and guidelines. Attraction to content, acceptance of the technology, as well as usability and novelty of the proposed solution have been validated in Katika et al. 2021, 2022a. The present study is organized as follows. First, we present related work in the field of object detection in AR. We then present the overall system design plus its most dominant feature, i.e., the object detection capability, and the system testing. Before concluding and describing the future research efforts, we present the performance of the AR app.

2 Related Work

AR is currently being utilized across disciplines for end-user engagement, and has been shown to enhance educational processes (Billinghurst and Dunser 2011) and overall motivation (Katika et al. 2022a). Given the adaptable nature of the technology, mobile AR can alleviate the limitations that other engagement tools face and may offer an inclusive environment for people having a wide range of specificities (Quintero et al. 2019).

Many existing approaches use object detection to recognize and track objects of the surroundings, and superimpose on them new media and content using smartphone cameras. Some of the challenges they face are the inability to determine a precise notion of their 3D pose or superimpose the virtual content on real images and objects (Gordon and Lowe 2006). Lin et al. 2018, developed a navigation AR application trained to recognize building doors. The application has been tested in a closed environment (one campus) with limited inputs in the database. Its main limitations are the effectiveness of the neural network and the performance on mobile devices. Tang et al. 2019 designed a mobile AR learning application for children with autism, which allows the detection of multiple items. The main limitation of their proposed design is its inability to perform offline, which limits its usability and portability. Other works merging AR with object detection report the inability to offer real-time artifact recognition, pertinent hardware-imposed limitations, and limited applications on commercially relevant fields (such as, Zhang et al. 2017).

3 Problem Definition

Context aware AR environments have the potential to provide a novel way of interfacing with everyday physical objects enabling seamless user-object interactions. Mobile AR applications can be imbued with context awareness by incorporating object detection capabilities. An AR user can point a smartphone camera to their physical surroundings, detect relevant objects and learn additional information (ranging from their use to their functionality) by following the spatial annotations and interaction cues.

In Dasgupta et al. 2020, the authors argue that providing such powerful functionalities through affordable and accessible smartphone devices in a real-time context can be expected to exponentially increase the user task performance and reduce cognitive load.

At the same time, experience inclusiveness and accessibility as well as user experience and system usability would be improved.

As powerful as current object detection technology can be, it still relies on resource hungry, computationally intensive algorithms. Achieving a seamless and realistic integration of the real and virtual worlds through an AR interface would require advanced optical and image sensors with a broad field of view, plus the computational resources needed to run the pertinent algorithms efficiently.

Building on previous research efforts in the field of mobile AR engagement tools, we aim to further expand the capabilities and address the limitations that commercially available solutions face by:

1. Ensuring smooth integration of object detection with AR technology.
2. Limiting the resources and computational power required by the AR device.
3. Broadening the application of mobile AR application and ensuring relevance to many fields of expertise.
4. Embedding a state-of-the-art object detection algorithm suitable for mobile devices with a proper balance between accuracy and speed ensuring that user data is not processed outside of the mobile device.
5. Using the detection algorithm results (2D on screen object detection's bounding box) as input for augmenting features in space, located at the detected object's location.

4   Methodology

In this section, we present the design and development efforts for the AR app coupled with object detection functionalities. We built on the model and designs of the AR application for end-user engagement developed by Katika et al. 2022a, and improved it by adding object detection capabilities to further enable the interaction of the end-user with their environment and intensify their experience. The mobile AR application presented in this section supports triggered AR content in three ways:

- A marker-based function which requires a marker (QR) to activate an augmentation related to media.
- A location-based AR functionality which uses the device's GPS location as a trigger to pair dynamic location with Points of Interest to augment relevant content.
- The object detection functionality which is a dynamic augmentation process based on trained deep learning models.

4.1   System Design

The overall system architecture of the AR components is designed to support two different users, the administrators of the AR Content Management System (AR-CMS), and the mobile application users (CirculAR). The administrators are considered the content owners. Their role is to produce and add content in the platform to create meaningful and educational experiences, so-called AR campaigns, that will be later enhanced with various gamification aspects and visualized by the mobile application end users. The platform and the two components have been presented in Katika et al. 2021, 2022a.

The mobile AR application previously reported, has undergone further improvements and now not only supports GPS localization and QR scanning for content attachment, but also supports object detection and image processing functionalities ensuring a more in-depth penetration of the end-user to their environment (Fig. 1). Gaming app UI research has been performed to ensure that the virtual agent (ARis) is present in most functionalities and offers helpful tips and comments upon execution. In addition, the AR app visuals and UI elements (such as the self-explanatory icons, call-to-action-buttons, visual graphics, and leaderboard tables) have been designed resulting to a custom UI footage focusing on an immersive, usable, and familiar user interface environment with a low cognitive load process to improve user engagement and avoid common usability errors (Katika et al. 2022a).

The main elements and features of the AR application have been studied separately to demonstrate their effect on the end-user engagement. The studies assessed the use of the mobile AR app for empowering and training citizens in Circular Economy and sustainability principles. The content, gamification features, the virtual agent, and the mobile AR usability were evaluated and validated using the Technology Acceptance Model (TAM) and the User Engagement Scale (UES) in Katika et al. 2021, 2022a, 2022b. All studies demonstrated significant improvements to the end-user engagement.

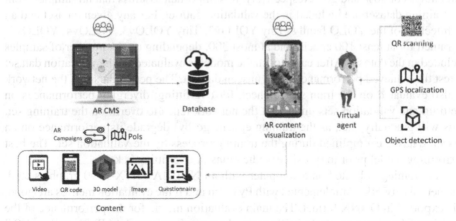

Fig. 1. The system design of the AR components adapted from Katika et al. 2021. The AR-CMS is the allows the content administrators to generate AR campaigns of specific content at their Points of Interest (PoIs). The content is augmented to the end-users via the mobile AR app which supports three means of interaction of the end-user with their environment shown to the right side of the image, including the object detection through recognition algorithms using the camera of the AR app.

4.2 Object Detection in AR

The AR app is using the smartphone's camera feed as input for the image processing with deep neural network (DNN). The DNN outputs the bounding box coordinates for each object of interest detected in the processed frame. The bounding boxes are drawn and displayed on the frame and a persistent AR anchor is created on each detected item.

In order to achieve the desired results for the application we used Unity3D (2020.3.23f1 LTS) and Barracuda (3.0). The Barracuda package is a lightweight cross-platform DNN inference library for Unity. Barracuda can run DNNs on both the GPU and CPU. For the image detection well known neural models were tested. Specifically, Tiny YOLO v2 and Tiny YOLO v3 were used for our implementation.

For the tested models we used pretrained versions located in the ONNX Model Zoo GitHub repository. Neural models imported in Unity and used by the Barracuda inference library must have the ONNX format. ONNX is an open format built to represent machine learning models. ONNX defines a common set of operators - the building blocks of machine learning and deep learning models - and a common file format to enable AI developers to use models with a variety of frameworks, tools, runtimes, and compilers. For the augmented reality part of the application, we are using Unity's AR foundation library (4.1.9) along with ARCore XR plugin on Android and ARKit XR plugin on iOS. AR Foundation allowed the work with augmented reality platforms in a multi-platform way within Unity.

Depending on the use-case, a different model must be trained on a corresponding annotated dataset. Assuming a fixed-use case and the availability of the dataset, the entire dataset is split in two disjoint sets called the train and the validation set, usually at percentages of 80% and 20%, respectively. It is important to stress that no samples from the training dataset are included in the validation dataset. For any given dataset and an architecture of the YOLO family (Tiny YOLOv2, Tiny YOLOv3, YOLOv4, YOLOv5) is trained for at least 100 epochs and at most 300, depending on the number of samples included in the dataset. After each epoch the model is evaluated on the validation dataset to test the achieved performance on an unseen dataset. The performance of the network is also evaluated on the train set, to check for overfitting; diverging performances on the train and validation sets imply that the network tends to overfit on the training set. This will gradually (i.e., as the training epochs go by) degrade its performance on an unseen dataset, exemplified during the training process by the validation set. The best performing model prior to (possible) indications of overfitting is kept.

The training is hosted on a computer with an NVIDIA's RTX-3090 graphics card. The neural network is implemented with PyTorch and if the evaluation metrics are good, it is exported in ONNX format. The main evaluation metric for the performance of the model is COCO's (Lin et al. 2018) mean Average Precision (mAP). A value of 0.3 and higher is considered sufficient for the purposes of the use-case. Furthermore, the confidence threshold determining the acceptance of a detection as a correct one was set at >0.6.

The object detection feature is introduced to the end-users via the AR campaigns. Specific learning blocks, require camera operation for scanning pre-defined items. As shown in Fig. 2, user is requested to scan for items in the surrounding area. Since the detection of the requested object class is achieved, the object's class and the user's GPS coordinates information are sent to the search engine to compare with the database. Then the output engine outputs the matching content on the screen of mobile devices. The content can be either contextual information or related 2D items which are presented as an augmented feature in space, located at the detected object. Figure 3 presents the journey of the user's experience through the mobile AR application. The virtual agent prompts the end-user to point the smartphone camera towards a nearest object. Upon selection, the AR application enables 5 localization rounds. Real-time testing of the overall system in scenes containing objects of interest demonstrated correct display of object-relevant information at an estimated rate of 90%. In the example of Fig. 3, we choose to overlay information related to the object's nature and location.

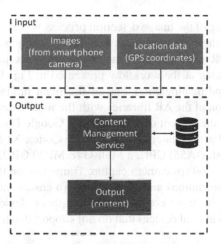

Fig. 2. Object detection structure

Fig. 3. The object detection functionality embedded in the mobile AR application. The object detection module starts with tips coming from the virtual agent, and ends with content superimposed on the physical object.

5   System Testing and Performance

To generate the real scenario for demonstration, we used pre-trained deep learning models which enables the detection of a variety specific specimens in good quality and great detail. Object detection models are available online for free, trained on general purpose annotated datasets such as Common Objects in COntext (COCO) or Visual Object Classes (VOC). For the demonstration we used Tiny YOLOv3 trained on the COCO dataset (Lin et al. 2018). Figure 4 demonstrates the mobile AR application localizing 3 items.

The whole processing of the image detection process is done on the mobile device's CPU in order to fulfill the system requirements and restrictions. Considering that the main objective of the AR app is to enable the end-users to get the "real time detection" experience while operating at the workflow presented in Fig. 1 and Fig. 3 related to content management and manipulation, one of the main limitations of our proposed design is the combination of the AR libraries with the mobile device's GPU.

For the purposes of the present demonstration a Google Pixel 6 mobile phone was used, which is equipped with Octa-core (2x2.80 GHz Cortex-X1 & 2x2.25 GHz Cortex-A76 & 4x1.80 GHz Cortex-A55) CPU, a Mali-G78 MP20 GPU, and a 50 MP camera. The smartphone supports 60 fps camera capture frame rate on the rear-facing camera, multiple GPU texture resolutions and Depth API. To ensure that the object detection feature is compatible with most commercial smartphone devices, the functionalities were also tested with additional devices that do not support depth API, such as Samsung s10 and Redmi note 9.

Fig. 4. Examples of specimens used for the demonstration of the object detection mechanism of CirculAR

The application performs at the following workflow. First, the latest CPU image from the AR camera is acquired. Unity transfers textures from the GPU to the CPU in order to access the pixel data from the device camera to be used by code that runs on the CPU DNN. Once the image is acquired, then it is preprocessed (crop, scale and rotate) to fit the DNN's input. Once the output is determined, the post processing commences. The bounding boxes that have been inferred with confidence less than the required confidence threshold (>0.6) are filtered out, the overlapping information is removed from the remaining and only the parts with the highest confidence are kept. To draw the bounding box on the screen, the bounding box data (X, Y, Width, Height) is translated to screen pixels. Upon acquisition of 6 or more continuous detections of high confidence for the same class item located on around the same area of the screen, then this is considered as the focus on the item and the AR part of the application is enabled. For this part of the application, the depth image from the Occlusion manager is requested and upon retrieval the center of the last drawn bounding box is translated to pixel of the depth image. The depth is then calculated at the specified position. As soon as the calculated depth is defined, we ray cast from the center of the last drawn bounding box and we detect the collision at the calculated depth. The collision point becomes the world position of the spawned object that contains the AR anchor.

6 Concluding Remarks and Future Studies

In this work, we reported on the development, design, and testing of a mobile application that couples AR technology with object detection mechanisms. The experimental results showed that the AR app successfully identified the items we stored in the database in advance. The object detection mechanisms performed seamlessly in various devices, in both offline and online modes, incorporating the AR functionalities for end-user engagement.

With in-app user permission, tasks related to content visualization and manipulation were determined by recognizing entities (such as QR codes and objects) and locations within the camera view of the user's device. So far, the application has been tested with a limited number of objects and images to support this AI feature and reported high accuracy and reliability.

Considering that the nature of our tool is to improve end-user engagement and interaction, integration of the object detection mechanism with the present functionalities of the AR app (including mobile AR and AR-CMS) should be achieved. The main aim is to dynamically pair the AR content curated through the authoring tool and displayed through the mobile AR app. Information regarding the number of classes related to the items to be detected will be fed from the AR-CMS, and the corresponding output of the DNN will be displayed to the mobile app. During such pairing, further testing and evaluation of the performance is required to meet any limitations related to the device and used hardware.

Additionally, expansion of the library of trained data is required to ensure a sound interaction of the end-user with their environment. Such an expansion should be thoroughly tested and evaluated both outdoors and indoors, as well as in other conditions (such as multiple detections and long distances) to ensure an uninterrupted user experience.

Considering that Tiny YOLO v2 and v3 were used for our implementation but the newest versions of the models (v4 and v5) need to be evaluated, although they are not fully supported by Barracuda inference library.

Finally, leveraging AI functionalities and semantic understanding technology, the virtual agent can transform into a virtual assistant to better understand user input, locate the required resource, and respond in an accurate, timely manner.

Funding. This research is based upon work supported by funding from the EU Horizon 2020 project under grant agreement No. 869474 (water-mining).

References

Dede, C.: Immersive interfaces for engagement and learning. Science **323**(5910), 66–69 (2009). https://doi.org/10.1126/science.1167311

Hall, S., Takahashi, R.: Augmented and virtual reality: the promise and peril of immersive technologies. In: World Economic Forum, vol. 2 (2017)

Sahu, C.K., Young, C., Rai, R.: Artificial intelligence (AI) in augmented reality (AR)-assisted manufacturing applications: a review. Int. J. Prod. Res. **59**(16), 4903–4959 (2021)

Church, S.: Photovoice as a community engagement tool in place-based sustainable neighborhood design: a review of literature (2020)

O'Brien, H.L., Toms, E.G.: What is user engagement? A conceptual framework for defining user engagement with technology. J. Am. Soc. Inf. Sci. Technol. **59**(6), 938–955 (2008)

Roesner, F., Kohno, T., Molnar, D.: Security and privacy for augmented reality systems. Commun. ACM **57**(4), 88–96 (2014)

Duguleană, M., Briciu, V.A., Duduman, I.A., Machidon, O.M.: A virtual assistant for natural interactions in museums. Sustainability **12**(17), 6958 (2020)

Dasgupta, A., Manuel, M., Mansur, R.S., Nowak, N., Gračanin, D.: Towards real time object recognition for context awareness in mixed reality: a machine learning approach. In: 2020 IEEE Conference on Virtual Reality and 3D User Interfaces Abstracts and Workshops (VRW), pp. 262–268. IEEE (2020)

Dünser, A., Billinghurst, M.: Evaluating augmented reality systems. In: Furht, B. (eds) Handbook of Augmented Reality. Springer, NY (2011). https://doi.org/10.1007/978-1-4614-0064-6_13

Quintero, J., Baldiris, S., Rubira, R., Cerón, J., Velez, G.: Augmented reality in educational inclusion. A systematic review on the last decade. Front. Psychol. **10**, 1835 (2019)

Edwards-Stewart, A., Hoyt, T., Reger, G.: Classifying different types of augmented reality technology. Annu. Rev. CyberTherapy Telemed. **14**, 199–202 (2016)

Gordon, I., Lowe, D.G.: What and where: 3D object recognition with accurate pose. In: Ponce, J., Hebert, M., Schmid, C., Zisserman, A. (eds.) Toward Category-Level Object Recognition. LNCS, vol. 4170, pp. 67–82. Springer, Heidelberg (2006). https://doi.org/10.1007/11957959_4

Katika, K., Karaseitanidis, I., Tsiakou, D., Makropoulos, C., Amditis, A.: Augmented reality (AR) supporting citizen engagement in circular economy. Circ. Econ. Sust. (2022). https://doi.org/10.1007/s43615-021-00137-7

Katika, T., Bolierakis, S.N., Tousert, N., Karaseitanidis, I., Amditis, A.: Building a mobile AR engagement tool: evaluation of citizens attitude towards a sustainable future. In: Bourdot, P., Alcañiz Raya, M., Figueroa, P., Interrante, V., Kuhlen, T.W., Reiners, D. (eds.) EuroXR 2021. LNCS, vol. 13105, pp. 109–125. Springer, Cham (2021). https://doi.org/10.1007/978-3-030-90739-6_7

Katika, T., Karaseitanidis, I., Amditis, S.A.: Coupling mobile AR with a virtual agent for end-user engagement. In: 1st International conference on eXtended reality, XR Salento (2022b)

Lin, C.-H., Chung, Y., Chou, B.-Y., Chen, H.-Y., Tsai, C.-Y.: A novel campus navigation APP with augmented reality and deep learning. In. 2018 IEEE International Conference on Applied System Invention (ICASI) (2018). https://doi.org/10.1109/icasi.2018.8394464

Tang, T.Y., Xu, J., Winoto, P.: Automatic object recognition in a light-weight augmented reality-based vocabulary learning application for children with autism. In: Proceedings of the 2019 3rd International Conference on Innovation in Artificial Intelligence, pp. 65–68 (2019)

Zhang, W., Han, B., Hui, P.: On the networking challenges of mobile augmented reality. In: Proceedings of the Workshop on Virtual Reality and Augmented Reality Network, pp. 24–29 (2017)

Lin, T.-Y., et al.: Microsoft COCO: common objects in context. In: Fleet, D., Pajdla, T., Schiele, B., Tuytelaars, T. (eds.) ECCV 2014. LNCS, vol. 8693, pp. 740–755. Springer, Cham (2014). https://doi.org/10.1007/978-3-319-10602-1_48

Modeling Scenes for XR

A Procedural Building Generator Based on Real-World Data Enabling Designers to Create Context for XR Automotive Design Experiences

Despoina Salpisti[1,2(✉)], Matthias de Clerk[1], Sebastian Hinz[1], Frank Henkies[1],
and Gudrun Klinker[2]

[1] Digital Design, BMW Group, Munich, Germany
{Despoina.Salpisti,Matthias.de-Clerk,Sebastian.Hinz,
Frank.Henkies}@bmw.de
[2] Informatics Department, Technical University of Munich, Garching, Germany
Klinker@in.tum.de

Abstract. Automotive design is inspired by certain experiences and is intended to evoke certain emotions in the user. To evaluate the ability of the design to facilitate such experiences, automotive designers need to experience not just any driving simulation, but one with the right environmental context. However, this comes with numerous challenges related to the amount of resources required to build such virtual environments and the communication between designers and developers. Therefore, we developed a procedural building generator based on real-world data to enable experiences that reflect reality, to create a common language between designers and developers and to enable designers to generate their own experience context. The generator consists of facade module generators that function based on a molecular design concept, using and combining the smallest basic elements of the facade modules. A range of architectural styles, found in three different cities, were chosen for their large automotive market and require only these basic elements for the facade module generators, making it easy, inexpensive and time-saving to add other architectural elements and consequently provide variety. The result is a building generator that provides highly stable outputs and makes designers independent in creating buildings for their design simulations.

Keywords: Automotive design · Mixed reality experience prototyping · Procedural building generation

1 Introduction

Procedural generation has reduced the modelling time of virtual environments during the development of many recently published games (e.g., Tom Clancy's Ghost Recon Wildlands [1] and Horizon Zero Dawn [2]). This algorithmic method of creating the data has also been the subject of many researchers with a great number of produced outputs, varying from 3D assets to complete levels. Another advantage of procedural generation

G. Zachmann et al. (Eds.): EuroXR 2022, LNCS 13484, pp. 149–170, 2022.
https://doi.org/10.1007/978-3-031-16234-3_9

is its adjustable level of control over the generated output and the resulting potential to provide this control to people with no programming skills.

One group of people who need such control are automotive designers. The rate at which the automotive industry advances leads to a frequent addition of new scenarios to present and evaluate the designs that are inspired by these advances [3]. Additionally, since the car design's characteristics are meant to provide a certain experience and elicit corresponding emotions to the user, the presentation method should aid the designer in testing this experience under the same conditions as the end user. For a car experience, these conditions are associated with the functional and aesthetic context of the surrounding environment [4]. The functional context is important for enabling the experience with a certain design feature. For example, testing the experience with the control of a car's center display requires that the driver is able to share their attention between the street and the middle console. Therefore, a suitable environment for testing such an experience would be a highway as opposed to a mountain street with many curves that require the driver's complete attention. The aesthetic context is crucial for focusing the designer's attention at the design during the presentation, as well as for creating an environment that represents the area of the target market and the vehicle's character. For example, the evaluation of colors on the car requires a neutral environment that does not influence the designer's perception of those colors and does not shift their attention to external elements.

These environments are needed often within a limited amount of time and can vary too much to use the same one for each test scenario. Furthermore, communication problems between the designers and the developers have been reported and are based on the oral description of such an environment, which is accompanied by many challenges of accuracy and time. Development time and cost quickly become an issue, as each of these environments is expensive and takes a long time to build. To solve these problems and offer the designers the right experience context for their presentations, we decided to use procedural generation and real map data. Using procedural generation, we can allow designers to customize and create their own experience context. By using real map data, these environments can provide the designers with real-world conditions for the functional aspect of the context and the ability to describe the environment based on a map. In this paper, we focus on the procedural generation of buildings with emphasis on representative architectural styles, minimal user effort for the generation inside a specific map area, and for increasing the variety. Consequently, we provide an application case for the procedural generation of buildings based on our own procedural methods and pipeline that we based on the designers' needs.

2   Background

In this section, we summarize the first phase of the Design Process and related previous work. We also collect information about different simulations created for automotive evaluations. Furthermore, we review the different approaches used for the procedural modelling of 3D buildings based on their methods, their use cases, and the potential to adjust the level of control over their output.

2.1 Forming Experience During the Design Process

Automotive designers aim at high aesthetic quality and the experience it can elicit [5]. Aesthetics and brand increase the desirability and appeal of the product leading the user to buy a car [6]. Consisting of many different features, the development of a vehicle is a complicated process [7–9]. According to Raabe's model [9], it contains three phases: 'Early', 'Concept' & 'Serial Production'.

The Early Phase contains the creation and subsequent presentation of several designs. The inspiration sources for these designs should be the user's requirements for innovation, usability and functionality. Simultaneously, these designs should fulfil the brand's values and respect the firm's resources [9, 10]. During this phase, mood boards and experience stories are created by designers based on a certain design concept. At the end of the Early Phase, the first sketches are produced, refined and rendered.

In previous work [11], we asked designers and developers about the new prototyping methods they have just started using to present and evaluate their designs in the Early Phase, the process used to prepare the prototype and the problems they experienced during this process. Based on their answers and the observations we conducted during their meetings [11], designers started presenting their design with the help of mixed reality driving experiences on a driving simulator. These simulations should depict certain experiences the designers intend to facilitate through their design. To achieve that, they should fulfill the right functional and aesthetic context of the design scenario [12]. The designers and developers interpret this into the following customizable parameters essential for the design experience (Table 1):

Table 1. The parameters of the virtual environments for UI design experiences and their available options.

Terrain geometry	• Urban/Suburban
	• Matching the corresponding street type
	• Matching the location of the target market
	• Functional context
	• Aesthetic context
	• Reflecting the character of the vehicle
Road geometry	• Urban/Suburban
	• Road Type
	• Road Form
	• Driving Maneuver
	• Realistic driving conditions
Building geometry	• Urban/Suburban
	• Road Type
	• Variety of facade elements inside and outside of the building category
	• Option for changing the building textures
	• Matching the location of the target market
Vegetation	• Matching the location of the target market

In addition, the process used for preparing these design experiences is characterized by a high number of feedback loops between designers and developers [11]. At first, information about the vehicle's character (e.g., MINI Gentleman) and the target market is provided to the designers by the market research department. This information is then used by the designers to create the corresponding design scenarios. These should match the aesthetic values of the users at the target market. Furthermore, they should offer the functional context to fulfill the user's needs during experiences that are common for the location of the target market and represent the vehicle's character. The designers start contacting the developers even before the details of the design scenarios are finalized to describe the required environment. According to the interview results, the main challenges of this process are caused by the high amount of resources required to create this large variety of environments and the difficulty of a detailed environment description. Combined with these challenges, the trial-and-error nature of the designers' process to find the right environment renders the development of a virtual environment for such design experiences even harder.

2.2 Related Work: Driving Simulations for Automotive Evaluations

As a product of high complexity, the car has many aesthetic and functional features which need evaluation. This has led to the development of tools for the creation of virtual environments to be used in the automotive research and evaluation. The development of these environments focuses on the generation of specific road systems which fulfill the purpose of autonomous driving-scenario evaluations [8, 13], training simulations [14], as well as in-vehicle user experience evaluations [15]. In addition, the automotive industry has shown the tendency to use procedural generation as a method to build virtual environments for empirical studies with the focus on the driving conditions [16]. Further studies focus on communication between the vehicle and pedestrians [17], as well as specific in-vehicle user experiences in Virtual Reality [18, 19].

In the automotive industry, Mixed Reality Prototyping is used in many cases. Today, it is common to use Augmented or Virtual Reality to evaluate design elements in the interior of already existing car models, to test the usability of certain automotive UI interaction methods or to help maintenance and manufacturing processes. In the development process of the automotive design, Mixed Reality Prototyping has been used to help designers bring the users closer to the new design concept and get their feedback about its aesthetic and ergonomic quality already in the early stages of the development [8, 20–22].

All these simulations regardless of their virtuality level focus on a certain situation, experience or series of interactions and the user's reactions, coping techniques and feedback. For all these simulations, the modelled virtual environments are only suitable for these specific studies. However, in automotive aesthetic design, the variety of use cases and the required graphics quality [11] cannot be covered by the same environments. This wide variety of environments is necessary due to the creativity of the designers and the sources of inspiration to be visualized. In addition, the vehicle's character and conveying messages should also be matched by its surroundings. Finally, the new design should be evaluated and presented in an environment that represents the target market.

The combination of all mentioned challenges has led to the conclusion that a new framework of procedural environment generation based on real world data would make the environment development process for design presentations more efficient [11].

2.3 Related Work: Procedural Building Generation

The Lindenmayer or L-system is most known for its ability to generate plants [23]. However, because of its ability to model an object hierarchy and mesh, it has been widely used to generate buildings [24, 25]. With the help of the L-system, the building's form can be modeled based on certain parameters. Facade details are added with a rendered texture.

Shape grammars have been used to create industrial architectural design. Rau Chaplin et al. [26] has produced a user-friendly interface to adjust an existing outside and inside design of a building and provide architects with a tool to reduce the design time and cost while retaining high quality. The split and control grammars have been used to design the facade by splitting it into compartments and processing them according to a set of rules [27]. This method can output highly detailed buildings, characterized by a correspondingly high polygon number and highly complex definition of rules to add new architectural styles. Other methods that also rely on shape grammar focus on generating walls [28], modelling cities [29, 30], increasing style diversity by allowing more building shapes [31], or importing vectorial shapes [32].

Mostly focused on the generation of floor plans, Tutenel et al. follows a semantic approach to design a consistent floor plan and model it based on shape grammar techniques [33]. For a similar output, another semantic approach requires the specific parameters written in XML format and the geometry of a 2D floor plan to create the building with pre-defined facade module positions [34].

Focused on the procedural generation of buildings based on real data, other approaches output floor plans by training Bayesian networks [35], and buildings with multiple Levels of Detail (LODs) by using a custom shape grammar [36]. For use cases, in which the exterior environment is more important, Open Street Map (OSM) data has been used for generating the roads and the Unity Asset, CityGen3D, for randomly creating the buildings along them [37]. On the other hand, Noghani et al. [38] focused on creating buildings that resemble architectural styles of certain real cities but did not use real map data as input.

A modern approach of procedurally generating buildings is based on the Wave Function Collapse (WFC) algorithm. It requires a sample pattern of the desired output, which is reconstructed and replicated with different variations [39].

Other methods include image-based procedural modelling of facades. Also based on shape grammar, this approach outputs a 3D facade without its connection to a building structure and creates realistic facade layout designs [40]. Moreover, model synthesis creates large-scale environments by providing a small example model [41, 42]. This example model should contain just the right amount of information to identify the repeating patterns and create a successful, more complex and naturally looking model [43].

Comparing the outputs of the existing methods for procedurally generating buildings, their level of complexity and the variety of their output with the use cases and needs of the automotive designers, we decided to make our own approach adjusted to their requirements. The use cases of automotive designers mostly include a driving simulation. Therefore, the driver can only clearly see the bottom part of the buildings through the car windows, as well as the more distanced buildings through the windshield. These conditions place the focus of the procedural generation on the sections of the buildings which are better seen by the driver. In addition, we decided to use Open Street Map (OSM) data, due to the requirement for realistic driving conditions and because it provides a satisfying amount of information (e.g., building type and height) and the building footprints. For important public buildings, it even includes the building's parts, thus offering a more detailed building form. This information also influences the focus of procedural generation, shifting it to other building details. Furthermore, since automotive designers usually do not have any technical skills, the generation of the buildings should only require a minimum amount of effort.

3   Materials and Methods

The building generator was developed using the software Houdini by SideFX. This decision was based on an engine-neutral solution and Houdini's ability to communicate with both most used game engines, Unity and Unreal, enabling further editing of the generator's output inside the game engine. Our implementation focused on the generation of buildings that match the chosen map area, but do not necessarily represent reality. Three cities were selected as the focus for the architectural styles implemented, based on three major automotive markets: Los Angeles, Munich, and Shanghai.

The generation process includes the following phases: a) Processing the OSM data, b) choosing an architectural style, c) reading the available facade parameters for the chosen architectural style, d) randomly choosing one parameter combination for each facade category, e) computing the right position for each facade module on the building walls, f) preparing the building walls to accommodate the facade modules and g) placing instances of the generated facade modules (Fig. 1).

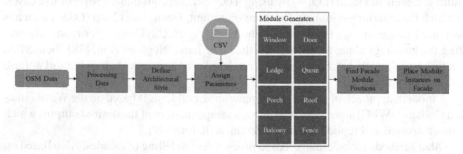

Fig. 1. Framework of the automotive procedural building generator.

3.1   Processing the OSM Data

The data provided by OSM are polygons that in most cases represent the footprints of the buildings. In other cases, these polygons are characterized by the attribute "multi-polygon". This information means that the outline represents a hollow space (e.g., inner garden) inside the building area. Additionally, the polygon may be part of a building and carry the corresponding attribute "building_parts". Moreover, some polygons symbolize the area covered by non-building elements such as swimming pools. To prepare this geometry for the next modelling steps, these non-building elements are first removed. Secondly, the "multipolygon"-footprints are filtered out since the driver cannot see the inner hollow spaces in a driving simulation. Thirdly, the building parts are extruded so that they get their individual height and are connected to the rest of the building after the main corresponding footprint polygon is also extruded.

An important attribute that must be calculated at the beginning of the modelling process is which building walls are facing a street. For this purpose, the footprint polygons and the street lines are first extruded in the z-axis (towards the sky). Then, a ray is cast from the top two points of each wall polygon towards the outside of the building. The wall polygons are grouped as *streetSide* when their ray hits a polygon that belongs to a street. This information is used to remove the buildings whose walls are all facing other buildings, i.e., they are not visible from the street. The street type (e.g., residential) which is also provided by OSM, can also be read from the street polygon hit by the ray and stored as an attribute in the wall polygon. This information helps, for example, to place the main door of the building on the side facing a street with a higher priority (primary > secondary > ...) in case more than one side faces a street.

3.2 Choosing an Architectural Style

The architectural style is chosen based on certain parameters that are either computed or provided by OSM. These parameters include the building's height and area, its type (e.g., apartments) and the geographic coordinates of the original data. Within this concept, the generation of architectural styles focuses on three specific cities: Los Angeles, Munich and Shanghai. Consequently, the following architectural styles were chosen as possible outputs: Skyscraper, Modern, Victorian, Craftsman, Spanish Colonial Revival, Beaux-Arts, Renaissance, Neoclassical, Tong Lau and Tang.

With the goal of modelling buildings that represent the character of each city, specific architectural styles were selected to create the facade modules. The following architectural styles define the character of Los Angeles:

- Skyscrapers: Often characterized by a steel framework that supports the curtain walls [44].
- Beaux-Arts: Demonstrates a great amount of decoration and a central focus element with characteristic coupled columns, corner elements and entablatures [45]. To show a more complicated bas-relief, the facade is decorated with sculptures and further decorative elements on the roof [45].
- Victorian: Among the most recognizable variants, Queen Anne buildings are characterized by multiple steep roofs, porches with decorative gables, octagonal or circular towers, intensively decorative windows, corbelled chimneys, and doors with glass panels [46].
- Craftsman: Bungalows in that style are characterized by a low-pitched, gabled roof, oversized eaves with massively exposed rafter tails, and grouped windows [47].

• Spanish Colonial Revival: Often recognized by a gabled, hipped, or flat roof and simple to no decoration at the cornices and eaves. Moreover, the windows, doors and balconies are deeply recessed [48].

Following the German architectural history, the following styles played an important role in the design of the city of Munich [49]:

• Neo-Renaissance: This style is highly diverse with a special focus on symmetry. It is characterized by a great amount of decorative elements, rusticated masonry, quoins, windows framed by architraves, as well as doors with pediments and entablatures. In a building with multiple floors, the top one usually has small square windows.
• Neoclassicism: This style presents simple geometric forms, the use of columns and blank walls.
• The skyscrapers, industrial and modern styles in Germany followed the same architectural concepts as the corresponding Western styles.

The Chinese architecture adopted many elements of Western styles [50]. These types of buildings were used as civil and industrial infrastructure as well as religious, educational, commercial, and entertainment facilities. Most urban and rural places were characterized by traditional styles, such as "Palace style" (gongdiau-shi), "Classical Chinese style" (Zhongguo guyou-shi) and "National style" (minzu-xingshi). Some of the characteristic buildings, like the Peking Union Hospital, were designed by European and American architects and combine elements of Neoclassicism and the traditional Chinese roofs. Modern Chinese architecture is also characterized by skyscrapers used for industrial purposes. Characteristic for the city of Hong Kong is the Tong Lau style, which was used in the construction of residential buildings in working-class districts. The shape of Tong Lau buildings is crystallized in a store on the ground floor and apartments on the upper floor. It is also known for its long and narrow wooden poles, integrated into the supporting structure. Furthermore, a common sight in both cities are tall apartment buildings with many windows, indicating that they are divided into many small tenants.

3.3 Facade Modules

The facade modules include the window, door, balcony, roof, ledge, quoin, fence, porch, and ground facade. For each of these modules, a generator was developed that models a module based on specific parameters. For each module, all possible values that can be assigned to its parameters are stored in CSV tables. When a new building is generated, the available values for each module are read for a specific architectural style at the corresponding row of the table. From these values, one is randomly chosen based on a uniform distribution. The module generators receive the final values for each parameter and generate the modules accordingly. The design of these generators was focused on the compatibility with future developments and the easy addition of assets to increase the diversity of an architectural style, as well as to facilitate further development.

The window generator is controlled by the following parameters:

a   Form: This parameter dictates the form of the window's glass and consequently also frame.

b   Grille: The grille separates the window glass into panes or lites [51]. This parameter can change the type of the window grille by processing a black and white image.

c   Frame: A toggle parameter which can be used to control whether a window frame is generated. It is a useful option, especially in case of a skyscraper window, which does not have a frame.

d   Number of additional windows: An important parameter for architectural styles that are characterized by grouped windows. The additional windows are automatically placed on the right and left side of the main one. They are also automatically assigned all the decorative elements chosen for the main window. An encapsulating wall pane is added around the group of windows and the whole model is considered as one window module.

e   Jamb: Consists of the two vertical sides of the window frame. This parameter is necessary to control the depth of the frame, with a higher value resulting in a more recessed window [51].

f   Sill: The horizontal bottom part of the window frame. With the help of this parameter, the type of sill can be adjusted among the options of no sill, a simple sill, i.e., without decorative elements, and a sill with decorative elements [51].

g   Sill Deco: Chooses the type of decorative elements placed under the sill.

h   Decorative Columns: Changes the type of columns decorating the sides of the window.

i   Pediment: A decorative element, usually in a triangular form, placed above the window. This parameter helps to control the pediment type to be modeled above the window, varying from none to a certain form (e.g., triangular, round) [51].

j   Glass Dimensions: Controls the size of the window glass. The frame and the rest of the window elements are added separately.

k   Wall dimensions: Controls the size of the wall parts on the four sides around the window glass. Decorative elements around the window do not cover part of this wall. The glass and wall dimensions are combined to manage the size of the window, as well as the distance between two adjacent windows.

l   Oriel Window: A form of a bay window that protrudes from the main wall. This parameter transforms any window into an oriel window [51].

For the form and grille parameters, the generator chooses one from a series of pre-imported images to use as the basis for their modeling. This method enables the extension of the existing dataset of window forms and grille patterns by simply adding a new black and white image. The decorative elements under the sill, the decorative columns and the pediments are provided as a 3D asset for the generator. Most photogrammetry assets were taken from Quixel Megascans. They were reduced to their smallest elements (e.g., decorative columns) and used as building blocks for the facade module generators. This method increased the diversity of buildings while reducing the required resources.

Some architectural styles include different window types for certain floors or the same window type spanning multiple floors. To enable the modeling of these windows, the same window generator was used (Fig. 2).

The door generator outputs doors based on the following parameters:

Fig. 2. A sample of the windows created by the window generator.

a Form: Like the window parameter, it chooses the form of the door.
b Entrance Frame: Can change the decorative elements surrounding the door.
c Single Door: Can be switched to false in case a double door is required.
d Panel Pattern: Controls the pattern of the panel on the door. The assigned material can be either glass or the material of the door.
e Jamb: Like the window parameter, it defines the depth of the door frame [51].

The concept of image processing was applied to the form and panel pattern parameters, whereas the entrance frame parameter requires an asset (Fig. 3).

Fig. 3. A sample of the doors created by the door generator.

The balcony generator is controlled by the following parameters:

a Form: Like the previous form parameters, it chooses the form of the balcony.
b Handrail: The type of hand support to place above the balcony's railing, varying from flat to cylinder form.

c Railing: The type of balcony railing, varying from thin cylinders to balustrade.
d Shed: Can add a shed to the balcony (Fig. 4).

Fig. 4. A sample of the balconies created by the balcony generator.

The next two module generators output decorative elements. One of them is a quoin, which decorates the corners of a building's exterior [51]. It can be adjusted based on the required quoin type, varying from none to a certain type. The other is a Ledge Generator that decorates the building facade with a protrusion on the wall and can divert rain from walls and windows. Two modelling methods are applied by the Ledge Generator: The first one allows the user to add only a cross-section of the ledge, which can be created either as a single polygon or as an imported image. This cross-section is then expanded along the building walls. The second method is based on a modular piece of ledge that is repeatedly placed along each side of the building. The first method is useful for creating a new ledge pattern quickly and easy, while the second method can be used if the ledge is more complicated (e.g., with decorative elements underneath) (Fig. 5).

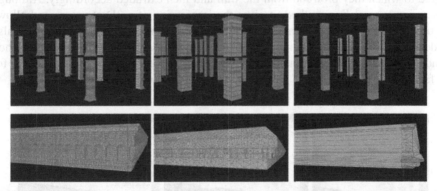

Fig. 5. A sample of the quoins (up) and the ledges (down) created by the Quoin and Ledge generators, respectively.

Furthermore, two more module generators were created, which provide elements not to the facade, but to the surroundings of the building: the Porch and Fence Generator. The Porch Generator models a porch around the building door using randomly distributed side panels in relation to the porch entrance. This randomness, combined with the adjustable railing type parameter, adds some diversity to the generated porches. New railings can be added by providing the corresponding modular part. The Fence Generator is controlled by parameters for the railing and fence door. An additional parameter provides the ability to turn the lower half of the railing into a wall. This generator also processes the modular railing and fence door assets. The railing could even be a hedge asset (Fig. 6).

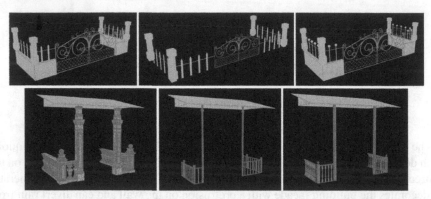

Fig. 6. A sample of the fences (up) and porches (down) created by the Fence and Porch generator, respectively.

The Ground Facade Generator was created to model the facade of the building's ground floor, which may be covered with windows, consist of a simple wall, or be a shop facade. Such a shop facade is processed from an image that contains the edges of the facade polygons in black and the rest in white. The white areas are grouped based on the degree to which they protrude from the wall and then extruded accordingly. Although it is a simple modeling method, it gives the impression of a 3D structure and allows the user to add more shop facades with little effort and resources. This generator also models signs based on the same method, as well as an awning at the top of the shop facade. Accordingly, the Ground Facade Generator is controlled by the parameters for the facade type (such as 'shop'), the sign type, and the awning type (Fig. 7).

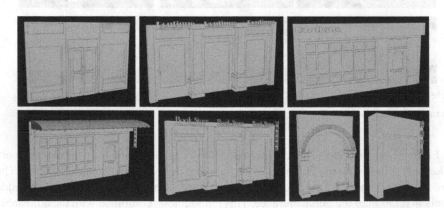

Fig. 7. A sample of the facades at the ground floor created by the Ground Facade generator.

Finally, the Roof Generator creates the following roof types: Hip, Gable, Mansard, Gambrel, Flat and Xieshan. Windows can be added to the roof by adjusting the corresponding parameter. The roof types can be adapted to any building, regardless of its shape (Fig. 8).

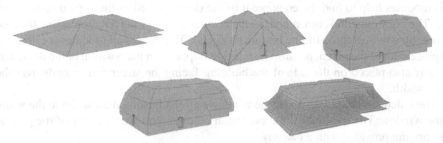

Fig. 8. A sample of the roofs created by the Roof generator.

3.4 Forming the Building's Facade

In every generator, the polygons of the generated modules that represent a part of the building wall are grouped accordingly using the "wall"-attribute. This is an important parameter that will be used in a later processing step.

After the outputs of the Window and Ground Facade Generators are created, their positions on each side of the wall are calculated using Houdini's building generator. This tool has been modified to allow for additional scenarios such as the exception of window columns. Moreover, the tool's division of each wall into modular pieces, which are placed at the areas of the facade that are not covered by other modules, are utilized. Their modular shape allows the exact removal of wall parts that are partially covered by other walls and therefore do not need to be modeled. In addition, no facade modules are assigned to the walls that do not face the street due to the previously calculated *streetSide* attribute. One output of the modified tool are points that serve as positions where the instances of the corresponding module are copied to. Each point is assigned an attribute containing the name of the corresponding module. The other output is the geometry that consists of the wall modules and only the polygons of the facade modules that are identified by the "wall"-attribute.

The height of the building is used to place the ledges at the top of each floor. The polygon of the building outline is used to create the points to which the modular ledge is copied as an instance, or to measure the length to which the cross-section of the ledge is expanded. The ledge corners are created by cutting the modular ledge at the angle of the corner.

For the quoins, the original polygon of the building footprint is transformed into a simple line primitive by computing the sequence of its points, based on which they are then connected with lines. In the next step the convex corners are found and the already calculated point sequence is used. For each convex corner, the quoins are copied as instances, leaving a space between the floors for the ledge.

The *streetSide* attribute from the original walls is transferred to the wall modules. If more than one wall module is selected based on this attribute, the modules with the highest priority street type (primary > secondary > ...) are preferred. From those, the middle wall module is selected as the one to which the door will be attached. If the width of the door exceeds the width of the wall module, the next one is gathered. The combined wall modules help to find the copy point of the door, as well as the copy direction and side. The copy direction corresponds to the normal vector of the polygon, while the side is computed by searching for the bottom right end. The same wall modules are used for the placement of the porch, because its position depends on the position of the door. The fence is also placed on the side of the building facing the street and extends over the entire width.

The balconies are placed under the windows after adjusting their width to the width of the window. The windows of the exception columns and the windows of the ground floor are not provided with a balcony.

After all copy point positions and their normal vectors have been found, the wall modules play a final important role: they serve as an orientation guide for the outlines of new uniform walls. Without them, the material assigned to each wall module would look inconsistent. After creating a new polygon for each wall by determining its four bounding points, the placed polygons identified by the "wall"- attribute are used to model specific structures. These structures represent the areas of the walls that will be opened to create space for the placement of the facade modules. These openings are created by a Boolean operation between the walls of the building and the generated structures. Before the facade modules are copied as instances to the corresponding points to fill these openings, the wall parts of the modules are removed and only the remaining parts are copied.

All UVs are projected orthographically and then scaled based on the area of each primitive. After this step, all building parts can be assigned with materials.

4 Results and Discussion

In this section, we present some generated buildings characteristic of each architectural style, the parameters that influenced their generation, and some of their possible variants. In addition, we analyze the expression range of the generator by examining the effects of its parameters on the output.

4.1 Results of the Automotive Building Generator

The following three tables show the outputs of our Automotive Building Generator based on the OSM data of Los Angeles, Munich and Shanghai, their architectural style, as well as a facade variation with the same building shape and style (Table 2).

Table 2. Generated buildings based on each architectural style and one variation.

City	Generated Building & Variations
Skyscraper (LA /Munich /Shanghai)	
Beaux-Arts (LA)	
Victorian (LA)	
Craftsman (LA)	
Spanish Colonial Revival (LA)	
Neo-Renaissance (Munich)	
Neo-Classicism (Munich)	
Modern (LA/Munich)	
Modern (Shanghai)	
Tong Lau (Shanghai)	
Tang (Shanghai)	

4.2 Discussion

To evaluate the generator's results, we selected specific criteria relevant to our goals and discussed the extent to which each outcome fulfils them. First, the definition of congruent buildings by Tutenel et al. [33] seemed appropriate to us. Their definition of consistent buildings is not in line with our goal, as we do not aim to produce "enterable" buildings or consequently complete buildings. Congruent buildings have consistent elements that correspond to a certain style. These elements should be placed in the right position and not overlap each other. Since we focus on achieving a resembling look of architectural styles, we have chosen as a second scale the presence of all the characteristic elements of the corresponding architectural style. In addition, the computation time, which depends on the number of buildings, and the number of polygons, are important parameters that determine the suitability of the generator. Finally, the effort that an automotive designer must spend to create the result, as well as the time and cost that a developer must spend to add additional architectural styles to the generator were also taken into consideration.

Congruent Buildings. 1000 buildings were generated using a laptop with following technical features: Intel(R) Core(TM) i7-8750H CPU (2.21 GHz), x64-based processor, 64bit operating system, 32.0 GB RAM and NVIDIA GeForce RTX 2080 with Max-Q Design. The generated buildings were examined for any geometry errors that would indicate incongruency, none of which were detected. The most important factor affecting this result is that the randomness of the generator is only in the parameters of the facade modules and the shape of the building. Due to the predefined selection of facade modules in the CSV tables, the exact mathematical determination of the position of each element based on the dimensions of the wall and the floor height, and the rules that prevent certain elements such as fences and porches from overlapping with other structures, the possibility of a facade module not fitting, being incorrectly positioned or overlapping remains minimal. This is one of our goals, as the generator is intended for automotive designers who do not have the programming skills to create their own virtual environment or correct such geometry errors.

Architectural styles. The generators for the facade modules were created based on the characteristic elements for each architectural style, with CSV tables defining the possible range for each style. From the results, it can be seen that the generated buildings are consistent with the assigned style by containing all characteristic elements, as they were presented in Sect. 3.2.

Computation time and polygon count: On the same laptop, for each building style, the computation time was calculated for a building with three floors and a footprint area of 991.146 m^2. The number of polygons of each building depends on the assets used for the facade modules. Photogrammetry assets typically have more polygons, which would result in a high total number if the repeating elements were not instances. Moreover, it took 45 min to generate a total of 1,000 buildings. This is not comparable to the time it would take a team to manually create them from scratch. In addition, an area of Los Angeles (2 km^2) was generated with streets, buildings and vegetation inside the Unreal Engine and tested for a design presentation on the driving simulator (Fig. 9) (Table 3).

Automotive Designer's effort: To generate the buildings, the generator only requires the.osm file with the data for the desired map area. The designer's only action is to select

Table 3. Computation time and polygon count for each architectural style for a building with three floors and an area of 991.146 m²

City	Architectural style	Computation time (s)	Polygon count
Los Angeles/Munich/Shanghai	Skyscraper	1.09	166
Los Angeles	Beaux-Arts	10.976	6000
Los Angeles	Victorian	1.725	4942
Los Angeles	Craftsman	2.408	32493
Los Angeles	Spanish Colonial Revival	2.351	14846
Munich	Neo-Renaissance	1.985	24629
Munich	Neo-Classicism	16466	17714
Los Angeles/Munich	Modern	19.593	15380
Shanghai	Modern	3.14	6617
Shanghai	Tong Lau	10.805	8898
Shanghai	Tang	8.068	5977

the area on a map and inform the developers. After that, designers just have to wait to receive the generated output.

Time and Cost for the addition of styles: Since automotive companies do not produce these driving simulations as their main product, but still need them to make crucial design decisions, the relationship between development cost and outcome is always particularly sensitive. If only images and small assets are needed, which can be produced at minimal cost to add new architectural styles, the overall cost of generating these valuable driving simulations is dramatically reduced compared to a manual approach.

The designers' and developers' feedback: We collected the qualitative feedback of designers and developers during a series of expert structured interviews. Accordingly, we contacted all designers and developers with the expertise in this new prototyping method and interviewed them while recording our sessions. By involving both perspectives represented by the two groups of participants, we aimed at increasing triangulation [52]. Due to the nature of the interviews and the limited number of experts in this new prototyping method, we sampled the participants based on the "n = 12 + 3" sample size principle for the collection of feedback [53]. To this end, we analyzed the interview results of twelve participants and cross-checked them with the answers of the rest three participants to ensure that no additional verbal codes arise, thus achieving saturation [53, 54]. Since this is only one of many generators creating the complete environment for the design experiences, we let the participants evaluate three different complete environments containing buildings by our generator with additional assets for terrain, streets and vegetation. The participants were asked the following questions: 1) What did they like or dislike in terms of the buildings' geometry and why? 2) Which elements would they add, change or remove regarding the buildings and why? 3) What are their thoughts on the Automotive Building Generator as a tool to generate their own environments based on a map area selection?

Content Analysis was used to analyze the collected data which were interpreted with the help of developers experienced in working with the designers and preparing design experiences. This method has been viewed as suitable for the interpretation and presentation of interview data [55]. The statements were categorized as follows:

Geometry: One developer stated that the buildings' facade variety is sufficient for their use cases. Another developer observed that the roofs do not extrude from the walls of a building and pointed that out as an optimization. The variety of architectural styles and the degree of the buildings' details with the example of the fences have fascinated a designer.

Materials: Three participants commented on the small variety of materials applied to the walls of the buildings. This is a comment we expected since we did not have the time to collect more materials.

Use cases: One participant mentioned the use case of a street full of shops with many neon signs shining in the night or a "party mile". From a developer point of view, we would interpret this use case as the need to have such an option available with the appropriate materials and ground floor facades. Consequently, some more shop and entertainment facades together with matching cube maps to visualize the interior would be an idea to bring more realism and liveliness.

The new Design Experience Development Process: All designers and developers were enthusiastic about this tool and expressed without even asked their positive impressions (e.g., "This is a very powerful tool"). One designer stated that designers changing their requirements about the virtual environment is part of a trial-and-error process to define it and is not going to change. He concluded that due to the nature of this process, having the ability with the help of this tool to create a result in a short amount of time in comparison to six months, is exactly the solution they need. In addition, he concludes that designers can get creative by using this system to test their design stories with different environments. Another designer also highlighted the advantage of being able to generate an environment in such a short amount of time. Two designers expressed the observation that the designers' needs have been heard and considered during the implementation of the framework.

The rest of the designers and developers did not have any comments to share about the buildings since they were content with the result. As for the whole idea of choosing an area in the world and getting the corresponding 3D environment in a short amount of time as opposed to either choose among only three environments or spend a big amount of resources to get the environment after 6 months, both designers and developers were very fascinated.

This Building Generator was created based on the needs of automotive aesthetic designers. However, it could also generate buildings for other groups of people inside the automotive industry who need virtual environments based on real map data (e.g., psychological or aesthetic evaluations with end users). Outside the automotive industry, potential users could be game designers who aim at creating a location-based game as well as people who need virtual environments for training simulations (e.g., fire department, military).

5   Conclusion and Future Work

There are many procedural methods for generating buildings, each with its own advantages and suitable use cases. In the case of automotive designers, several needs led to the development of a new building generator. These include the need to reduce environment development resources to achieve the right experience context for design evaluations, to find better methods to describe the right environment to developers, and to have power over the creation of their own experience context. This generator meets all of these requirements by using a set of molecular facade module generators, selecting an appropriate architectural style, and placing the modules on the right positions of the building's facade. The generation for a given area of the world map is done automatically, without the designers having to do anything except choosing the area. Thanks to the Houdini pipeline with one of the two most used game engines, Unity and Unreal, changes can be made after the generation. Thus, developers can add more elements directly inside the game engine in case some last-minute changes or finer details are needed. With this approach, we strive to demonstrate the use of procedural generation to enable automotive designers to create their own context for automotive design experiences upon which they can evaluate and present their design.

There are still many steps to be taken on the way to a complete virtual world in which automotive design scenarios can be simulated. We have also developed a street generator and already started to create a suitable interface that can support automotive designers in defining the environment. For the building generator, a concept is being implemented for randomly assigning materials from a material library depending on the architectural style and city. According to this concept, each building part (e.g., roof, balcony) has an available palette of materials, one of which is randomly chosen to be assigned, based on the same concept applied for choosing the facade modules (described in Sect. 3.3).

Fig. 9. A generated area of Los Angeles created with our building generator.

References

1. Procedural Technology in Ghost Recon: Wildlands (80.lv). https://80.lv/articles/procedural-technology-in-ghost-recon-wildlands/. Accessed 20 Apr 2022
2. The Procedural Nature of the Horizon Zero Dawn (80.lv). https://80.lv/articles/the-procedural-nature-of-the-horizon-zero-dawn/. Accessed 20 Apr 2022
3. Weber, M., Giacomin, J., Malizia, A., Skrypchuk, L., Gkatzidou, V., Mouzakitis, A.: Investigation of the dependency of the drivers' emotional experience on different road types and driving conditions. Transp. Res. F: Traffic Psychol. Behav. **65**, 3 (2019). https://doi.org/10.1016/j.trf.2019.06.001
4. Satake, I., et al.: A comparative study of the emotional assessment of automotive exterior colors in Asia. Prog. Org. Coat. **72**, 528–540 (2011). https://doi.org/10.1016/j.porgcoat.2011.06.013

5. Ranscombe, C., Hicks, B., Mullineux, G., Singh, B.: Characterizing and evaluating aesthetic features in vehicle design. In: Proceedings of the 3rd International Conference on Research into Design Engineering (ICORD 2011), Bangalore, India (2011)
6. Warell, A.: Multi-modal visual experience of brand-specific automobile design. TQM J. **20**(4), 356–371 (2008). https://doi.org/10.1108/17542730810881348
7. Argyris, C.: Reasoning, Learning, and Action: Individual and Organizational. Sage Publications, Thousand Oaks, CA (1982). https://doi.org/10.1177/017084068400500316
8. Bordegoni, M., Caruso, G.: Mixed reality distributed platform for collaborative design review of automotive interiors. Virtual Phys. Prototyp. **7**(4), 243–259 (2012). https://doi.org/10.1080/17452759.2012.721605
9. Raabe, R.: Ein rechnergestütztes Werkzeug zur Generierung konsistenter PKW-Maßkonzepte und parametrischer Designvorgaben. Universität Stuttgart (2013)
10. Braess, H.-H., Seiffert, U. (eds.): Vieweg Handbuch Kraftfahrzeugtechnik. A, Springer, Wiesbaden (2013). https://doi.org/10.1007/978-3-658-01691-3
11. Salpisti, D., de Clerk, M., Hinz, S., Henkies, F., Klinker, G.: Requirements for 3D environments as the context for mixed reality automotive design experiences. In: Proceedings of the Driving Simulation Conference (DSC 2022), Strasbourg, France (2022)
12. Obrist, M., Tscheligi, M., De Ruyter, B., Schmidt, A.: Contextual user experience: how to reflect it in interaction designs? In: Proceedings of the 28th International Conference on Human Factors in Computing Systems (CHI 2010) Association for Computing Machinery, Atlanta, Georgia, USA, pp. 3197–3200 (2010). https://doi.org/10.1145/1753846.1753956
13. Burch, M., Wallner, G., Arends, S.T.T., Beri, P.: Procedural city modeling for AR applications. In: Proceedings of the International Conference on Information Visualisation, Institute of Electrical and Electronics Engineers Inc., pp. 581–586 (2020). https://doi.org/10.1109/IV51561.2020.00098
14. Krueger, H., Grein, M., Kaussner, A., Mark, C.: SILAB – a task oriented driving simulation. In: Driving Simulation Conference (DSC 2005), Orlando, FL, pp. 323–331 (2005)
15. Alvarez, I., Rumbel, L., Adams, R.: Skyline. In: Proceedings of the 7th International Conference on Automotive User Interfaces and Interactive Vehicular Applications. ACM, New York, NY, pp. 101–108 (2015). https://doi.org/10.1145/2799250.2799290
16. Barz, A., Conrad, J., Wallach, D.: Advantages of using runtime procedural generation of virtual environments based on real world data for conducting empirical automotive research. In: Stephanidis, C., Duffy, V.G., Streitz, N., Konomi, S., Krömker, H. (eds.) HCII 2020. LNCS, vol. 12429, pp. 14–23. Springer, Cham (2020). https://doi.org/10.1007/978-3-030-59987-4_2
17. Colley, M., Walch, M., Rukzio, E.: For a better (simulated) world: considerations for VR in external communication research. In: Proceedings of the 11th International Conference on Automotive User Interfaces and Interactive Vehicular Applications: Adjunct Proceedings (AutomotiveUI 2019) Association for Computing Machinery, NY, pp. 442–449 (2019). https://doi.org/10.1145/3349263.3351523
18. McGill, M., Brewster, S.: Virtual reality passenger experiences. In: Proceedings of the 11th International Conference on Automotive User Interfaces and Interactive Vehicular Applications: Adjunct Proceedings (AutomotiveUI 2019) Association for Computing Machinery, NY, pp. 434–441 (2019). https://doi.org/10.1145/3349263.3351330
19. Li, J., George, C., Ngao, A., Holländer, K., Mayer, S., Butz, A.: An exploration of users' thoughts on rear-seat productivity in virtual reality. In: 12th International Conference on Automotive User Interfaces and Interactive Vehicular Applications (AutomotiveUI 2020) Association for Computing Machinery, NY, pp. 92–95 (2020). https://doi.org/10.1145/3409251.3411732

20. Bordegoni, M., Cugini, U., Caruso, G., Polistina, S.: The role of mixed prototyping in product design assessment. In: Proceedings of the 2nd International Conference on Research into Design, pp. 427–434 (2009)
21. Caruso, G.: Mixed reality system for ergonomic assessment of driver's seat. Int. J. Virtual Real. **10**(2), 69–79 (2011). https://doi.org/10.20870/ijvr.2011.10.2.2813
22. de Clerk, M., Dangelmaier, M., Schmierer, G., Spath, D.: User centered design of interaction techniques for VR-based automotive design reviews. Front. Robot. AI **6**, 13 (2019). https://doi.org/10.3389/frobt.2019.00013
23. Prusinkiewicz, P.: Graphical applications of L-systems. In: Proceedings of Graphics Interface/Vision Interface 1986, pp. 247–253 (1986)
24. Marvie, J.-E., Perret, J., Bouatouch, K.: The FL-system: a functional L-system for procedural geometric modeling. Vis. Comput. **21**(5), 329–339 (2005). https://doi.org/10.1007/s00371-005-0289-z
25. Parish, Y. I. H., Pascal, M.: Procedural modeling of cities. In: Proceedings of the 28th Annual Conference on Computer Graphics and Interactive Techniques (SIGGRAPH 2001) Association for Computing Machinery, NY, pp. 301–308 (2001). https://doi.org/10.1145/383259.383292
26. Rau-Chaplin, A., MacKay-Lyons, B., Spieremburg, P.F.: The LaHave house project: towards an automated architectural design service. Technical University of N.S., School of Computer Science, Architecture and Urban Design, Halifax, Canada (1996)
27. Wonka, P., Wimmer, M., Sillion, F., Ribarsky, F.: Instant architecture. ACM Trans. Graph. **22**(3), 669–677 (2003). https://doi.org/10.1145/882262.882324
28. Larive, M., Gaildrat, V.: Wall grammar for building generation. In: Proceedings of the 4th International Conference on Computer Graphics and Interactive Techniques in Australasia and Southeast Asia (GRAPHITE 2006) Association for Computing Machinery, NY, pp. 429–437 (2006). https://doi.org/10.1145/1174429.1174501
29. Kelly, T.: CityEngine: an introduction to rule-based modeling. In: Shi, W., Goodchild, M.F., Batty, M., Kwan, M.-P., Zhang, A. (eds.) Urban Informatics. TUBS, pp. 637–662. Springer, Singapore (2021). https://doi.org/10.1007/978-981-15-8983-6_35
30. Jesus, D., Coelho, A., Rebelo, C., Cardoso, A., de Sousa, A.A.: A pipeline for procedural modelling from geospatial data. In: 33rd Annual Conference of the European Association for Computer Graphics, Eurographics 2012, pp. 9–10 (2012)
31. Schwarz, M., Müller, P.: Advanced procedural modeling of architecture. ACM Trans. Graph. **34**(4), Article 107 (2015). https://doi.org/10.1145/2766956
32. Jesus, D., Coelho, A., Sousa, A.A.: Layered shape grammars for procedural modelling of buildings. Vis. Comput. **32**(6–8), 933–943 (2016). https://doi.org/10.1007/s00371-016-1254-8
33. Tutenel, T., Smelik, R.M., Lopes, R., de Kraker, K.J., Bidarra, R.: Generating consistent buildings: a semantic approach for integrating procedural techniques. IEEE Trans. Comput. Intell. AI Games **3**(3), 274–288 (2011)
34. Silveira, I., Camozzato, D., Marson, F., Dihl, L., Musse, S.R.: Real-time procedural generation of personalized facade and interior appearances based on semantics. In: Proceedings of the 14th Brazilian Symposium on Computer Games and Digital Entertainment (SBGames), pp. 89–98 (2015). https://doi.org/10.1109/SBGames.2015.32
35. Merrell, P., Schkufza, E., Koltun, V.: Computer-generated residential building layouts. ACM Trans. Graph. **29**(6), Article 181 (2010). https://doi.org/10.1145/1882261.1866203
36. Biljecki, F., Ledoux, H., Stoter, J.: Generation of multi-LOD 3D city models in CityGML with the procedural modelling engine Random3Dcity. In: ISPRS Annals of the Photogrammetry, Remote Sensing and Spatial Information Sciences 4 (4W1), pp. 51–59. ScholarBank@NUS Repository (2016). https://doi.org/10.5194/isprs-annals-IV-4-W1-51-2016

37. Dam, P., Duarte, F., Raposo, A.: Terrain generation based on real world locations for military training and simulation. In: Brazilian Symposium on Games and Digital Entertainment (SBGAMES), IEEE Computer Society, Rio de Janeiro, Brazil, pp. 173–181 (2019). https://doi.org/10.1109/SBGames.2019.00031
38. Noghani, J., Liarokapis, F., Anderson, E.F.: Procedural generation of urban environments through space and time. In: Poster Proceedings of the 31st Annual Conference of the European Association for Computer Graphics, Eurographics 2010 (2010)
39. Gaisbauer, W., Raffe, W.L., Garcia, J.A., Hlavacs, H.: Procedural generation of video game cities for specific video game genres using wavefunctioncollapse (WFC). In: Extended Abstracts of the Annual Symposium on Computer-Human Interaction in Play (CHI PLAY 2019) Association for Computing Machinery, Inc, pp. 397–404 (2019) https://doi.org/10.1145/3341215.3356255
40. Müller, P., Zeng, G., Wonka, P., Gool, L.V.: Image-based procedural modeling of facades. ACM Trans. Graph. **26**, 3 (2007). https://doi.org/10.1145/1276377.1276484
41. Merrell, P.: Example-based model synthesis. In: Proceedings of the 2007 Symposium on Interactive 3D Graphics and Games (I3D 2007) Association for Computing Machinery, NY, pp. 105–112 (2007). https://doi.org/10.1145/1230100.1230119
42. Merrell, P., Manocha, D.: Continuous model synthesis. ACM Trans. Graph. **27**(5), Article 158 (2008). https://doi.org/10.1145/1409060.1409111
43. Merrell, P., Manocha, D.: Constraint-based model synthesis. In: 2009 SIAM/ACM Joint Conference on Geometric and Physical Modeling (SPM 2009) Association for Computing Machinery, NY, pp. 101–111 (2009). https://doi.org/10.1145/1629255.1629269
44. Ambrose, G., Harris, P., Stone, S.: The Visual Dictionary of Architecture. AVA Publishing SA, Switzerland, p. 233 (2008). ISBN 978-2-940373-54-3
45. GPA Consulting: Architecture and Engineering, 1850–1980: Beaux Arts Classicism, Neoclassical, and Italian Renaissance Revival Architecture, 1895–1940. Los Angeles Citywide Historic Context Statement, City of Los Angeles Office of Historic Resources (2016)
46. Dixon, R., Muthesius, S.: Victorian Architecture: With a Short Dictionary of Architects and 251 Illustrations. Thames and Hudson (1978). ISBN 978-0-500-18163-8
47. GPA Consulting. Architecture and Engineering, 1850–1980: Arts and Crafts Movement, 1895–1930. Los Angeles Citywide Historic Context Statement, City of Los Angeles Office of Historic Resources (2016)
48. GPA Consulting. Architecture and Engineering, 1850–1980: American Colonial Revival, 1895–1960. Los Angeles Citywide Historic Context Statement, City of Los Angeles Office of Historic Resources (2016)
49. London, J.: A review of the Cambridge Companion to modern German culture, edited by Eva Kolinsky and Wilfried van der Will. Contemp. Theatre Rev. **12**(1–2), 269–271 (2002). https://doi.org/10.1080/10486800208568668
50. Chang, Q.: Architectural models and their contexts in China's 20th-century architectural heritage: an overview. Built Heritage **3**, 1–13 (2019). https://doi.org/10.1186/BF03545715
51. Davies, N., Jokiniemi, E.: Architect's Illustrated Pocket Dictionary. Taylor & Francis (2012). 9781136444067
52. Carter, N., Bryant-Lukosius, D., DiCenso, A., Blythe, J., Neville, A.J.: The use of triangulation in qualitative research. Oncol. Nurs. Forum **41**(5), 545–547 (2014). https://doi.org/10.1188/14.ONF.545-547
53. Mason, M.: Sample size and saturation in PhD studies using qualitative interviews. In: Forum Qualitative Sozialforschung/Forum: Qualitative Social Research **11**(3) (2010)
54. Baker, S.E., Edwards, R.: How many qualitative interviews is enough. National Center for Research Methods. http://eprints.ncrm.ac.uk/2273/. Accessed 20 Apr 2022
55. Elo, S., Kyngäs, H.: The qualitative content analysis process. J. Adv. Nurs. **62**(1), 107–115 (2008)

Generating VR Meeting Rooms
with Non-rectangular Floor Plans Using
Cost Optimization and Hard Constraints

Katja Tümmers[1,2]([✉]), Tobias Kemper[2], and Arnulph Fuhrmann[1] [iD]

[1] Computer Graphics Group TH Köln, Cologne, Germany
katja.tuemmers@smail.th-koeln.de, arnulph.fuhrmann@th-koeln.de
[2] World of VR GmbH, Cologne, Germany
{katja,tobias}@worldofvr.de

Abstract. This paper describes a method to generate 3D meeting rooms
for virtual reality (VR) applications using a greedy cost minimization.
Our algorithm can create unique meeting rooms during runtime efficiently enough that its suitable for commonly used stand-alone consumer
VR Headsets. First, it extracts information about the room, such as its
volume and shape. Then it iteratively generates a layout by altering
the furniture and subsequently evaluating it. Changes that lead to inferior layouts are reversed, and those that improve the layout are kept.
The algorithm takes the functionality of furniture into consideration as
well as design guidelines. In contrast to previous research, the algorithm
focuses on non-rectangular rooms. For this purpose, we propose improved
cost terms. Additionally, hard constraints were implemented at the end
of the algorithm to enforce functional and aesthetic standards. To test
our generated rooms we conducted a user study, comparing our proposed algorithm with previous work. Results of this study show that our
algorithm generates rooms that were consistently preferred by users.

Keywords: Immersive environments · Furniture arrangement ·
Content generation · Optimization algorithm · Greedy cost
minimization

1 Introduction

As virtual reality (VR) becomes more and more accessible to consumers and
wider audiences, the demand for a large variety of virtual environments increases.
Since the time spent in virtual realities increases, the need for not just varied
content but personal spaces matching individual preferences grows rapidly. But,
creating such 3D environments is time-intensive and requires a specific skill set.
Contrary, algorithms for automatic content generation meet this demand on
the click of a button. Furthermore, as virtual spaces grow into fully fledged
alternatives for real life meetings for recreational and professional purposes alike,
it is important that these spaces are well designed and comfortable to reside in.

© The Author(s), under exclusive license to Springer Nature Switzerland AG 2022
G. Zachmann et al. (Eds.): EuroXR 2022, LNCS 13484, pp. 171–188, 2022.
https://doi.org/10.1007/978-3-031-16234-3_10

The aim of this paper is to build a system that would allow generation of interior spaces quickly and observable with a stable framerate on virtual reality devices. Instead of using pre-build meeting rooms, users are supposed to be able to generate individual rooms at run time. This newly generated unique meeting room can then be used for virtual coaching sessions. Especially in virtual reality it is important that the meeting room's layout is plausible, as spacial perception and awareness are far higher in virtual reality applications as opposed to viewing 3D scenes on a screen. The furniture needs to be placed in the room in manner that facilitates free movement through the virtual space and makes for a sensible meeting room that is being used by several users at the same time. Therefore, direct evaluation in virtual reality by the user is important. By allowing users to generate their own room and observe the whole process, a sense of ownership over the space is supposed to be transferred. The generated room is the users personal space as opposed to using the same room as everyone else.

Based on an optimization algorithm, various kinds of furniture are picked and placed into an empty room. Our algorithm explores various constellations and evaluates their worth through a mathematical cost function. This function considers functionality and aspects of design to determine the quality of the generated room. Previous work considered mainly simple rectangular rooms [8]. Our algorithm, however, produces well designed layouts for rooms with complex shapes, that allow modern and dynamic architecture. While optimized for convex rooms, it even produces pleasant layouts for concave rooms. For our evaluation, we modelled three different complex room shapes to assess our algorithm and its limitations. This paper focuses on the generation of furniture layouts for virtual meeting rooms, but the described system should be able to generate any kind of interior space. For the purposes of this paper, the generation or assigning of suitable textures and materials is not being considered. The algorithm was implemented using the Unity Engine. The resulting application can be run in two ways: first as a VR Version on a stand-alone VR Headset like the Oculus Quest, or second as a non-VR version developed for Windows PCs.

2   Related Work

Several methods to generate the contents of a virtual space have been proposed. Each of them approaches the subject from a different angle, often tied to the application they might be used in. While some methods can combine elements of different approaches, in general one can divide the approaches into three different categories.

2.1   Procedural

Procedural methods have the benefit that they can be highly efficient and quick, making them very suitable for working in real-time. The generation of large-scale scenes especially benefits from this approach, as not just the layout for a single room but whole building blocks, including their geometry, can be generated. The generation process is driven by rules or hard constraints. Procedural methods to generate the geometry for whole building blocks were proposed on the concept of formal grammars [12]. Procedural methods can be used to assist users in creating a furniture layout [13] but can also generate the layouts without user input. Approaches to solve the complete generation of interior layouts, as opposed to the generation of architecture driven by rule sets and constraints, were proposed by Nakamura et al. [11] and Germer and Schwarz [5]. In the latter, each furniture object is its own agent and finding its own place in the layout by following a set of rules that informs its decision process. The efficiency of these methods can partly be explained by the nature of the decision-making process based on rules. While first considered as a viable approach, procedural attempts are also limited by this characteristic. Furthermore, a procedural method can have trouble expanding its use case. Each furniture object, or room, is under the control of its ruleset or constraints. In turn, they might not be easily applicable to all kinds of rooms and all kinds of furniture. Especially when approaching the subject from the angle of design, procedural methods are often lacking as they tend to focus on the functionality of their individual objects [11]. To create pleasant interior layouts, the layout as a whole has to be considered having design principles in mind.

2.2   Data or Example-Based

Another approach to generate furniture layouts works on the basis of data of already existing rooms. In example-based methods, 3D objects are arranged by reproducing patterns found in data describing existing layouts [3]. Using already designed rooms gives such methods an advantage, as design guidelines used by interior designers to create those rooms are reproduced. While advantageous, it consequently limits its scale. Most of the time these layouts have to be created manually. Data-driven methods can use data from already existing rooms but also integrate other kinds of data to drive their algorithm. Data modelling human behavior and its influence on the room can be used as data point informing the generation process [9]. For example, the algorithm could use the data to first identify typical activities recorded in the room and then arrange the objects to specifically facilitate those activities. Some approaches mix example-based and data-driven approaches that use 3D scans of real rooms to create the room layouts [4]. Either way, manual creation of layouts or finding ways to generate data through other means is needed. This can be a labor-intensive process or might not be feasible at all when access to real rooms is required.

2.3   Optimization

Optimization methods work by evaluating room layouts through mathematical functions that quantify concepts of interior design. These concepts can range from functional requirements to aesthetic considerations. They explore the possibility space of the room by changing it, and sampling a said function. An optimization algorithm repeats this process until a certain number of repetitions is reached. By then, it should have produced an interior design that approaches an optimum defined by the mathematical model used.

Optimization algorithms can be used to generate a layout either from an empty room or based on a starting point. The latter method can require the user to choose for example all furniture. It subsequently optimizes the room only constrained by the chosen furniture and modifies only the furniture placement. It is also possible to generate the furniture layout with no or little user input. A method like that picks the furniture for the room itself and can be fully automatic. One disadvantage of an optimization algorithm is the possibility of local extrema. In a user assisted method with already chosen furniture [10], the possible room layouts are explored using Monte Carlo sampling. Another possibility is a genetic algorithm that integrates user input during its generation process to make adjustments during runtime [1]. A fully automatic method that also uses a genetic algorithm for its optimization was proposed by Kán and Kaufmann [7]. Both the genetic algorithm and the Monte Carlo sampling prevent local extrema by generating multiple layouts at the same time. This allows exploring the possibility space more broadly, as all layouts would have to get stuck in the same local extrema. Furthermore, the layouts do not explore the possibility space strictly independent but can influence each other, which also prevents local extrema. Generating two or more layouts simultaneously requires considerable performance optimization. In Merrell et al.'s implementation [10] the algorithm needs 10000 iterations for each individual layout, the process taking roughly 1 s. While efficient, this algorithm requires all furniture and their quantity to be chosen as well as placed in the room by a user. In Kán and Kaufmann's version [8] 100 iterations might be needed depending on the type of room. This takes up to 51 s. Both methods run on PCs with dedicated GPUs. Our goal, however, is to be able to produce acceptable results and runtimes on an Oculus Quest VR headset which is limited by its Qualcomm Snapdragon 835 system on a chip (SoC), the onboard GPU, and 4GB memory capacity.

A more viable method is a greedy optimization algorithm [8]. Only one layout is created and optimized. The number of iterations is higher compared to the genetic algorithm, but its performance is vastly improved. The greedy optimization algorithm has more trouble avoiding local extrema, but its rapid exploration of the possible layouts makes it the most fitting match to implement on a mobile VR device. Therefore, this paper bases its proposed implementation on the work of Kán and Kaufmann [8]. The greedy optimization algorithm allows for design considerations and does not require existing data, while being efficient enough to run on the Oculus Quest.

3 Modified Greedy Optimization Minimization

The greedy optimization algorithm follows a simple structure. It alters the layout by a set of so-called moves. Those moves can be random changes of position or rotation. They can also include more elaborate changes like spawning or deleting an object, or even automatically placing an object with its back against a wall.

After these changes are made, a cost function evaluates if the room's layout has improved. If it has improved the changes are kept, if not they are undone. The optimization algorithm runs for 500 to 650 iterations. To encourage more variety, and to explore more possible layouts, this basic structure was slightly altered. In this implementation, there is a chance for an alteration which slightly worsens the current layout to be kept. For this to happen, the difference between the currently considered lowest cost and the new value has to be below 0.1. If this is the case, there is a 35

Furthermore hard constraints were added to the algorithm, and are applied after the minimization process has ended. By enforcing hard constraints the viability of the room is guaranteed as the constraints prevent placements of furniture that would make the room implausible.

In addition to our own contributions, we will summarize previous research that was adapted in the following sections for coherency's sake.

3.1 Categorization

Like in previous research [7,8] for the optimization, furniture is assigned a designated category. This category describes certain properties defining how it should be assessed in the design layout by the cost function. It also influences its behavior and probability when being altered by the moves changing the layout. The properties used are as follows:

- Clearance constraints
  A list of vectors defining in which direction the object should clear the space around it. A shelf category only has the vector $[0, 0, 1]^T$ as clearance constraint, since a functional shelf only needs an accessible front. Some objects might not have such constraints as they do not need to clear space around them. A table does not have to clear any of its sides, since it should be surrounded by chairs. The vector also defines the amount of space needed to be cleared.
- Probability of standing against a wall
  Describes how important it is for an object to stand with its back against a wall.
- Possible parents
  List of names of categories that can serve as possible parents to the object.
- Probability parents
  Importance of the object having a different object as parent.
- Room importance
  How important is the presence of an object of this category in the room layout. A meeting room for example needs a table, therefore it is set to 1.
- Desired Count
  The minimum and maximum number of objects in a category

3.2   Moves

Based on the approach of Kán and Kaufmann [7,8], during the optimization process the layout of our furniture is altered in each iteration by 10 possible moves. The first 8 moves are executed on each furniture object in each iteration. Moves 9 and 10 add or remove objects and are only executed at most once each iteration. Moves 1 to 6 change the furniture in rotation and position:

1. Assign a random position
2. Assign a random rotation
3. Align with the closest object
4. Align with the closes wall
5. Snap to the closest other furniture object
6. Snap to the closest wall

These moves are executed per object with a probability of 0.3. During development we found that with move 6, furniture that needed to stand against a wall would often not find a spot alongside its closest wall segment. To achieve consistently good results, especially in rooms with a high number of wall segments, or rooms in which many objects need to stand against a wall move 6 had to be extended compared to Kán and Kaufmann [7,8]. We first search the closest wall segment and then the object is rotated to match its forward vector. Afterwards an algorithm checks for an empty spot alongside either direction of the wall, iterating step by step using the object's bounding box to determine whether a big enough free space is found. For a position to be viable, the back of the object has to completely stand against the wall. If such a space cannot be found at the closest wall segment, the algorithm iterates through all other wall segments until one is found, or all wall segments have been checked and no available spot was found. By extending this move to check against all wall segments, viable positions were found quicker and more consistently. Moves 7 to 9 concern themselves with spawning new objects into the design layout or parentage of the objects.

7. Connect furniture to a possible parent object
8. Spawn a possible child object of a furniture object based on its category
9. Spawn a random furniture object into the layout

Move 7 is executed with the probability defined by the object's category. Move 8 is executed with a probability of 0.6 and move 9 with the probability of 0.5. Additionally moves 7, 8 and 9 can also cause a more extensive change by triggering a heuristic that places children appropriately around their parents and rotates them. If the algorithm can find a suitable implemented heuristic for a given parent-child pair it will trigger it, if the parentage of an object is modified, or an object spawned as a child during the moves 8 and 9. It re-calculates appropriate spacing around the parent and the appropriate direction the objects should face. In previous research [7,8] this heuristic is only triggered in move 8 and 9. By triggering it more often the algorithm produces viable rooms more consistently.

The last move executes with a probability of 0.2:

10. Delete a random object

The moves are executed as numbered and a move is executed on all objects before applying the next move. The order of objects in which the moves are used on is defined by their categories. Move 1 is first executed on all chairs, then on all tables. The order of objects does not change during an iteration. This means the order of applying move 1 to all objects is the same as the order with which all objects are modified with move 2. Newly spawned objects are not changed until the next iteration. They are only added to the list of objects to be changed at the end of an iteration. This is necessary, as moves have to be undone in the reverse order in which they were applied. Each move retains the state from just before its application, and moves are undone move by move.

3.3 Cost Function

For the optimization algorithm to decide whether the room is furnished better or worse after the moves were applied, the abstract concepts of "better" and "worse" have to be quantified. This is achieved by using a cost function f. The cost function is defined as the summation of terms that are mathematical representations of design guidelines or other aspects of interior decoration. It assesses how well these guidelines are being fulfilled in the current state of the interior design.

$$f = \sum_{i=1}^{n} w_i g_i \qquad (1)$$

The different terms g_i model aspects of design or function and are weighted individually by w_i. One such term could evaluate and assign a cost to where in the room the objects are placed while another assess which objects are present in the room. Each room weights these terms differently to accommodate its specific needs, as certain aspects are more important to one room shape than others. After each iteration, the set of terms is evaluated. Their results are summed up and compared to the cost of the previous iteration. Should the summed up cost have risen, the changes made to the interior design are reversed, if the cost is lower than previously the changes are kept. For the terms g_i we adopted several terms from Kán and Kaufmann: [7,8]:

- Alignment
- Distribution and Rhythm
- Group Relationships
- Golden Section

Additionally, we propose the following cost terms which are improved versions of previously published research:

Circulation. Many furniture objects need to be physically accessible to be used, which is expressed by the circulation term g_r which quantifies whether certain furniture can be reached from a defined starting point. Kán and Kaufmann [7,8] proposed that all furniture should be accessible from the entrance, which seemed too generalized as certain objects do not need to be accessed directly. Examples of this are a meeting room table surrounded by chairs, a wall mounted clock or picture frames that hang over a cupboard. To accommodate this, furniture that needs to be accessed is specifically marked as such by a child object which can be visually placed by the user. This child object is placed at where the access point of the furniture is supposed to be, and ignored for any other purposes but being used as a target for the pathfinding algorithm. For pathfinding, Unity's own pathfinding system is used which operates by using the A* algorithm on a navigation mesh defining the surface. As only certain objects need to be accessible, the circulation term g_r is proposed to be:

$$g_r = \begin{cases} 1 - \frac{n_{pa}}{n_{pt}} & n_{pt} > 0 \\ 0.5 & n_{pt} \leq 0 \end{cases} \tag{2}$$

The value n_{pt} is the number of possible targets and n_{pa} is the number of possible targets reached. With no target currently in the scene, a cost of 0.5 is assigned. This is important to not overly punish a layout by increasing the cost from 0 to 1, when placing the first furniture object that needs to be accessed.

Clearance. According to their clearance constraints, furniture objects might need to have open space around them to be functional. The value of the clearance term g_c increases when an object does not have sufficient free space in the direction defined by this constraint. The constraint is realized as an array of vectors defining the direction and amount of space. To calculate the clearance term, the bounding boxes of the furniture objects are extended according to the values of the constraint. These extended bounding boxes b_i, in addition to the bounding boxes of the walls, doors and windows, make up the set $\mathcal{A}$. Kán and Kaufmann [7,8] define the clearance term as such:

$$g_c = \frac{1}{|\mathcal{A}|(|\mathcal{A}| - 1)} \sum_{b_1, b_2 \in \mathcal{A}: b_1 \neq b_2} \frac{V(b_1 \cap b_2)}{V(b_1)} \tag{3}$$

The function V returns the volume of a 3D shape. As opposed to the originally proposed function, for efficiency instead of calculating the exact volume of the overlap between two 3D volumes b_1 and b_2 an approximation is used. The cost function does not need exact results, it only needs to increase and decrease proportionally to the degree the guideline was disregarded or followed. Instead of iterating through a nested loop that checks a possible intersection between all possible pairs of elements, the set is only iterated over once. Each element b_1 is checked for possible collisions. Should it overlap with other elements, the approximated overlap between the two colliders involved is calculated. The approximation uses the minimal translation required to separate any two colliders. With this information the volume of a box is calculated. The box uses the resulting distance for its width and length and the smallest height of one of the colliders as its height. Furthermore, we use this term not just for functionality but also aesthetics. For pleasant placement across the room some furniture objects might need a minimum of cleared space around them. A whiteboard hanging at a wall should clear some space to its right and left side, to not distract visually from the whiteboard and its contents.

Functional Needs. The functional needs term ensures that items vital for the functionality of a room are present in the layout. A meeting room requires certain furniture to be present to function, a meeting table, and chairs for example.

$$g_f = k_1 \frac{\sum_{i_o \in I} 1 - i_o}{|I|} + k_2 \frac{\sum_{o_c \in O} \Delta(o_c)}{|O|} \tag{4}$$

The term g_f covers two aspects: First, how important objects are for a given room. This is defined by the importance values assigned to each object category. The importance values i_o for all individual objects in the current layout are contained in the set I. Secondly, the desired count of the objects. The set O contains the categories of objects o_c that are intended to be in the room layout. The function Δ calculates the difference between the present count of objects of a category and the desired count. As opposed to previous research [7,8] that sets the value of k_1 and k_2 to 0.5, equally weighing both aspects, we propose values of $k_1 = 0.5$ and $k_1 = 2$. A meeting room, for example, should have exactly one meeting table, but the table also has the highest importance value. For the table this would result in more leniency regarding deviations from the desired count when both aspects of the term are weighted equally. This tended to lead to layouts containing multiple tables and the term had to be modified. The modification puts greater weight on the desired count of the object.

Proportions. For the proportion term, an ideal proportion between empty space and furniture is chosen. The proportion is calculated as the ratio between the volume of the room and the volume of all furniture objects in the scene. The value r_v defines the desired ratio and Kán and Kaufmann [7,8] set it at 0.45. In this work varying values below 0.07 were chosen. The proportion term g_p calculates how much the ratio between furniture and room volume in the current layout deviates from the desired r_v. The values V_o and V_r are the volume of all furniture and the room volume, respectively. The equation proposed by Kán and Kaufmann [7,8] only assigns a cost to a layout which has a summed-up volume of furniture below the desired ratio. Higher ratios than the desired one are not assigned a cost, i.e. overly full rooms are not penalized. Since this is not desirable, we modified the equation to the following:

$$g_p = \frac{|r_v - \frac{V_o}{V_r}|}{r_v} \tag{5}$$

Viewing Frustum. Certain objects need to be visible from the position of other objects. A TV screen for example should be visible from the couch in a living room. Whether an object needs to be visible from another object is defined by the object's hierarchy. A child furniture object should always have an uninterrupted line of sight to their parent object. The value n_t is the total number of parent-child pairs and the value n_i the number of occluded parent-child pairs. Occlusion is checked by using a raycast to check whether direct line of sight is possible without hitting any other objects. At certain points of the generation process layouts might not contain a parent-child relationship. Therefore the following term g_v is proposed:

$$g_v = \begin{cases} \frac{n_i}{n_t} & n_t > 0 \\ 0.5 & n_t \leq 0 \end{cases} \tag{6}$$

In contrast to the version Kán and Kaufmann [7,8] propose, the additional case ensures that layout changes that introduce parent-child pairs for the first time are not punished too harshly.

Visual Balance. Based on the approach proposed by Merrell et al. [10], a Visual Balance term was included. This term is supposed to make sure that the distribution of objects is focused around the visual center.

$$g_b = \left\| \frac{\sum_{f \in \mathcal{F}} D(f)}{\sum_{f \in \mathcal{F}} A(f)} - \mathbf{p}_c \right\| \tag{7}$$

$$D(f) = A(f)(p_w \mathbf{c}_{x,z} + (1 - p_w)\mathbf{p}_c) \tag{8}$$

All furniture in the layout is contained in the set $\mathcal{F}$. Function $A(f)$ returns the area the object takes up in the x, z plane. $\mathbf{c}_{x,z}$ is the position of the furniture, also in the x, z plane. Vector $\mathbf{p}_c$ is the position of the chosen visual center of the room in the x, z plane. The term is normalized by the room's diagonal length d_r. Furthermore, the wall probability constraint of an object is being taken into account. The wall probability p_w is used as a weight to balance how important it is that the object stands close to the visual center $\mathbf{p}_c$. An object that should stand close to a wall does not need to be standing close to the visual center of the room.

3.4   Hard Constraints

To ensure a certain standard for the generated room hard constraints based on our furniture categories were added to the algorithm. The categories properties are used to decide whether a hard constraint will be enforced. The two implemented hard constraints concern themselves with objects that have to stand against a wall and parent-child relationships.

If a furniture object has to stand against a wall with a wall probability of p_w then a hard constraint is enforced at the end of algorithm. First the algorithm checks whether the object with a p_w of 1 stands against a wall, if not, the algorithm will use move 6 to look for a place spot against a wall. If no such free spot can be found, the object is deleted. This is important as wall-mounted objects such as picture frames are included in the algorithm. Without this hard constraint it could be possible that the algorithm places such an object not against a wall giving it the appearance to be floating.

Another hard constraint is enforced in the case of parent-child relationships. As mentioned before, a heuristic can place a group of children properly around its parent. If such a heuristic exists for a given parent-child pair it is enforced through a hard constraint if the probability of having a parent is 1 for the child. After the minimization the algorithm will look for these cases, and then try to use the heuristic to properly set the placement of children one more time. If too many children are attached to the parent that the heuristic can not place the children properly, the algorithm will delete as many children as necessary until the heuristic can position them around the parent.

4   Implementation

The system was implemented using the Unity Engine and can be run as a desktop version, or a stand-alone VR Version for the Oculus Quest. Both versions have a UI that lets the user choose from three rooms to generate their meeting rooms. Room layouts can be saved and loaded by the user. Saves are stored as JSON files on the device. To easily include new room types or furniture, the implementation uses Unity's addressable system for its asset management. This allows on the air updates as everything needed for the optimization algorithm is downloaded during runtime, including the 3D models, category information and settings for the room.

To give users control over their generated room, they can choose between different kinds of tables and chairs for their meeting room at the start of each generation. As the size of the table defines how many chairs are appropriate for the room, the chairs' desired count is always modified dynamically to match the chosen table. After choosing the desired table and chair, the generation starts. Two random categories are picked to spawn one object each as a starting point. Then the greedy optimization algorithm goes through 500 to 650 iterations depending on room size. We also tested multiple categories and larger rooms. Then, the iterations had to be increased to allow the room to fill up.

4.1   Information Extraction from 3D Meshes

Standardization. Similarly to the categories, to make it possible for the algorithm to engage with the different kind of furniture, all 3D models had to be standardized. One example of this is that the 3D models should be correctly scaled and furniture needs to be correctly oriented so that their front points to the positive z axis of their local coordinate system. In the case of tables which have no clearly defined front and back, it is required for the shorter side to be aligned with the z axis.

Volume. To calculate the cost function properly the volume of both the room and furniture objects is needed. For both of these an approximation is used. While one could calculate it directly [15], these methods would require a certain amount of preprocessing of the assets and the assets would have adhere to a strict standard in regards to their topology. Furthermore, in the case of furniture the exact volume of their mesh is not an accurate representation of the space they take up. The perception of space taken up by the object includes negative spaces such as the insides of a vase or the space between a tables legs. While the convex hull would represent such negatives spaces for the furniture quite well, we found it sufficient to use the volume of the bounding box as an approximation. For the room's volume, first the area of the polygon describing the floor is calculated. Then the height of the vertices making up the ceiling are averaged to retrieve the average height of the room. The volume is then approximated by multiplying those two. Both approximations lead to sufficiently accurate results for the optimization to work.

5   Results

Our research aimed at an algorithm which generates consistently plausible rooms. The rooms should not have floating objects or shelves turned with their face towards a wall. The meeting rooms should be functional and contain at least one table, chairs, and a whiteboard. This was achieved through improved cost terms and extended moves, that places objects against walls, as well as enforcing hard constraints that would ensure acceptable results every time. We found all of our generated rooms to appear plausible and livable spaces.

We created three rooms, each with its own characteristic and floor plan. Notably Room 3 is not a convex shape, as seen in Fig. 1. Because it was important that the algorithm can handle more than just simple rectangular layouts we included one concave room shape to test that even such complex room shapes are possible and can produce satisfying room layouts but will result in less exact calculations of the cost function driving the algorithm.

The weights used for the terms in the cost function vary, as well as the properties for the object categories. Table 1 shows the final weights chosen for the individual rooms and the number of iterations.

When experimenting with the different rooms, it became clear that the rooms' architecture plays a vital role in what designs appear pleasant and why the cost term weights should be modified to meet the needs of the room. Room 2 favors centered designs and needs certain considerations. For this reason, the Golden Section weight was set to zero and the Visual Balance weight to one. The cost terms can favor crowding objects in the same area. As a result, the wall between the windows in Room 2 was often neglected. The Group Relationship as well as the Distribution and Rhythm term especially cause crowding. As most wall space is in the front of the room, any object placed on the single wall

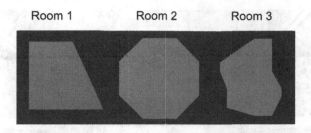

Fig. 1. The different floor plans of the rooms. Rooms 1 and 2 are convex while Room 3 is concave.

Table 1. Parameters and cost term weights used to generate the three rooms.

	Room 1	Room 2	Room 3
Clearance	10.00	5.00	7.00
Circulation	2.0	1.1	2.0
Alignment	3.0	5.0	3.5
Group relationships	1.0	0.3	1.0
Distribution and Rhythm	2.0	0.7	2.0
Viewing frustum	1.0	1.0	1.0
Proportion	2.0 with $r_v = 0.062$	0.7 with $r_v = 0.043$	1.0 with $r_v = 0.07$
Functional needs	5.0	8.5	5.0
Golden section	0.5	0.0	1.0
Visual balance	0.6	1.0	0.0
Iterations	500	650	650

in front is a deviation assigned cost. Only the whiteboard can be placed there without extra cost. While this could lead to a pleasant design, the wall was often left empty. To combat this the weights were adjusted. Similarly, Room 3 is not suitable for centered designs. It is elongated and contains a pillar blocking space around the centroid. The Golden Section term works very well for it, but the Visual Balance term does not. Therefore, the latter was assigned a zero weight. Furthermore, testing showed that certain terms in the cost function might not actually be helpful to generating good designs. An example for this is the Group Relationship term: By design, the term rewards placing objects of the same category in proximity to one another. This can be useful for chairs or other objects that benefit from such crowding, but decorations for example should be spread across the room.

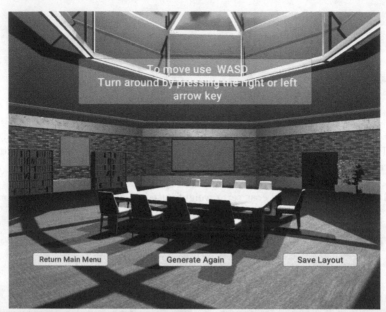

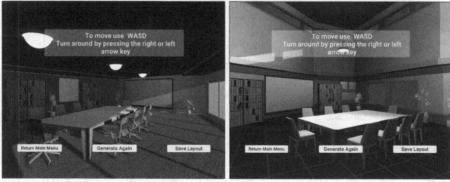

Fig. 2. Results for room 2 (top), room 1 (left) and room 3 (right)

5.1 Performance

As the user is supposed to be able to observe the process, an important goal was a smooth execution on limited hardware, as the system is supposed to generate rooms at runtime on the Oculus Quest system. Therefore, the algorithm deliberately interrupts the optimization after each iteration to allow for rendering and a stable framerate. This slows down the performance and creates a certain bottleneck but is necessary for the program to be usable on a standalone VR System. On a windows PC equipped with an Intel(R) Core^{TM}i7-8750H CPU, a dedicated NVIDIA GeForce RTX 2030 GPU and 16GB RAM the generation process took 8 s on average for Room 1, 11 s for Room 2, and 11 s for Room 3. On the Oculus Quest the generation process took 16 s on average for Room 1, and 25 s for Room

2 and Room 3. Differences can be explained by the increased number of iterations in Room 2 and 3, but also by the amount of furniture in the room. With these results the performance of the algorithm is similar to that of the genetic algorithm [7]. Since most of the collision handling is delegated to Unity's physics simulation, the algorithm could be optimized by manually handling collision checks. Furthermore instead of using Unity's pathfinding algorithm using costly generation of navigation meshes, a more lightweight algorithm could increase performance greatly.

5.2   User Study

To test the results we conducted a user study. Several rooms were generated for each room type, to investigate whether the algorithms produce consistent results each generation. This was an important aspect as the algorithm should be used by users themselves and preferably never result in non-viable rooms. For this user study we generated 30 rooms, 15 with the algorithm proposed in this paper and another 15 rooms using cost terms and weights proposed by Kán and Kaufmann [8]. For each of these 15 rooms, we generated 5 samples of one of the three room floor plans. Furthermore, the rooms generated using Kán and Kaufmann's settings uses the move set as proposed in their paper, so the move snapping furniture to walls was reduced to only snap the furniture to the closest wall as opposed to look for a spot along all walls. Regardless both versions trigger the heuristic with move 7, 8, 9 to make the results comparable.

Our study follows a within group design and we asked the participants to rate all 30 rooms with regard to two different aspects. First, whether they think they could conduct a virtual meeting in this room, and second whether they find the furniture layout pleasant. The first aspect asks for functionality while the second interrogates the aesthetics of the rooms. Due to the COVID-19 pandemic the survey was conducted exclusively online. Through a panoramic image viewer 33 users were shown 360° images of the rooms. 16 of the participants claimed to have a lot of experience using VR, with 12 participants only having some experience and 5 participants having none. The participants were aged 20 to 54 with 19 participants identifying as male, 12 participants as female and 2 as other. The order of presented rooms was randomized with respect to algorithms and room type. Then, all users were shown the rooms in that same order. For each room they rated whether they agreed with two statements on a scale from "Strongly Agree" to "Strongly Disagree". The two statements were as following:

- Statement 1: "I could hold a virtual meeting in this room"
- Statement 2: "The furniture layout is pleasant"

Figure 3 shows an overview of the ratings given by the participants. To test our hypothesis that the users rated the rooms generated by our algorithm better we employed the Wilcoxon Signed Rank test to test for significance in the results for the two statements. For this we used the median rating of the 15 rooms for each algorithm per participant as data points.

Table 2 shows the p-values as well as the effect sizes. For both statements there was a significant difference between the two algorithms and we can safely reject the null hypothesis for both statements. Therefore, it can be assumed that the algorithm proposed in this paper outperforms the previously proposed one in the matter of aesthetics and functionality. In conclusion our algorithm creates viable rooms that are preferred by users more often than the ones created with previously proposed algorithms.

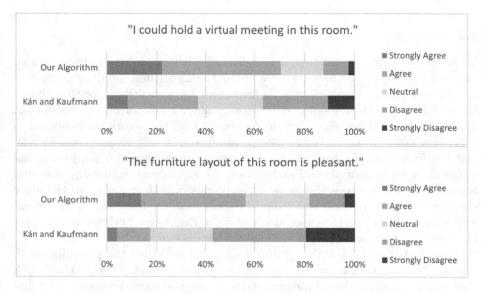

Fig. 3. All ratings for statement 1 (top) and statement 2 (bottom) on the rooms generated by our algorithm and the algorithm by Kán and Kaufmann

Table 2. Effect size and p-values of the wilcoxon signed rank test for each statement

	Effect size r	p-value
Statement 1	0.73	< 0.001
Statement 2	0.76	< 0.001

6   Conclusion

With the proposed algorithm plausible VR meeting rooms can be consistently generated at runtime while letting the user observe the process on limited hardware. The hard constraints ensure a functional standard and together with the improved cost terms produce visually pleasant rooms. We refer to the accompanying videos of the generation process for a demonstration captured live on a

VR headset during runtime. The user study shows that the rooms generated are preferred by users when compared to those generated using algorithms proposed in previous research.

There are two aspects of the algorithm that could be improved in the future: The performance, and the end results of the generation process itself. Issues with the performance could be reduced by using dedicated algorithms for collision detection and not relying on a general purpose physics engine. More importantly, one point of improvement could be the cost function itself. During development, it became apparent that certain cost terms did not have the desired effect, especially the term Group Relationship. Re-implementing the term to analyze the distances between child objects of a parent could result in major improvements. Experimenting with deeper hierarchies might be worthwhile as well. Instead of only grouping furniture by function, furniture could be grouped to be visually interesting. Another area of improvement is the process of finding the right settings. This is currently done on a trial-and-error basis. By implementing aspects of data-driven or example-based methods, these settings could be found automatically. Yu et al. [14] proposes an optimization algorithm which extracts the information about relationships of furniture from already existing rooms. Finally, the algorithm could be extended to consider the lighting and the material of furniture. Adding an algorithm such as to assign suitable materials as done in Jain et al. [6] and Chen et al. [2] would directly improve the visual appearance of the end product.

Letting the user observe the process opens up many possibilities for expanding on the algorithm. Future work could explore involving the user further in the process by allowing the user to directly manipulate the generation algorithm. As the whole process is observed live by the user, one could let the user intervene and direct the process by rejecting changes, or modifying the current layout to match personal preferences, before letting the algorithm continue. This way the user can steer the process to generate a room suitable for their needs and taste.

Furthermore, to aid the user in such modifications the algorithm could provide feedback to the user on the basis of the cost function. Should for example the user proceed to move a chair to a less suitable position haptic feedback could alert the user of the rising cost.

For this paper only VR meeting rooms were generated, but the implemented system can be used to generate many other interior spaces. Adding new kinds of objects and rooms is fast and only requires writing simple JSON files that can be added over the air. Our algorithm can handle complex room layouts, and produces satisfying results for not just rectangular room shapes. Hence, it can be easily extended to include new types of furniture and room designs.

References

1. Akase, R., Okada, Y.: Automatic 3d furniture layout based on interactive evolutionary computation. In: Proceedings - 2013 7th International Conference on Complex, Intelligent, and Software Intensive Systems, CISIS 2013, pp. 726–731 (2013). https://doi.org/10.1109/CISIS.2013.130

2. Chen, K., Xu, K., Yu, Y., Wang, T.Y., Hu, S.M.: Magic decorator: automatic material suggestion for indoor digital scenes. ACM Trans. Graph. **34**(6), 1–11 (2015). https://doi.org/10.1145/2816795.2818096

3. Fisher, M., Ritchie, D., Savva, M., Funkhouser, T., Hanrahan, P.: Example-based synthesis of 3d object arrangements. ACM Trans. Graph. **31**(6), 1–11 (2012). https://doi.org/10.1145/2366145.2366154

4. Fisher, M., Savva, M., Li, Y., Hanrahan, P., Nießner, M.: Activity-centric scene synthesis for functional 3d scene modeling. ACM Trans. Graph. **34**(6), 1–13 (2015). https://doi.org/10.1145/2816795.2818057

5. Germer, T., Schwarz, M.: Procedural arrangement of furniture for real-time walk-throughs. Computer Graphics Forum **28**(8), 2068–2078 (2009). https://doi.org/10.1111/j.1467-8659.2009.01351.x

6. Jain, A., Thormählen, T., Ritschel, T., Seidel, H.P.: Material memex: automatic material suggestions for 3d objects. ACM Trans. Graph. **31**(6), 1–18 (2012). https://doi.org/10.1145/2366145.2366162

7. Kán, P., Kaufmann, H.: Automated interior design using a genetic algorithm. In: Proceedings of the 23rd ACM Symposium on Virtual Reality Software and Technology, VRST '17, pp. 1–10, no. 25. ACM, New York (2017). https://doi.org/10.1145/3139131.3139135

8. Kán, P., Kaufmann, H.: Automatic furniture arrangement using greedy cost minimization. In: IEEE Conference on Virtual Reality and 3D User Interfaces (IEEE VR), pp. 1–8. IEEE Computer Society (2018). https://doi.org/10.1109/VR.2018.8448291

9. Ma, R., Li, H., Zou, C., Liao, Z., Tong, X., Zhang, H.: Action-driven 3d indoor scene evolution. ACM Trans. Graph. **35**(6) (2016). https://doi.org/10.1145/2980179.2980223

10. Merrell, P., Schkufza, E., Li, Z., Agrawala, M., Koltun, V.: Interactive furniture layout using interior design guidelines. ACM Trans. Graph. **30**(4), 1–10 (2011). https://doi.org/10.1145/2010324.1964982

11. Nakamura, N., Akazawa, Y., Takano, S., Okada, Y.: Virtual space construction based on contact constraints using robot vision technology for 3d graphics applications. In: RO-MAN 2007 - The 16th IEEE International Symposium on Robot and Human Interactive Communication, pp. 469–474 (2007). https://doi.org/10.1109/ROMAN.2007.4415129

12. Schwarz, M., Müller, P.: Advanced procedural modeling of architecture. ACM Trans. Graph. **34**(4), 1–12 (2015). https://doi.org/10.1145/2766956

13. Xu, K., Stewart, J., Fiume, E.: Constraint-based automatic placement for scene composition. In: Proceedings of the Graphics Interface 2002 Conference, 27–29 May 2002, Calgary, Alberta, Canada, pp. 25–34 (2002). https://doi.org/10.20380/GI2002.04

14. Yu, L.F., Yeung, S.K., Tang, C.K., Terzopoulos, D., Chan, T.F., Osher, S.J.: Make it home: automatic optimization of furniture arrangement. ACM Trans. Graph. **30**(4) (2011). https://doi.org/10.1145/2010324.1964981

15. Zhang, C., Chen, T.: Efficient feature extraction for 2d/3d objects in mesh representation. In: Proceedings 2001 International Conference on Image Processing (Cat. No.01CH37205), vol. 3, pp. 935–938 (2001). https://doi.org/10.1109/ICIP.2001.958278

Scientific Posters

Controlling Continuous Locomotion in Virtual Reality with Bare Hands Using Hand Gestures

Alexander Schäfer[1]() [iD], Gerd Reis[2], and Didier Stricker[1,2]

[1] TU Kaiserslautern, Gottlieb-Daimler-Strasse Building 47,
67663 Kaiserslautern, Germany
`Alexander.Schaefer@dfki.de`
[2] German Research Center for Artificial Intelligence, Trippstadter str. 122,
67663 Kaiserslautern, Germany
`{Gerd.Reis,Didier.Stricker}@dfki.de`

Abstract. Moving around in a virtual world is one of the essential interactions for Virtual Reality (VR) applications. The current standard for moving in VR is using a controller. Recently, VR Head Mounted Displays integrate new input modalities such as hand tracking which allows the investigation of different techniques to move in VR. This work explores different techniques for bare-handed locomotion since it could offer a promising alternative to existing freehand techniques. The presented techniques enable continuous movement through an immersive virtual environment. The proposed techniques are compared to each other in terms of efficiency, usability, perceived workload, and user preference.

Keywords: Virtual Reality · Locomotion · Hand gestures · Bare hand

1 Introduction

Recent advances in hardware development of Head Mounted Displays (HMDs) provide affordable hand tracking out of the box. In the future, a hand held controller as input modality could be replaced by using hand gestures in many scenarios. Therefore, the potential of this technology should be explored. The use of hand tracking is already widely acknowledged and research is being conducted in many different areas of human computer interaction. For example, hand tracking can be used to pick up virtual objects in more natural ways than with a controller such as done by Schäfer et al. [30,33] or Kang et al. [21]. Moving around in Virtual Reality (VR) is one of the essential interactions within virtual environments but the capability of this technology for moving around in VR is largely unexplored.

Generally, there are two ways to move in virtual environments: Teleportation based locomotion and continuous locomotion. Teleportation locomotion instantly changes the position of the user. Continuous locomotion on the other hand is more like a walk, where the user gradually moves in the desired direction.

© The Author(s) 2022
G. Zachmann et al. (Eds.): EuroXR 2022, LNCS 13484, pp. 191–205, 2022.
https://doi.org/10.1007/978-3-031-16234-3_11

Teleportation based locomotion is known to cause less motion sickness compared to continuous locomotion, but the latter is more immersive [2,14,25]. It is a trade off between immersion and motion sickness. Therefore, if the application scenario permits, care should be taken to allow the user to choose between the two methods. Games and other commercial applications using a controller usually allow for an option to choose which locomotion method is desired. In this work, three novel locomotion techniques using bare hands for continuous locomotion are proposed and evaluated. A technique which uses index finger pointing as metaphor was implemented. Steering is performed by moving the index finger into the desired direction. A similar technique using the hand palm for steering was implemented. The third bare handed technique utilizes a thumbs up gesture to indicate movement. Compared to other freehand locomotion techniques which involve rather demanding body movements, locomotion using hand gestures could be a less stressful and demanding technique. This assumption arises from the fact that only finger and hand movements are required for locomotion, whereas other techniques require large parts of the body to be moved. The three techniques are compared to each other and to the current standard for moving in VR, the controller. This work aims to provide more insights into hand gesture based locomotion and whether it is applicable and easy to use by users. In particular, the research gap of continuous locomotion with hand gestures should be addressed, as most existing techniques use teleportation. In addition, it is not yet clear which hand gestures are suitable for the locomotion task in VR, and further research should be conducted to find suitable techniques. The contributions of this paper are as follows:

- Introducing three novel locomotion techniques for VR using bare hands
- A comprehensive evaluation of these techniques

2   Related Work

2.1   Locomotion Techniques in VR Without Using Controllers

Several techniques for moving in VR have been proposed by researchers. Some of these techniques involve rather large and demanding body movements such as the well established technique Walking in place (WIP). To move virtually with this technique, users perform footsteps on a fixed spatial position in the real world. This technique is already widely explored and a large body of existing work can be found in the literature. Templeman et al. [34] attached sensors to knees and the soles of the feet to detect the movements, which are then transmitted to the virtual world. Bruno et al. [8] created a variant for WIP, Speed-Amplitude-Supported WIP which allows users to control their virtual speed by footstep amplitude and speed metrics.

Another technique for moving without controllers is leaning. This technique uses leaning forward for acceleration of the virtual avatar. Buttussi and Chittaro [9] compared continuous movement with controller, teleportation with controller, and continuous movement with leaning. Leaning performed slightly worse compared to the other techniques. Langbehn et al. [24] combined WIP with leaning where the movement speed of the WIP technique is controlled by the leaning angle of the user. Different techniques for leaning and controller based locomotion was evaluated by Zielasko et al. [37]. The authors suggest that torso-directed leaning performs better than gaze-directed or virtual-body-directed leaning. In another work, Zielasko et al. [36] compared leaning, seated WIP, head shaking, accelerator pedal, and gamepad to each other. A major finding of their study is that WIP is not recommended for seated locomotion. A method that pairs well with WIP is redirected walking. With this method, the virtual space is changed so that the user needs as little physical space as possible. Different techniques exist to achieve this, for example manipulating the rotation gains of the VR HMD [16] or foldable spaces by Han et al. [17]. More redirected walking techniques are found in the survey from Nilsson et al. [27]. Since a large body of research work exists around locomotion in virtual reality, the reader is referred to surveys such as [1,3,13,26,28,31] to gain more information about different locomotion techniques and taxonomies.

Physical movement coupled with virtual movement offers more immersion, but hand gesture-based locomotion is expected to be a less strenuous and demanding form of locomotion than those mentioned above. Furthermore it is a technique that requires minimal physical space and can be used in seated position as well as standing.

2.2 Locomotion in VR Using Hand Gestures

Early work on how hand gestures can be used for virtual locomotion was conducted by Kim et al. [22,23]. The authors presented Finger Walking in Place (FWIP), which enables virtual locomotion through the metaphor of walking triggered by finger movements. Four different locomotion techniques for teleportation using hand gestures are compared to each other by Schäfer et al. [32]. Two two-handed and two one-handed techniques are proposed. The authors came to the conclusion that palm based techniques perform better than index pointing techniques but overall the user should decide which technique to use. Huang et al. [20] used finger gestures to control movement within virtual environments. The gestures are used to control the velocity of moving forward and backwards. Four different locomotion techniques are proposed by Ferracani et al. [15]. The techniques are WIP, Arm Swing, Tap, and Push. Tap uses index finger pointing and Push involves closing and opening the hand. The authors conclude that the bare handed technique Tap even outperformed the well established WIP technique. Zhang et al. [35] proposes a technique to use both hands for locomotion. The left hand is used to start and stop movement while the right hand uses the thumb to turn left and right. Cardoso [12] used hand gestures with both hands as well for a locomotion task. Movement was controlled by opening/closing both hands, speed was controlled by the number of stretched fingers, and the rotation of the avatar was mapped to the tilt angle of the right hand. The authors concluded that the hand-tracking based technique outperformed an eye gaze based technique but was inferior to a gamepad. Hand gestures were also used by Caggianese et al. [11] in combination with a navigation widget. Users had to press a button to move through a virtual environment whereas with the proposed technique, users can move by performing a hand gesture. In subsequent work, Caggianese et al. [10] compared three freehand and a controller based locomotion technique. In their experiment, participants had to follow a predefined path. The authors show that freehand steering techniques using hand gestures have comparable results to controller. While Caggianese et al. [10] uses hand gestures to start/stop movement, this work compares two techniques with a 3D graphical user interface, a one-handed gesture to start movement. The direction of movement was also tied to the direction of the hand, whereas in this work the direction of movement is tied to the direction of the user's VR HMD. Bozgeyikli et al. [4,5] compared Joystick, Point and Teleport, and WIP. The results showed that the hand gesture based teleportation technique is intuitive, easy to use, and fun.

3   Proposed Locomotion Techniques

Four different locomotion techniques were developed: Controller, FingerUI, HandUI, and ThumbGesture. The proposed locomotion techniques are depicted in Fig. 1. The implementation of each technique is briefly explained in this section.

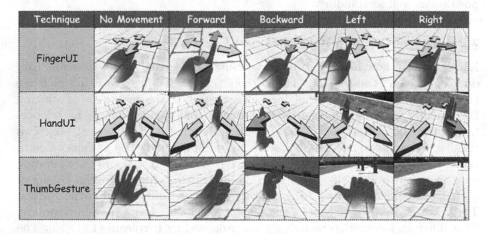

Fig. 1. The proposed one-handed locomotion techniques. Users could move by moving the hand to a designated zone for moving forward, backward and rotating left and right. The arrows to control movement all had the same size.

Controller. This technique uses the standard implementation for continuous locomotion with the Software Development Kit (SDK) of the chosen VR HMD. The thumbstick on the left controller is used for acceleration and the thumbstick on the right controller can be used to rotate the user. Using the right thumbstick is optional since the user can turn normally by just moving the head.

FingerUI. If the user points the index finger forward, a 3D graphical user interface will be shown. A 3D arrow for the four different directions Forward, Backward, Left, and Right are shown. While the user is maintaining the index finger forward pose with the hand, locomotion is achieved by moving the hand to one of the arrows depending on which movement is desired. The arrows are only for visualisation purposes. The actual movement is triggered when the index finger enters invisible zones which are placed around the 3D arrows indicating the movement direction. Only touching the arrows would be too strict, whereas the introduction of movement zones allows more room for user error. For this reason, zones are actually larger than the arrows shown to the user. This is depicted in Fig. 2. Furthermore, the zones for moving left and right are generally bigger than for moving forward and backward. The reason for this is that during first pilot testing it was found that users generally made wide movements to the left and right. If the hand moves out of a zone, movement will unintentionally stop. Moving the hand forward was restricted due to arm length and moving backwards was restricted because the own body was in the way. Furthermore, with the design showed in Fig. 2, users could move forward by putting the hand forward and then swiped to the left/right to rotate instead of moving the hand to the center and then to the left/right. Once the UI is shown, the zones are activated for all movement directions and the center can be used to indicate that no movement is desired.

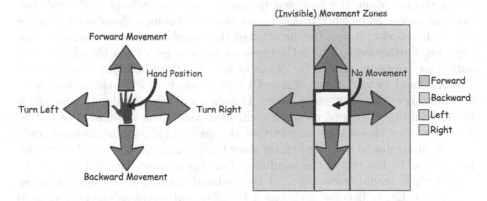

Fig. 2. The 3D graphical user interface which is visible once a specific hand gesture is detected. The interface will be shown around the hand of the user. The left image shows the possible movement actions. The right image shows zones which are invisible to the user. If the hand/index finger enters one of these zones, the respective movement is triggered. The two techniques FingerUI and HandUI use different sizes for the zones (smaller zones for the IndexUI).

HandUI. This technique is similar to FingerUI. The difference is the hand pose to enable the user interface. A "stop" gesture, i.e. palm facing away from the face and all fingers are up, is used to show the user interface. Instead of the index finger, the palm center needs to enter a zone to enable movement. The size of the zones is also adjusted (bigger and more space in the center for no movement).

ThumbGesture. A thumbs up gesture is used to activate movement. The four movement directions are mapped to different gestures. Thumb pointing up = Forward; Thumb pointing towards face = Backward; Thumb left = Left; Thumb right = Right.

All hand based locomotion techniques used a static gesture to activate locomotion and no individual finger movement was necessary. Furthermore, while the gestures and controller had a dedicated option to rotate the virtual avatar, users could also rotate by looking around with the VR HMD. Users can not change the locomotion speed but once the user enters a zone with their hand to enable movement, the users locomotion speed increases over the first second up to a maximum of 28.8 km/h (8 m/s). The time it takes a user to rotate their body about 90° using hand gestures or the controller is 1.5 s. Movement is immediately stopped if the users' hand is no longer in a movement zone.

3.1 Explanation of Chosen Techniques

Techniques with different input modalities such as controller can be adapted or serve as metaphor to implement bare handed techniques for locomotion. With this in consideration, the proposed techniques were implemented. ThumbGesture was implemented since it is quite similar to rotating a thumbstick into the desired direction as it uses the direction of the thumb to indicate the movement direction. Furthermore, ThumbGesture can be seen as a variation of the locomotion technique introduced by Zhang et al. [35]. ThumbGesture however uses only one hand instead of two. FingerUI was developed to use the metaphor of pointing forward to enable movement. The shown 3D graphical user interface is similar to a digital pad on common controllers that allow movement of virtual characters. Previous studies suggest that the gesture for pointing forward could be error-prone due to tracking failures since the index finger is often obscured for the cameras by the rest of the hand [33]. For this purpose, HandUI was implemented which should be easy to track by the hand tracking device since no finger is occluded. Controller was added as a baseline and serves as the current gold standard for locomotion in VR. Only one-handed techniques were implemented, as one hand should be free for interaction tasks.

4   Evaluation

4.1   Objectives

The goal of this study was to compare the three locomotion techniques using bare hands. Controller was added as a baseline, to generally compare hand gesture locomotion with the gold standard. It was anticipated that a controller will outperform the bare handed techniques. However, the main objective was to find out which of the three bare handed techniques is best in terms of efficiency, usability, perceived workload, and subjective user rating. The efficiency of the different techniques was measured by the task completion time. The well known System Usability Scale (SUS) [6,7] was used as usability measure. The perceived workload was measured by the NASA Task Load Index (NASA-TLX) [18,19]. Since hand tracking is still a maturing technology and tracking errors are expected, NASA-TLX should give interesting insights into possible frustration and other measures. It was deliberately decided not to use more questionnaires to keep the experiment short. This was because it was expected that some participants would suffer from motion sickness and might decide to abort the experiment if it takes too long. It was also decided not to include any questionnaire for motion sickness as it can be expected that the proposed techniques are similar in this regard.

4.2 Participants

A total number of 16 participants participated in the study and 12 completed the experiment. Four participants cancelled the experiment due to increased motion sickness during the experiment. The participants' age ranged between 18 and 63 years old (Age $\mu = 33.38$). Six females participated in the study. All participants were laypeople to VR technology and wore a VR HMD less than five times.

4.3 Apparatus

The evaluation was performed by using a gaming notebook with an Intel Core I7-7820HK, 32 GB DDR4 RAM, Nvidia Geforce GTX 1080 running a 64 bit Windows 10. Meta Quest 2 was used as the VR HMD and the hand tracking was realized using version 38 of the Oculus Integration Plugin in Unity.

4.4 Experimental Task

The participants had to move through a minimalistic, corridor-like virtual environment and touch virtual pillars. The environment is 10m wide and 110m long. A total of ten pillars are placed in the environment about 10m apart from each other. The pillars are arranged in a way that users had to move left and right to reach the pillars (See Fig. 3). After a pillar was touched, its color changed to green, indicating that it was touched. Once ten pillars were touched, a trial was completed.

4.5 Procedure

The experiment had a within-subject design. Each participant had to move twice through the virtual environment with each technique. This allowed the subjects to understand and learn the technique in one trial and the latter trial can be used

Fig. 3. The virtual environment used for the experiment. Users had to move in a large corridor-like environment, touching 10 pillars. After all pillars are touched once, the experiment continues with the next step.

more reliable as measure for task completion time. A short video clip was shown to the participant to inform them how to move with the current technique. The experiment was conducted in seating position and users could rotate their body with a swivel chair. The order of locomotion techniques was counterbalanced using the balanced latin square algorithm. After a participant touched all ten pillars in the virtual environment twice, the participant was teleported to an area where questionnaires should be answered. Participants first filled in the NASA-TLX and then the SUS. The answers could be filled in with either the controller or using bare hands in VR. This was repeated for each locomotion technique. After the last, a final questionnaire was shown to the participant were they could rate each technique on a scale from 1 (bad) to 10 (good). One user session took about 30 min.

5   Results

5.1   Task Completion Time

For the task completion time, the time between touching the first and the last pillar is measured. The average time to touch all ten pillars in a trial is depicted in Fig. 4. Levene's test assured the homogeneity of variances of the input data and therefore one-way ANOVA was used. The result $F(3,47) = 8.817$ with p value < 0.01 showed significant differences between the techniques. The post-hoc test TukeyHSD revealed the following statistically significant differences between technique pairs: Controller-FingerUI $p < 0.001$; Controller-HandUI $p < 0.05$; ThumbGesture-FingerUI $p < 0.01$.

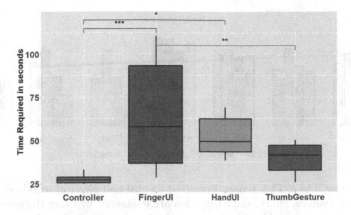

Fig. 4. Average time taken by users to touch all ten pillars. Significance levels: *** = 0.001; ** = 0.01; * = 0.05;.

5.2 NASA Task Load Index (NASA-TLX)

The NASA-TLX questionnaire was answered after performing the experimental task with a technique. A task took about two minutes to complete and the completion of the questionnaires allowed a break of about two minutes between each successive task. The raw data of the NASA-TLX is used without additional subscale weighting in order to further reduce the amount of time required by participants to spend in VR (Questionnaires were answered within the virtual environment). Using the raw NASA-TLX data without weighting is common in similar literature [10,33]. The questionnaire measures the perceived mental and physical workload, temporal demand, performance, effort, and frustration of participants. The overall workload of the proposed techniques is calculated by the mean of the six subscales. The overall score for each technique in order from high to low: The highest perceived workload was using HandUI (M = 53.72), followed by FingerUI (M = 46.13), a slightly lower workload by using ThumbGesture (M = 41.55), and finally Controller (M = 37.92).

5.3 System Usability Scale (SUS)

The SUS gives insight into the subjective perceived usability for the different techniques. Generally, a higher value means better perceived usability and a value above 69 can be considered as above average according to Sauro [29]. It is to note that the SUS scores of this evaluation are only meaningful within this experiment and should not be compared to SUS scores of techniques within other research work. The following SUS scores were achieved: Controller 66.1; FingerUI 62.9; HandUI 61.4; ThumbGesture 76.8. The scores are depicted in Fig. 6.

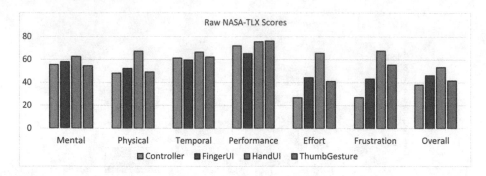

Fig. 5. The raw NASA-TLX scores. Perceived mental and physical workload, temporal demand, performance, effort, and frustration are measured by using the questionnaire. The overall perceived workload is shown on the far right of the bar charts.

5.4　Subjective Ranking of Techniques

Participants were asked to rate each technique on a scale from 1 (bad) to 10 (good). The techniques got the following average rating from users: Controller 8.5; FingerUI 6.42; HandUI 5.21; ThumbGesture 7.57. The scores are depicted in Fig. 6.

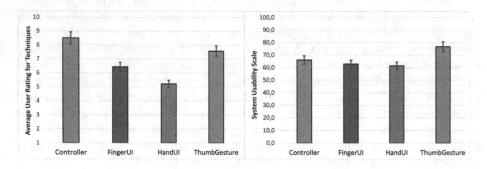

Fig. 6. Left: Average user rating for the proposed techniques. Users could rate each technique on scale from 1(bad) to 10(good). Right: results of the system usability scale.

6　Discussion and Future Work

It was anticipated that the controller outperforms the hand gesture based techniques in task completion time. However, no statistically significant difference was found between Controller and ThumbGesture. Another noteworthy observation is that ThumbGesture received a better SUS score than Controller. This could be explained by the fact that all participants were laypeople to VR and therefore have minimal experience with using a controller which lead to a better usability rating.

No significant differences were found in the overall scores regarding the perceived workload of the techniques. However, it can be observed in Fig. 5 that controller required less effort and led to lower frustration by the participants.

Ranking of techniques was also in favor of Controller but ThumbGesture received similar results. Overall it can be said that ThumbGesture was the winner out of the three proposed one-handed locomotion techniques as it got the best SUS scores, highest user rating, and fastest task completion time. This leads to the conclusion that a one-handed technique for continuous locomotion should use a simple gesture for moving without an additional user interface.

Interestingly, some participants exploited the fact that turning the head also rotated the virtual character. Thus, only the gesture for moving forward was necessary to achieve the goal. A follow-up study could investigate whether gestures to change the direction of movement offer added value or if they are unnecessary.

It was also interesting that three out of four subjects who stopped the experiment, stopped during the controller condition (the last participant interrupted at HandUI). This could be a hint that the controller actually causes more motion sickness than gesture-based locomotion. However, more data is required to support this hypothesis.

7   Limitations

Little research has been performed on how bare hands can be used to move in virtual environments. Therefore, it is not yet clear which bare handed technique is performing well enough to compare it to other freehand techniques which are widely researched and acknowledged such as WIP. In that regard, once suitable bare handed locomotion techniques have been found, they should be compared to sophisticated techniques such as WIP. Only then can a well-founded insight be gained into whether hand gestures are a valid alternative.

The robustness of the bare handed techniques is highly dependent on the quality of the hand tracking solution. Some participants had problems with the gestures, even though they were quite simple. This was particularly noticeable with the ThumbGesture technique, where the virtual hand sometimes had an index finger pointing outwards, even though the physical hand was correctly shaped. Similar false hand configurations occurred once the index finger pointed outwards because the finger was covered by the cameras. Furthermore, no questionnaire for motion sickness was used. The experiment was designed without a questionnaire on motion sickness in order to keep it as short as possible, also so that subjects would not have to spend much time in VR. However, since some subjects dropped out due to motion sickness, an evaluation in this regard would have been useful.

Another limitation is the number of participants. Only a limited number of participants could be recruited due to the COVID-19 pandemic. More participants would be required in order to be able to draw stronger conclusions about the proposed techniques.

8 Conclusion

This work presents three one-handed techniques for continuous locomotion in VR. The techniques are compared with a standard controller implementation and the respective other techniques. The techniques are compared with respect to task completion time, usability, perceived workload, and got ranked by the participants. Controller was fastest in task completion time and got the highest rating from participants. In the other measurements, however, there is no clear winner between the use of a controller and one of the presented one-handed techniques for continuous locomotion. ThumbGesture even got a higher SUS score than Controller. Overall, it can be said that out of the three one-handed techniques, ThumbGesture was the winner in this experiment. This technique received the highest scores in the SUS and ranking by participants. Furthermore, it got lowest perceived workload out of the three one-handed techniques. It was also the fastest in task completion time among the bare handed techniques. This work aims towards using natural hand gestures for moving around in VR. The techniques presented show promising results overall, but further techniques should be evaluated to find potential suitable hand gestures for the locomotion task. This is especially important if physical controllers are to be replaced by hand tracking in the future or if controllers are not desired for an application.

Acknowledgement. Part of this work was funded by the Bundesministerium für Bildung und Forschung (BMBF) in the context of ODPfalz under Grant 03IHS075B. This work was also supported by the EU Research and Innovation programme Horizon 2020 (project INFINITY) under the grant agreement ID: 883293.

References

1. Al Zayer, M., MacNeilage, P., Folmer, E.: Virtual locomotion: a survey. IEEE Trans. Visual. Comput. Graph. **26**(6), 2315–2334 (2020). https://doi.org/10.1109/TVCG.2018.2887379. ISSN 1941–0506
2. Berger, L., Wolf, K.: Wim: Fast locomotion in virtual reality with spatial orientation gain & without motion sickness. In: Proceedings of the 17th International Conference on Mobile and Ubiquitous Multimedia, MUM 2018, pp. 19–24. Association for Computing Machinery, New York (2018). ISBN 9781450365949. https://doi.org/10.1145/3282894.3282932
3. Bishop, I., Abid, M.R.: Survey of locomotion systems in virtual reality. In: Proceedings of the 2nd International Conference on Information System and Data Mining - ICISDM 2018, pp. 151–154. ACM Press, Lakeland (2018). ISBN 978-1-4503-6354-9. https://doi.org/10.1145/3206098.3206108
4. Bozgeyikli, E., Raij, A., Katkoori, S., Dubey, R.: Locomotion in virtual reality for individuals with autism spectrum disorder. In: Proceedings of the 2016 Symposium on Spatial User Interaction, SUI 2016, pp. 33–42. Association for Computing Machinery, New York (2016a). ISBN 9781450340687. https://doi.org/10.1145/2983310.2985763

5. Bozgeyikli, E., Raij, A., Katkoori, S., Dubey, R.: Point & teleport locomotion technique for virtual reality. In: Proceedings of the 2016 Annual Symposium on Computer-Human Interaction in Play, CHI PLAY 2016, pp. 205–216. Association for Computing Machinery, New York (2016b). ISBN 9781450344562. https://doi.org/10.1145/2967934.2968105

6. Brooke, J.: SUS: a quick and dirty' usability. Usability Eval. Ind. 189 (1996)

7. Brooke, J.: Sus: a retrospective. J. Usability Stud. 8(2), 29–40 (2013)

8. Bruno, L., Pereira, J., Jorge, J.: A new approach to walking in place. In: Kotzé, P., Marsden, G., Lindgaard, G., Wesson, J., Winckler, M. (eds.) INTERACT 2013. LNCS, vol. 8119, pp. 370–387. Springer, Heidelberg (2013). https://doi.org/10.1007/978-3-642-40477-1_23

9. Buttussi, F., Chittaro, L.: Locomotion in place in virtual reality: a comparative evaluation of joystick, teleport, and leaning. IEEE Trans. Visual. Comput. Graph. 27(1), 125–136 (2021). https://doi.org/10.1109/TVCG.2019.2928304. ISSN 1941-0506

10. Caggianese, G., Capece, N., Erra, U., Gallo, L., Rinaldi, M.: Freehand-steering locomotion techniques for immersive virtual environments: a comparative evaluation. Int. J. Human-Comput. Inter. 36(18), 1734–1755 (2020). https://doi.org/10.1080/10447318.2020.1785151

11. Caggianese, G., Gallo, L., Neroni, P.: Design and preliminary evaluation of freehand travel techniques for wearable immersive virtual reality systems with egocentric sensing. In: De Paolis, L.T., Mongelli, A. (eds.) AVR 2015. LNCS, vol. 9254, pp. 399–408. Springer, Cham (2015). https://doi.org/10.1007/978-3-319-22888-4_29

12. Cardoso, J.C.S.: Comparison of gesture, gamepad, and gaze-based locomotion for VR worlds. In: Proceedings of the 22nd ACM Conference on Virtual Reality Software and Technology, VRST 2016, pp. 319–320. Association for Computing Machinery, New York (2016). ISBN 9781450344913. https://doi.org/10.1145/2993369.2996327

13. Cardoso, J.C.S., Perrotta, A.: A survey of real locomotion techniques for immersive virtual reality applications on head-mounted displays. Comput. Graph. 85, 55–73 (2019). https://doi.org/10.1016/j.cag.2019.09.005. ISSN 0097-8493

14. Clifton, J., Palmisano, S.: Comfortable locomotion in VR: teleportation is not a complete solution. In: 25th ACM Symposium on Virtual Reality Software and Technology, VRST 2019. Association for Computing Machinery, New York (2019). ISBN 9781450370011. https://doi.org/10.1145/3359996.3364722

15. Ferracani, A., Pezzatini, D., Bianchini, J., Biscini, G., Del Bimbo, A.: Locomotion by natural gestures for immersive virtual environments. In: Proceedings of the 1st International Workshop on Multimedia Alternate Realities, pp. 21–24. ACM, Amsterdam The Netherlands (2016). ISBN 978-1-4503-4521-7. https://doi.org/10.1145/2983298.2983307

16. Grechkin, T., Thomas, J., Azmandian, M., Bolas, M., Suma, E.: Revisiting detection thresholds for redirected walking: combining translation and curvature gains. In: Proceedings of the ACM Symposium on Applied Perception, SAP 2016, pp. 113–120. Association for Computing Machinery, New York (2016), ISBN 9781450343831. https://doi.org/10.1145/2931002.2931018

17. Han, J., Moere, A.V., Simeone, A.L.: Foldable spaces: an overt redirection approach for natural walking in virtual reality. In: 2022 IEEE Conference on Virtual Reality and 3D User Interfaces (VR), pp. 167–175 (2022). https://doi.org/10.1109/VR51125.2022.00035

18. Hart, S.G.: Nasa-task load index (NASA-TLX); 20 years later. Proc. Hum. Factors Ergon. Soc. Annu. Meet. **50**(9), 904–908 (2006). https://doi.org/10.1177/154193120605000909
19. Hart, S.G., Staveland, L.E.: Development of NASA-TLX (task load index): results of empirical and theoretical research. In: Hancock, P.A., Meshkati, N. (eds.) Human Mental Workload, Advances in Psychology, North-Holland, vol. 52, pp. 139–183 (1988). https://doi.org/10.1016/S0166-4115(08)62386-9
20. Huang, R., Harris-adamson, C., Odell, D., Rempel, D.: Design of finger gestures for locomotion in virtual reality. Virtual Reality Intell. Hardware **1**(1), 1–9 (2019). https://doi.org/10.3724/SP.J.2096-5796.2018.0007. ISSN 2096–5796
21. Kang, H.J., Shin, J.h., Ponto, K.: A comparative analysis of 3D user interaction: how to move virtual objects in mixed reality. In: 2020 IEEE Conference on Virtual Reality and 3D User Interfaces (VR), pp. 275–284 (2020). ISSN 2642-5254. https://doi.org/10.1109/VR46266.2020.00047
22. Kim, J.-S., Gračanin, D., Matković, K., Quek, F.: Finger walking in place (FWIP): a traveling technique in virtual environments. In: Butz, A., Fisher, B., Krüger, A., Olivier, P., Christie, M. (eds.) SG 2008. LNCS, vol. 5166, pp. 58–69. Springer, Heidelberg (2008). https://doi.org/10.1007/978-3-540-85412-8_6
23. Kim, J.-S., Gračanin, D., Matković, K., Quek, F.: The effects of finger-walking in place (FWIP) for spatial knowledge acquisition in virtual environments. In: Taylor, R., Boulanger, P., Krüger, A., Olivier, P. (eds.) SG 2010. LNCS, vol. 6133, pp. 56–67. Springer, Heidelberg (2010). https://doi.org/10.1007/978-3-642-13544-6_6
24. Langbehn, E., Eichler, T., Ghose, S., Bruder, G., Steinicke, F.: Evaluation of an omnidirectional walking-in-place user interface with virtual locomotion speed scaled by forward leaning angle. In: GI AR/VR Workshop, pp. 149–160 (2015)
25. Langbehn, E., Lubos, P., Steinicke, F.: Evaluation of locomotion techniques for room-scale VR: joystick, teleportation, and redirected walking. In: Proceedings of the Virtual Reality International Conference - Laval Virtual, VRIC 2018. Association for Computing Machinery, New York (2018). ISBN 9781450353816. https://doi.org/10.1145/3234253.3234291
26. Marie Prinz, L., Mathew, T., Klüber, S., Weyers, B.: An overview and analysis of publications on locomotion taxonomies. In: 2021 IEEE Conference on Virtual Reality and 3D User Interfaces Abstracts and Workshops (VRW), pp. 385–388 (2021).https://doi.org/10.1109/VRW52623.2021.00080
27. Nilsson, N.C., et al.: 15 Years of research on redirected walking in immersive virtual environments. IEEE Comput. Graph. Appl. **38**(2), 44–56 (2018). https://doi.org/10.1109/MCG.2018.111125628. ISSN 1558–1756
28. Nilsson, N.C., Serafin, S., Steinicke, F., Nordahl, R.: Natural walking in virtual reality: a review. Comput. Entertainment **16**(2), 1–22 (2018). https://doi.org/10.1145/3180658
29. Sauro, J.: A practical guide to the system usability scale: background, benchmarks & best practices. Measuring Usability LLC (2011)
30. Schäfer, A., Reis, G., Stricker, D.: The gesture authoring space: authoring customised hand gestures for grasping virtual objects in immersive virtual environments. In: Proceedings of Mensch und Computer 2022. Association for Computing Machinery, New York (2022). ISBN 978-1-4503-9690-5/22/09. https://doi.org/10.1145/3543758.3543766
31. Schuemie, M.J., van der Straaten, P., Krijn, M., van der Mast, C.A.: Research on presence in virtual reality: a survey. CyberPsychology Behav. **4**(2), 183–201 (2001). https://doi.org/10.1089/109493101300117884. ISSN 1094–9313

32. Schäfer, A., Reis, G., Stricker, D.: Controlling teleportation-based locomotion in virtual reality with hand gestures: a comparative evaluation of two-handed and one-handed techniques. Electronics **10**(6), 715 (2021). https://doi.org/10.3390/electronics10060715. ISSN 2079-9292

33. Schäfer, A., Reis, G., Stricker, D.: Comparing controller with the hand gestures pinch and grab for picking up and placing virtual objects. In: 2022 IEEE Conference on Virtual Reality and 3D User Interfaces Abstracts and Workshops (VRW), pp. 738–739 (2022). https://doi.org/10.1109/VRW55335.2022.00220

34. Templeman, J.N., Denbrook, P.S., Sibert, L.E.: Virtual locomotion: walking in place through virtual environments. Presence **8**(6), 598–617 (1999). https://doi.org/10.1162/105474699566512

35. Zhang, F., Chu, S., Pan, R., Ji, N., Xi, L.: Double hand-gesture interaction for walk-through in VR environment. In: 2017 IEEE/ACIS 16th International Conference on Computer and Information Science (ICIS), pp. 539–544 (2017). https://doi.org/10.1109/ICIS.2017.7960051

36. Zielasko, D., Horn, S., Freitag, S., Weyers, B., Kuhlen, T.W.: Evaluation of hands-free HMD-based navigation techniques for immersive data analysis. In: 2016 IEEE Symposium on 3D User Interfaces (3DUI), pp. 113–119 (2016). https://doi.org/10.1109/3DUI.2016.7460040

37. Zielasko, D., Law, Y.C., Weyers, B.: Take a look around - the impact of decoupling gaze and travel-direction in seated and ground-based virtual reality utilizing torso-directed steering. In: 2020 IEEE Conference on Virtual Reality and 3D User Interfaces (VR), pp. 398–406 (2020). https://doi.org/10.1109/VR46266.2020.00060

An Augmented Reality Solution for the Positive Behaviour Intervention and Support

Mariella Farella[1]([⊠])(iD), Marco Arrigo[1], Crispino Tosto[1], Davide Taibi[1],
Luciano Seta[1], Antonella Chifari[1], Sui Lin Goei[2], Jeroen Pronk[2,3],
Eleni Mangina[4], Paola Denaro[1], Doriana Dhrami[1], and Giuseppe Chiazzese[1]

[1] National Research Council of Italy - Institute for Educational Technology,
Palermo, Italy
mariella.farella@itd.cnr.it
[2] Faculty of Behavioural and Movement Sciences, Vrije Universiteit Amsterdam,
Amsterdam, Netherlands
[3] Department of Child Health, The Netherlands Organization for Applied Scientific
Research, Leiden, The Netherlands
[4] School of Computer Science, University College Dublin, Dublin, Ireland

Abstract. The spread of Augmented Reality (AR) and the recent technological developments, provide innovative techniques and tools that
show a growing potential in education. One of the pilots of the European
Horizon 2020 project ARETE (Augmented Reality Interactive Educational System) aims to investigate and evaluate for the first time the
introduction of an AR solution to support a behavioral lesson in schools
where the Positive Behaviour Intervention and Support (PBIS) methodology is adopted. Specifically in this paper, we describe the architectural
design and implementation of a PBIS-AR application as a component of
the ARETE ecosystem. It describes the functionality of the system and
the teaching process that the AR solution will support.

Keywords: Augmented Reality · Positive Behaviour · Behavioural
learning

1 Introduction

Augmented Reality (AR) is changing the way people experience physical and
virtual environments. In particular, AR has expanded widely in the field of education. The concept of AR dates back to the 1960 s s and is focused on improving user perception and interaction with the real world. According to [2], AR
combines the real world and virtual objects and provides simultaneous interaction between them. Through AR, users in real time can see their environment
enriched with virtual elements (textual information, images, videos or 3D elements) through the camera of the device used, either it is a mobile device, a

G. Zachmann et al. (Eds.): EuroXR 2022, LNCS 13484, pp. 206–212, 2022.
https://doi.org/10.1007/978-3-031-16234-3_12

headset or a smart glasses specifically designed for AR. Several studies demonstrated that Augmented Reality has the potential to enhance student motivation and make learning a more engaging, challenging, and dynamic activity [7,13]. In addition, it can stimulate creativity, collaborative skills, and critical thinking in students. In the context of behavioral education, which is related to the study of how the environment stimulates changes in students' behavior, AR technologies have been integrated into interventions delivered in school and clinical settings to teach social skills (e.g. [1,10]). However, the use cases of AR in school-based behavioral education are very few.

In the Horizon 2020 European project ARETE[1](Augmented Reality Interactive Educational System), the use of Augmented Reality in behavioral education is explored for the first time [12]. Specifically, the project pilot #3 aims for the first time at developing and testing an AR system that supports teachers during behavioral lessons in teaching and practicing behavioral expectations following the guidelines provided by the Positive Behaviour Intervention and Support (PBIS) framework[2]. First, a short introduction of the PBIS framework is given; following, the design process of the AR based application to support teachers during behavioral lessons is described.

2   The PBIS Framework

School-Wide Positive Behaviour Intervention and Support (SWPBIS) is a school-wide educational approach aimed at supporting students' behavior and school outcomes by stimulating the creation of safe learning environments [11]. Specifically, SWPBIS provides schools with a framework for implementing evidence-based educational interventions that promote students' (and all school stakeholders') prosocial behaviour, thus contributing to the emergence of a positive and safe school climate.

SWPBIS interventions delivered at the primary-tier level are usually applied to all school members and across all school settings (e.g. classroom, hallway, corridor, et cetera) to create and guide a positive social culture. This primary interventions get the foundation for delivering regular, proactive support and preventing unwanted behaviors. SWPBIS interventions also includes systematic rewards of students' accuracy in adhering to the defined behavioral expectations and systematic interventions to address problem behaviours [9]. At the same time, second-tier interventions are still delivered as group interventions but are designed to address problem behaviour of those students who do not positively respond to first-tier interventions. Finally, the third tier comprises interventions specifically designed to be delivered individually to students who exhibit exceptionally challenging behavior and do not profit from interventions delivered in the first two tiers. Safer and more positive learning environments at school, as promoted by SPWPBIS interventions, have been proved to account for a set of positive outcomes, including reduced problem behavior [4] and improved school

---

[1] https://www.areteproject.eu/.
[2] https://www.pbis.org/.

climate [3] among others; more in general, literature has extensively confirmed the effectiveness of SWPBIS in improving students' learning engagement and educational outcomes across different grade levels [8].

3   Design of the AR Based Application for PBIS

In the framework of pilot #3 of the ARETE project, named Augmented Reality for promoting Positive Behaviour Intervention and Support, an application is designed to support educational interventions delivered within the first tier of a multi-tiered system of support [5].

The research and development process towards universal implementation of PBIS-AR was based on data collection through focus groups with stakeholders (i.e., PBIS experts and PBIS teachers). The design process envisaged the involvement of the stakeholders in construction and validation of the ARETE PBIS Behavioural Expectation matrix and PBIS-AR application content. In this way, the design phase would take into account the needs highlighted by the PBIS teachers. This process was affected by the pandemic phase from covid-19 forcing the application of contingency plans to complete the process. Therefore, a review was created to the literature on PBIS school values, behavioral expectations, common school contexts, and reinforcement systems as a contingency plan. In addition, an online questionnaire was created and administered to students (N = 209) and teachers (N = 135), which results allowed the selection of behavioral expectations, settings, and values for the construction of AR lesson content.

Taking into consideration the requests of PBIS teachers and the outputs obtained from the various focus groups, an app for smart devices (mobile phone and tablet) was designed specifically oriented to support PBIS practice of students and teachers during the behavioural lesson. This application aims to support the definition, modeling and practice of expected behaviors and to provide support for the recognition and reinforcement of students' compliance with expected behaviors. Students are guided through a learning path that, leads them toward practicing PBIS methodology in a real environment, to finally reinforce their experience with PBIS. In order to interleave the effects of the PBIS behaviours with the real context in which students actually are, the Augmented Reality technology has been leveraged.

3.1   PBIS-AR Application Architecture

The architecture of the PBIS-AR application integrates different modules, each of them devoted to a specific functionality. Users of the application are students or groups of students (depending on the number of available devices). An App Controller module manages activities, user profile and data synchronization and interacts with:

- the tracking system, which is responsible for managing the AR-content tracking.

– the data controller to manage user data and leader board. It takes care of the authentication procedure and manages the reward system including the leader board system.
– the xAPI for learning analytics.
– the student module, to control interactions during the PBIS phases (teach, practice and reinforce) performed by students through the application.

Moreover, the 3D objects as well as 3D animations, are stored in a repository of a ARETE Moodle[3] server using ARLEM[4] standards. Finally, the Orkestra library will be used as a multi-user orchestrator.

3.2   AR Objects for the PBIS-AR App

A series of virtual characters were designed and developed to show students the execution of expected behaviors. The main character is an alien, Arpro, from the space who is completely unfamiliar with life on Earth, so that he can be considered as a neutral behavioral coach. In fact, an alien is new to planet Earth and must explicitly learn all the values, procedures and routines. The alien is only one of the characters that can be involved in creating examples and non-examples of a behavioral routine in the PBIS-AR application. In fact, at school it should have relationships with other characters, such as teachers, the administrator, and classmates.

3.3   Students' Activities in the PBIS-AR App

The PBIS-AR application supports students during the training, practice and reinforcement activities. Taking into account the outline of the PBIS framework, the functionalities that the PBIS-AR application will have to offer to its users have been identified and will be implemented using Augmented Reality:

– Interactive introduction to the system in which the main character, the alien Arpro, is introduced to the student through an interactive presentation. The interactive dialogue will be developed in AR mode using the balloon system and allowing students to become familiar with the user interface of the application and making them more involved in the learning process.
– Setting up of the environment where the user will be led to a simple configuration of the working environment by entering a nickname that will be used to anonymously track all student interactions and to set the necessary parameters to launch the application in a personalized way.
– Reproduction of behavioral routines related to the school environment and specific setting. Content will be offered through 3D AR animations directly in the school environment in which students are about to learn.

---

[3] https://arete.ucd.ie.
[4] https://standards.ieee.org/ieee/1589/6073/.

- Behavioral AR reflection game where a gamification learning content will be provided to students. Using this feature, students participate in a behavioral reflection game in AR. Through a series of markers located in various settings, examples and non-examples of behavior are shown to students to facilitate learning of expected behaviors.
- Multi-user interactive behavioral activity where students will have the opportunity to practice behavioral tasks through augmented reality, using 3D objects and characters to interact with in a mixed environment. An in-development library, the Orkestra library, will be used for the implementation, allowing the application to create a multi-user behavioral activity.
- Leaderboards and rewards where the student will be able to view leaderboards, and combined points according to different behavioral expectations experienced in the AR environment.

3.4   Behaviour Tracking with xAPI

PBIS behavioral lessons will be developed and piloted to investigate the efficacy of integrating AR technology within PBIS interventions and supports to encourage expected behaviors at the school and classroom level. The learning process will be monitored through the integration of the Experience API[5] (xAPI) standard that will send the data to a Learning Locker platform that is a Learning Record Store (LRS). The activities described in the Sect. 3.3, create xAPI statements to track the student's interaction with the system and are sent to the chosen LRS to store them.

   The use of the xAPI standard provides an interoperable layer to track student activities and to simplify the design of learning analytics tools that support teachers in making decisions about educational processes in school settings. One of the advantages of the xAPI standard is the ability to define specific profiles related to a domain of interest. This also makes it appropriate in our context where innovative AR-based approaches are used in learning and practice of the PBIS framework. As described in [6], the use of xAPI standards promote the development of Learning Analytics approaches to monitor PBIS experiences. A comprehensive xAPI vocabulary will be defined for modeling the AR-based PBIS experience.

4   Conclusion and Future Steps

This paper presents the architecture of the PBIS-AR application prototype. It is an application designed to support a behavioural lesson with the use of AR learning contents. The main effort to obtain an innovative app able to involve and engage children and young students is devoted to encourage the adoption of the PBIS methodology and sustain teachers and students in the behavioural teaching and learning process. This result will be pursued by adopting new

---

[5] https://xapi.com.

AR standards and technologies permitting the authoring of context-aware and purpose-aware AR objects and animations, the tracking of the user's experience with AR learning objects and the use of AR multi users interactions learning activities. The next steps include the development of the application prototype and the testing of PBIS-AR application with children in the age group of 9–12 in the school year 2022–2023.

Acknowledgment. The following paper has been supported by European Union's Horizon 2020 research and innovation programme, ARETE project under grant agreement No 856533.

References

1. Alqithami, S., Alzahrani, M., Alzahrani, A., Mostafa, A.: Modeling an augmented reality game environment to enhance behavior of ADHD patients. In: Liang, P., Goel, V., Shan, C. (eds.) BI 2019. LNCS, vol. 11976, pp. 179–188. Springer, Cham (2019). https://doi.org/10.1007/978-3-030-37078-7_18
2. Azuma, R.T.: A survey of augmented reality. Presence: Teleoperators Virtual Environ. **6**(4), 355–385 (1997)
3. Bradshaw, C.P., Koth, C.W., Thornton, L.A., Leaf, P.J.: Altering school climate through school-wide positive behavioral interventions and supports: findings from a group-randomized effectiveness trial. Prev. Sci. **10**(2), 100 (2009). https://doi.org/10.1007/s11121-008-0114-9
4. Bradshaw, C.P., Waasdorp, T.E., Leaf, P.J.: Effects of school-wide positive behavioral interventions and supports on child behavior problems. Pediatrics **130**(5), e1136–e1145 (2012)
5. Chiazzese, G., et al.: Teaching behavioural routines using augmented reality in the arete project. In: International Science Fiction Prototyping conference, SCIFI-IT, pp. 60–64 (2021)
6. Farella, M., Arrigo, M., Chiazzese, G., Tosto, C., Seta, L., Taibi, D.: Integrating xAPI in AR applications for positive behaviour intervention and support. In: 2021 International Conference on Advanced Learning Technologies (ICALT), pp. 406–408. IEEE (2021)
7. Farella, M., Taibi, D., Arrigo, M., Todaro, G., Chiazzese, G.: An augmented reality mobile learning experience based on treasure hunt serious game. In: ECEL 2021 20th European Conference on e-Learning, p. 148. Academic Conferences International limited (2021)
8. Freeman, J., Simonsen, B., McCoach, D.B., Sugai, G., Lombardi, A., Horner, R.: Relationship between school-wide positive behavior interventions and supports and academic, attendance, and behavior outcomes in high schools. J. Positive Behav. Interv. **18**(1), 41–51 (2016)
9. Lynass, L., Tsai, S.F., Richman, T.D., Cheney, D.: Social expectations and behavioral indicators in school-wide positive behavior supports: a national study of behavior matrices. J. Positive Behav. Interv. **14**(3), 153–161 (2012)
10. Sahin, N.T., Abdus-Sabur, R., Keshav, N.U., Liu, R., Salisbury, J.P., Vahabzadeh, A.: Case study of a digital augmented reality intervention for autism in school classrooms: associated with improved social communication, cognition, and motivation via educator and parent assessment. In: Frontiers in Education, vol. 3, p. 57. Frontiers (2018)

11. Sugai, G., Horner, R.H.: Defining and describing schoolwide positive behavior support. In: Sailor, W., Dunlap, G., Sugai, G., Horner, R. (eds.) Handbook of positive behavior support. Issues in Clinical Child Psychology, pp. 307–326. Springer, Boston (2009). https://doi.org/10.1007/978-0-387-09632-2_13
12. Tosto, C., et al.: The potential of AR solutions for behavioral learning: a scoping review. Computers **11**(6) (2022). https://doi.org/10.3390/computers11060087, https://www.mdpi.com/2073-431X/11/6/87
13. Wu, H.K., Lee, S.W.Y., Chang, H.Y., Liang, J.C.: Current status, opportunities and challenges of augmented reality in education. Comput. Educ. **62**, 41–49 (2013)

The Reality of Virtual Experiences: Semantic and Episodic Memory Formation in VR

Alena Kostyk[1] ⓘ, Laurence Dessart[2] ⓘ, and Kirsten Cowan[3(✉)] ⓘ

[1] University of Glasgow, Glasgow G12 8QQ, UK
[2] HEC Liege, 4000 Liege, Belgium
[3] University of Edinburgh, Edinburgh EH8 9LL, UK
Kirsten.cowan@ed.ac.uk

Abstract. While we understand how consumers attend to and process information in VR, research has yet to explore how consumers store information from virtual experiences in memory and recall it later. However, memory is important for developing knowledge about something, like a destination, and later decision-making. In fact, VR (vs. other information channels) are more persuasive in decision-making. Yet we know very little about the role of VR and memory on these decisions. Thus, we seek to understand how VR experiences affect memory and specifically episodic versus semantic memory systems. Findings from a series of interviews and an online survey documented a constant comparison of reality and virtuality. Virtual experiences create rich semantic memories, moreso for individuals where more time had passed. However, semantic and episodic memories formation was at odds with one another. While those who had not visited the destination previously reported higher semantic and episodic details, the experience was overwhelming for individuals who had not visited previously. Additionally, those who had not experienced the destination received the experience with skepticism and downplayed their expectations of real future interactions. Finally, the results reveal the imperfect nature of memory, including misremembering.

Keywords: Virtual reality · Memory · Semantic · Episodic · Tourism

1 Introduction

In times of technological transformation, brand experiences, increasingly take new forms, such as virtual forms. This follows VR adoption trends, propelled by the COVID-19 pandemic (Schiopu et al. 2021). Different from augmented (AR) and mixed reality, which overlay the physical environment with virtual annotations, enabling interactions with the environment in real time, VR fully transports users to virtual worlds. Hence, VR offers greater immersion and presence, and notably, is not tied to a physical location (Cowan and Ketron 2019). While past research has made initial efforts to understand how consumers process information in VR (e.g. Orth et al. 2019), scholarship is rather limited (see Cowan and Ketron 2019). As a result, while VR is exciting for consumers, marketers have yet to understand how to make the most efficient use of VR that evokes

G. Zachmann et al. (Eds.): EuroXR 2022, LNCS 13484, pp. 213–217, 2022.
https://doi.org/10.1007/978-3-031-16234-3_13

positive sentiments toward the brand. For example, Orth et al. (2019) use construal level theory to argue that processing style preference (e.g. preference for verbalizing versus visualizing) influences presence from a virtual servicescape. Additionally, Cowan et al. (2021) also explain differences in presence and consumer responses from semantic and narrative information processing. Yet, both studies fail to examine how the information processed affects memory, and thus, decision-making. This begs a question: how do VR experiences impact brand memories?

2 Literature Review

The literature provides conflicting insights regarding consumer memory of VR versus real-world experiences. Some research suggests that VR experiences are better remembered than those in the real world. Particularly, virtual environments are free from external distractions and "noise", encouraging uninterrupted attention (Kang 2018; Optale et al. 2010). Consequently, more focused cognitive processing should result in better memory of the experience (Fassbender et al. 2012). However, other literature suggests that excessive levels of emotional arousal, typical for a VR experience, hinder memory (e.g. Kim et al. 2014). In a cognitively demanding virtual experience, consumers' ability to "record" information into their memory structures might be lowered. One enquiry examined the effect of different media on memory recall (Mania and Chalmers 2001), and found higher recall when information was presented in the real world (vs. VR).

Further, classic literature distinguishes between episodic and semantic memory. Semantic memory is a "mental thesaurus" of symbols, concepts, and relations, and is sometimes contrasted with "experience knowledge" (Ofir et al. 2008; Park et al. 1994), suggesting that it is somewhat independent of a specific brand experiences. For some brands, semantic memories are paramount, especially where prior experiences are scarce. Indeed, non-users tend to hold more semantic than episodic memories of brands (Herz and Brunk 2017). In contrast, episodic memory stores information about "autobiographical" events (e.g. specific brand interaction). As such, episodic memory involves "memory markers" recording multiple sensory and environmental changes during the experience (Ahn et al. 2009). It is possible that in VR brand experiences, the multitude of recorded "memory markers" results in a better episodic memory (Optale et al. 2010). At the same time, each channel of human information-processing has limited capacity (Mayer and Moreno 2003), and the excessive amount of memory markers to "catalogue" might hinder the formation of semantic memory in VR experiences. Hence, 1) how do consumers relate their memories formed by the VR experience to prior brand experience memories? 2) to which extent are the (a) episodic and (b) semantic memories of formed by the VR experience, and retained?

3 Study 1: Semi-structured Interviews

The first study undertook a phenomenological approach by collecting and analyzing first-hand accounts of VR destination brand experiences (Thompson et al. 1989) using semi-structured interviews. A snowball sample was used to obtain participants who owned head-mounted displays and had watched a VR experience focused on a tourism brand within the past four months. In total, 15 individuals were interviewed. Interviews were audio-recorded, and the 6.5 h of audio were transcribed for the purposes of analysis. Thematic analysis with NVivo 12 software was employed. Open coding was carried out until coding reached maturity, resulting in thirty-five codes (Weber 1990; Braun and Clarke 2006) and eleven major themes. The interview guide included questions covering the choice of the brand (e.g. why did you choose to watch the VR experience by this brand?) time passed since the experience, device information, the sequence of events that took place within the VR experience, the aspects of the experience that stood out the most, and comparing the experience to real life (e.g. imagined visit or actual visit, depending on whether they had visited the site in real life).

Most participants chose VR experiences based on their past experiences (e.g. Schacter et al. 2015). Motivations for selecting VR experiences reflected choices not only to enrich or deepen prior memories but also to compare real-world memories with virtual encounters. Participants with prior experiences were more likely to pay attention to details or look for specific objects in their environment, experiencing greater presence and immersion. When consumers formed brand-related memories, they recalled aspects that tapped into pre-existing brand knowledge but sometimes led to inaccurate reconstruction (e.g. Bartlett 1932).

The VR experience itself contributes to generating two types of memories. VR experience richness puts episodic and semantic memory at odds. Specifically, some consumers form strong semantic memories, but weak episodic memories, while others experience the opposite. This is likely due to the limited capacity of human information-processing, or the amount of time lapsing from the brand VR experience. Concerning semantic memory, the findings show that VR experiences created or reinforced semantic memories (e.g. Ochsner and Lieberman 2001; Johnson et al. 2011). This richness of the information experienced in VR facilitated episodic memory creation.

4 Study 2: Online Survey

Participants (n = 101; 68% male; Mage = 32.39) on Prolific Panel who own a VR headset took part in a survey asking them to recall a VR experience. These participants were recruited from a VR panel that two of the authors had created previously for another research project. All participants provided images of their devices with the date hand written on a piece of paper to ensure that they owned their device and to confirm the device type. Individuals' ownership varied from devices that required mobile phones (n = 504) to systems like Oculus Quest and more. Only panel members who owned head mounted displays that required use of their phones but were not Google Cardboard, were invited and qualified to participate in this questionnaire. Participants reported on a recent destination (e.g. museum, city, distillery, etc.) that they had visited using their VR headset. Then, they were asked whether they had experienced the destination directly beforehand and the time that lapsed between the VR experience and present. Then, they completed open-ended questions assessing their semantic and episodic memories. Specifically, they were asked what came to mind first about the destination brand. Then, they were asked to recall and type the sequence of events that took place within the VR experience. We coded the memories using the volume of the text to create an index of both semantic and episodic memories. Lastly, participants provided demographics.

Using t-tests to examine differences between groups, results indicated that following the VR experience, those without prior experiences reported slightly more semantic memories (p = .047) and greater episodic memories (M = 2.10 vs. 1.87; p = .03) compared to individuals who had experienced the brand prior. Interestingly, some of the narratives involved cases of misremembering. For example, as the authors were aware of some of the destination brand experiences, some of the detailed text over exaggerated the content that was provided within the semantic memories. In one case, there was one house in the VR experience shown but the participant recalled a village of houses. Finally, the data suggested that semantic memories "solidify" as more time passed, resulting in more detailed semantic memories for those who had their experience more than 3 months ago. These results were also assessed using a t-test with time as the independent variable (0 = less than 3 months ago, 1 = 3 or more months) and the volume of each of the memory indices as the dependent variables.

5 Conclusion

We demonstrate that in VR, semantic memories can be formed at the expense of episodic memories, and vice versa. Though individuals without prior direct brand experiences struggled with an 'overwhelming' experience, they were more likely to pick up on new semantic memories of the brand. This might corroborate the account of stronger semantic brand memories held by the non-users (e.g. Herz and Brunk 2017). And while the results of the survey indicate that these individuals likewise form stronger episodic memories, they involve misremembered markers. This research also has implications. Prior literature suggests that marketers should develop experiences to make them more memorable (Ezzyat and Davachi 2011; Latour and Carbone 2014). Current research indicates that excessive memory markers in VR experiences can impair memory formation. It follows that these experiences need to be carefully designed. Moreover, marketers should design VR experiences with particular customers in mind - those who have prior direct brand experience, and those who do not.

This research has its limitations due to its exploratory nature. Experimental designs might provide opportunities for further investigation, especially to better understand recall inaccuracies. While this study provides insight into the impact of prior memories on the VR experience memory, the influence in the opposite direction was not investigated.

References

Ahn, H.K., Liu, M.W., Soman, D.: Memory markers: how consumers recall the duration of experiences. J. Consum. Psychol. **19**(3), 508–516 (2009)

Bartlett, F.C.: Remembering: A Study in Experimental and Social Psychology. Cambridge University Press, Cambridge (1932)

Braun, V., Clarke, V.: Using thematic analysis in psychology. Qual. Res. Psychol. **3**(2), 77–101 (2006)

Cowan, K., Ketron, S.: Prioritizing marketing research in virtual reality: development of an immersion/fantasy typology. Eur. J. Mark. **53**(8), 1585–1611 (2019)

Cowan, K., Spielmann, N., Horn, E., Griffart, C.: Perception is reality... How luxury brands can use presence and haptic factors to augment digital environments. J. Bus. Res. **123**, 86–96 (2021)

Ezzyat, Y., Davachi, L.: What constitutes an episode in episodic memory? Psychol. Sci. **22**(2), 243–252 (2011)

Fassbender, E., Richards, D., Bilgin, A., Thompson, W.F., Heiden, W.: VirSchool: the effect of background music and immersive display systems on memory for facts learned in an educational virtual environment. Comput. Educ. **58**(1), 490–500 (2012)

Herz, M., Brunk, K.H.: Conceptual advances in consumers' semantic and episodic brand memories: a mixed methods exploration. Psychol. Mark. **34**, 70–91 (2017)

Johnson, R., Simon, E.J., Henkell, H., Zhu, J.: The role of episodic memory in controlled evaluative judgments about attitudes: an event-related potential study. Neuropsychologia **49**, 945–960 (2011)

Kang, J.: Effect of interaction based on augmented context in immersive virtual reality environment. Wirel. Pers. Commun. **98**, 1931–1940 (2018)

Kim, K., Park, K.K., Lee, J.-H.: The influence of arousal and expectation on eyewitness memory in a virtual environment. Cyberpsychol. Behav. Soc. Netw. **17**(11), 709–713 (2014)

LaTour, K.A., Carbone, L.P.: Sticktion: assessing memory for the customer experience. Cornell Hospitality Q. **55**(4), 342–353 (2014)

Mania, K., Chalmers, A.: The effects of levels of immersion on memory and presence in virtual environments: a reality centered approach. Cyberpsychol. Behav. **4**(2), 247–264 (2001)

Mayer, R.E., Moreno, R.: Nine ways to reduce cognitive load in multimedia learning. Educ. Psychol. **38**(1), 43–52 (2003)

Ochsner, K.N., Lieberman, M.D.: The emergence of social cognitive neuroscience. Am. Psychol. **56**(9), 717–734 (2001)

Ofir, C., Raghubir, P., Brosh, G., Monroe, K.B., Heiman, A.: Memory-based store price judgments: the role of knowledge and shopping experience. J. Retail. **84**(4), 414–423 (2008)

Optale, G., et al.: Controlling memory impairment in elderly adults using virtual reality memory training: a randomized controlled pilot study. Neurorehabil. Neural Repair **24**(4), 348–357 (2010)

Orth, U.R., Lockshin, L., Spielmann, N., Holm, M.: Design antecedents of telepresence in virtual service environments. J. Serv. Res. **22**(2), 202–218 (2019)

Park, C.W., Mothersbaugh, D.L., Feick, L.: Consumer knowledge assessment. J. Consum. Res. **21**, 71–82 (1994)

Schacter, D.L., Benoit, R.G., De Brigard, F., Szpunar, K.K.: Episodic future thinking and episodic counterfactual thinking: intersections between memory and decisions. Neurobiol. Learn. Mem. **117**, 14–21 (2015)

Schiopu, A., Hornoiu, R.I., Padurean, M.A., Nica, A.-M.: Virus tinged? Exploring the facets of virtual reality use in tourism as a result of the COVID-19 pandemic. Telematics Inform. **60**, 101575 (2021)

Thompson, C.J., Locander, W.B., Pollio, H.R.: Putting consumer experience back into consumer research: the philosophy and method of existential-phenomenology. J. Consum. Res. **16**(2), 133–146 (1989)

Weber, R.P.: Basic Content Analysis. Sage Publications, Thousand Oaks (1990)

Author Index

Printed in the United States
by Baker & Taylor Publisher Services

Printed in the United States
by Baker & Taylor Publisher Services